THE CONVERSATION OF ECONOMIC DEVELOPMENT

THE CONVERSATION OF ECONOMIC DEVELOPMENT

Historical Voices, Interpretations, and Reality

WILFRED L. DAVID

Routledge
Taylor & Francis Group
LONDON AND NEW YORK

First published 1997 by M.E. Sharpe

Published 2019 by Routledge
2 Park Square, Milton Park, Abingdon, Oxon OX14 4RN
52 Vanderbilt Avenue, New York, NY 10017

Routledge is an imprint of the Taylor & Francis Group, an informa business

Library of Congress Cataloging-in-Publication Data

David, Wilfred L.
The conversation of economic development : historical voices, interpretations, and reality / Wilfred L. David.
p. cm.
Includes bibliographical references and index.
ISBN 0-7656-0116-8 (hardcover : alk. paper)
1. Economic development. 2. Development economics.
3. Dependency. I. Title.
HD75.D378 1997
338.9—dc21 97-10367
CIP

ISBN 13: 978-0-7656-0116-2 (hbk)

To the memory of my two great teachers and mentors,
LADY URSULA HICKS and SIR JOHN HICKS

Contents

PART V: COUNTER-REVOLUTION AND BEYOND

Tables

Preface

The idea of "development" is as old as history itself and is embedded in all the hopes and contradictions of the human condition. Throughout the ages, the belief has persisted that everything could be better than it actually is if all human potentials were to be fully realized. This is reflected in the fact that, unlike lower animals, all human beings are bequeathed with certain qualities and powers that could enable them to live an enjoyable or "good" life. Such an existential condition can be broadly defined as one in which people are free to the greatest extent possible from the forces of anti-development, such as fear, want, misery, and oppression. It also connotes a positive "freedom to choose," or a life that is being lived in accordance with the "essence," or true nature, of the human personality.

Ever since the days of classical political economy, the pattern of human concerns has been linked to the optimistic expectation that it is possible to explain and understand why some peoples and countries are poor and others rich, and how an authentic transformation can be effected from poverty to riches. In modern times, the professional field known as the "economics of development" or "development economics" has emerged out of this concern. While it has undoubtedly matured as an intellectual discipline, development economics might have failed in its original purpose, and there is a widespread perception that the field is no longer viable. One reason is that its dominant ideas remain an "intellectual chess game" in academia, but in the real world their significance ultimately depends on the degree to which they affect people's lives for the better, or make a positive contribution to human betterment.

Thus, the human development potential is inextricably linked with the nature of our truth claims, or what purports to be valid knowledge. Historically, the consciousness of *homo sapiens* has developed alongside essential human needs, and the quest for knowledge and truth has always reflected the optimistic belief that human beings would be freed from the constant struggle to meet their survival needs. From a development perspective, therefore, greater significance should be attached to the level of consciousness or people's awareness of their own potentials, rather than to some abstract conceptualization of such potentials.

The perceptible failure of development economics is traceable in part to the fact that its analytical core has become increasingly distanced from the realities and everyday struggles facing the majority of humankind. The conceptual structure undergirding its dominant discourse has consistently turned a blind eye to the concrete conditions of abject poverty, inequality, social injustice, and hopelessness that continue to define the lot of billions of people living in the less developed sector of the world. This is an integral part of an apparently endemic antinomy that has engulfed the structure and functioning of the world order, that is, the globalization of both economic progress and human misery.

On the one hand, the past three centuries have witnessed a veritable revolution in various dimensions of human progress. The growth and spread of industrialization, technological progress, mass communications, and related aspects of socio-economic change have transformed the way people live throughout the globe. A new world of knowledge has been created, a wealth of information is now available about economies and societies, and hitherto unknown analytical tools are now used for explaining economic behavior and the application of empirical knowledge to the study of human, social, and economic problems. On the other hand, despite the new vistas and laudable transformations in the material and knowledge bases of societies, multiple sets of contradictory forces have produced a dampening effect on the human striving for a more joyful life and corresponding improvements in the life chances of the human species.

The global antithesis of economic prosperity and human misery has marched in tandem with a plethora of development theories based on different interpretations of human nature, ontologies of social life, value-orientations and epistemological presuppositions. More often than not, dominant theoretical and empirical findings about development are constantly incorporated into policies designed to change people's lives in one way or another, or otherwise have become integral parts of a social, economic, and political commentary that persuades members of society to adopt a particularly narrow view of themselves, their capabilities, and relations to others.

The deep cathexy of underdevelopment and forces of antidevelopment that continue to engulf the majority of poor nations and their inhabitants clearly indicates an urgent need for critical interpretation and reinterpretation of the dominant theorems of development economics. As an interpretive endeavor, this book humbly attempts to lay bare the belief patterns and truth conditions underlying alternative perspectives or paradigms of development thought and policy, and their implications for the achievement of authentic development. The latter revolves around the possibilities of making sustainable improvements in the overall quality of life. The ultimate aim is individual freedom or the fullest realization of the human potential.

The problem posed for the study of development, as for all forms of social and economic inquiry, is that interpretation of the truth is *perspectival*. Accordingly, most answers to the question of why some people and countries are so rich and others so poor rely on different conceptions of truth, theories of causation, and criteria for explanatory adequacy. As the book demonstrates, alternative clusters of development theories, empirical generalizations, and germane policy prescriptions rest on rival belief systems, preconceptions, and assumptions about human nature and behavior. These are normally implicit, but even when made explicit, they are not amenable to empirical corroboration.

The assumptions underlying development theories and policies reflect fundamental belief systems that tend to bias interpretation of human activity and goals. The significance of this is that the policy conclusions and preferred development strategies generated from the assumptions and preconceptions invariably suggest desirable forms of economic, social, and political organization. From this perspective, particular sequences of theories and policy mixes are able to perform what is essentially an ideological role of justifying particular ways of life.

The book utilizes the metaphor of *conversation* in order to: (a) highlight the pivotal role of discursive acts in the acquisition of knowledge; and (b) to sensitize a diverse readership--students, economists, policymakers, and those with a general interest in economic development--to the need to understand fundamental differences among development economists. Correlatively, the starting point of understanding and the possibilities for unravelling the truth tend to hinge on three related imperatives: the need for a continuous critique of the conventional wisdom; the juxtaposition of rival perspectives and interpretations against each other; and a constant adjustment or dynamic synergy between theoretical precepts and practical reality. This implies a "back and forth" process of alignment between the "pure" theses of academic discourse and everyday experiences.

A conversation can be carried out in many locations and in diverse ways. In general, it refers to the formal and informal exchange of ideas through the spoken or written word. In the strict academic sense, it connotes the discourse taking place in a professional field such as development economics. As such, it can be viewed as a pragmatic tool for discovering, interpreting, and reinterpreting truths about particular aspects of social and economic reality. The *Shorter Oxford English Dictionary on Historical Principles* defines a conversation as "intercourse, the action of living or having one's being *in* and *among* . . . the action of consorting with others." In other words, the primary focus is on "dialogue" as distinct from "monologue." Like plays, dramas, or dances, dialogical acts are orchestrated through social understandings and depend on the sharing of human agency. They are different from "games" in which dominant players tend to consort with each other primarily through the corridors of academia and other institutional channels.

This practice, albeit parochial, can generate useful knowledge if tenets such as originality of insight, a willingness to weigh all evidence, and abiding by scientific principles such as validity, coherence, and objectivity are upheld. However, since conversations usually take place in a plurivocal world, that is, one with many voices, they tend to be open-ended and indeterminate. As a result, they are prone to degenerate into dogmatism or negative-sum games. This underscores the fact that there are always contradictory interests at the heart of understanding. One normative lesson is that representatives of different interpretive communities, schools of thought, or research programs should always be willing to listen to each other, and constantly modify their own viewpoints. This entails a retreat from totalitarian perspectives or absolutism.

At another level, it should be recognized that enlightened conversations about development take place not only behind academic walls, but also in the street, in unemployment lines, on farms, in villages, on river banks, and under palm trees. This means that the masses of people in the so-called developing world can no longer remain misunderstood "objects" of development, or otherwise silent listeners to a discourse they cannot decipher. The point of emphasis is that knowledge about development is not merely an act of comparing given ideas with "facts," but more a dynamic process of mutual interaction between the would-be "knower" and the "known," or between "subject" and "object."

This signifies a need for sympathetic acquaintance with things in the real world and to effect correspondence between theory construction, on the one hand, and understanding human conduct in terms of people's own life experiences and self-understandings, on the other. From the very inception, theory should be grounded in the immediacy and plurality of life experiences. With the latter as the point of departure, and working back to theory, the findings can then be juxtaposed against the concrete practices of human social agents. This would ensure that critical interpretation of the economy and society eventually generates a self-liberating, emancipatory, and enlightened social, economic, and political practice.

Acknowledgments

Acknowledging all of one's personal and intellectual debts is an impossible task. Of course, the author must be prepared to bear the ultimate responsibility for what he creates. But even admitting this, the network of wider and more specific obligations cannot be denied. In the former case, the list of intellectual debts is endless, so I simply thank in a general way those who over the years have encouraged my efforts in one way or another, either through published works or sharp criticism via correspondence or personal contact.

During the period of preparing this book, Professor Ken Cole of the University of East Anglia, U.K., has been a prolific correspondent and an invaluable source of ideas and insights. I am particularly grateful to him and Professor Cedric Grant of Clark-Atlanta University for their incisive comments on earlier drafts.

Helen Watkins has done a superb job of word-processing successive versions of the manuscript. Her tenacity and endeavors, while coping with all her other tasks, have been superlative. The technical support provided by Steve Dalphin, Wendy Muto, Esther Clark, and the production team at M. E. Sharpe is also gratefully acknowledged.

Last, but not least, I wish to thank my wife, Peggy Ann, for her sympathetic support, companionship, criticism, and almost everything else.

The usual caveat should be added that all errors remain the author's own responsibility.

THE CONVERSATION OF ECONOMIC DEVELOPMENT

I

INTRODUCTION

Chapter 1

The Interpretation of Development

The meaning attached to the concept of development is not purely neutral nor descriptive, but is essentially linked to values about which reasonable people can disagree. All theoretical, empirical, and policy perspectives are in principle contestable not so much because of problems of logic or observation, but more because of differences in values or the presence of value heterogeneity. The differences ultimately boil down to alternative perceptions about human nature. It is necessary to have some prior understanding about who human beings are before answering questions about human betterment, the constitution of the good society, and how a full and enjoyable life can be achieved. In turn, different understandings about human motivation lead to different definitions of economic development and policies for promoting it.

From a human perspective, the idea of development may be interpreted in two broad, but related, senses. At one level, it can be conceptualized as a valuable end-state, level of well-being, or quality of life that has either been achieved, or is achievable, in principle. At another level, it connotes a process of change from conditions of life widely perceived to be undesirable, to others that are much more desirable in human terms. In the former case, the question becomes whether it should be valued as an end in itself (intrinsic) or as a proximate or instrumental end (extrinsic) geared toward achieving higher-order ends or core human values. The intrinsic valuation of development makes it coterminous with certain moral and psychological states that typically reflect essential conditions of human well-being. The extrinsic valuation entails that development is desired more because it presumably helps in the evaluation or promotion of other things that people value. The latter range from subjective feelings of pleasure and happiness to more tangible things such as money and the acquisition of material possessions.

In any event, the quality of life that people succeed in living is the result of a multidimensional process, which is itself a reflection of the complexity of human nature. The possibilities for attaining authentic development are inherently linked to the nature of outcomes generated by the complex interactions taking place among the component parts - that is, economic, socio-cultural, political, and ecological - of the quality of life and related human attributes. The component parts may interact in unpredictable ways that cannot be generalized. The causal linkages are not necessarily linear or unidirectional, but are typically embedded in a multiplicity of heterogeneous processes that are rife with tensions, ambiguities, and even contradictions.

The conventional wisdom is predicated on a strong belief in a positive and direct relationship between the quality of life and individual economic achievement. Throughout history, this expectation has been linked to a universal belief that human development is a basic right, and as a corollary, that all human beings are entitled to some minimal level of *economic welfare or development* below which it becomes impossible to sustain any form of human dignity, decency, or self-respect. Contextually, the provision of higher material well-being is expected to expand individual choices and enable people to better control their environment, thereby enlarging the possibilities of human freedom.

Accordingly, improvements in material economic welfare are expected to offer better avenues for the satisfaction of human wants and needs by enabling people to escape unbearable forms of economic deprivation and servitude. Needless to say, the competitive struggle for economic survival tends to be much more acute when basic material needs are not met because the majority of people will be locked into a constant struggle to escape the forces of anti-development and the related pursuit of freedom from want, misery, joblessness, excessive government coercion, and fear.

The mere struggle for survival that takes place at this level not only results in social and economic divisiveness, but also various forms of militarism, political dissension, and violence. For example, violent struggle remains a foremost cause of world hunger. It is estimated that about 100 million people are trapped in violent settings, such as Bosnia and Rwanda, that militate against normal food production and distribution. According to the Bread for the World Institute (1995), famine is a result not so much of natural disaster but more because of human choices related to civil violence, uprooted people, and failing nation states. In these "complex emergencies," warring factions loot and deliberately destroy crops, draw labor resources away from food production, and use food as a weapon.

We hasten to add that the general argument is not predicated on a deterministic view about the economic components of development. The seemingly straightforward story about the prerequisite of improved economic welfare is by no means conclusive. There is ample historical evidence as well as plausible theoretical speculations supporting the thesis that an inverse relationship may sometimes exist between economic dimensions of the quality of life and individual achievements. This may arise, for example, when successful macro-economic growth performance of an economy is accompanied by a worsening of income and wealth distribution, increased poverty rates, and therefore a limited access by some individuals and groups to the basic necessities of life.

In other circumstances, a conflict may also arise between economic improvements and the march of freedom. The evidence suggests that the process of macroeconomic development may be accompanied by the atomization of people and the statistical manipulation of society by powerful central governments and state elites. In some instances, this has culminated in a pervasive condition of alienation in which people have come to forget that they can potentially live in a world of their own creation. Rather, human abilities have been construed as economic resources to be owned and disposed of at will. As a result, the larger majority of people in the developing world have become passive role-players or institutional decision makers who are incapable of changing their historical or socio-economic conditions.

Values and Ideology in Interpretation

There is still a lack of consensus about the actual or potential constitution of development, its underlying processes, and the appropriate policies and strategies for achieving it. This underscores the fact that its true meaning remains a matter of interpretation, and helps to highlight the hermeneutic tension that has historically suffused the development discourse. As a general proposition, there can be no appeal to knowledge, truth, meaning, or experience that escapes hermeneutics - the art and science of interpretation. Complex arrays of interpretive acts are embodied not only in formal academic and policy discourse, but in all facets of everyday life. They traverse a wide spectrum ranging from people's definitions of their own situations, how they express themselves, the rationality or irrationality of their actions, to their encounters with other people, societies, and cultures.

Thus, interpretation is a ubiquitous feature of all human activity and therefore lies at the heart of our entire approach to the social sciences and the study of development. In this context, the following pertinent questions can be asked about the value-orientations of social scientists and the conceptions of development to which they variously subscribe. First, are they disciples of Jesus, Mohammed, Confucius, Adam Smith, or Karl Marx? Second, do they identify with the poor, the rich, or the middle classes? Third, are they elitist, technocratic, or populist in orientation? Fourth, do they believe that authentic development is achievable under capitalism, socialism, or a social market economy?

Thus, while the search continues for universally acceptable or "objective" truths about the development phenomenon, the task remains inherently difficult, if not impossible, for no other reason than the fact that beliefs and evaluative standards tend to vary among development analysts, individuals and groups in society, and across societies and cultures. As Amartya Sen (1988: 1) eloquently remarks:

> There are many fundamentally different ways of seeing the quality of living, and quite a few of them have some immediate plausibility. You could be *well off* without being *well*. You could be *well*, without being able to live the life you *wanted*. You could have got the life you *wanted*, without being *happy*. You could be *happy*, without having much *freedom*. You could have a great deal of *freedom*, without achieving much (emphasis in original).

From this angle, the interpretation of development can be located within the age-old epistemological debate about the validity of "objective" vis-à-vis "subjective" or relativistic dimensions of truth. The issue boils down to whether social and economic reality is a mere concoction in the minds of social scientists, that is, a social construct, as distinct from the claim that there is a possibility of discovering objective truth. At one extreme, it is believed that all knowledge about development and related matters is contextual, that is, based on preconceptions that are conditioned by ideological, cultural, linguistic, and historically relative influences. This entails that the "reality" of development or underdevelopment does not exist apart from our psychological, socio-cultural, and mental forms of representation.

At the other end, the claim is that there might be an independent reality, or "brute facts" about the development-underdevelopment nexus, that is utterly indifferent to, and totally unaffected by, the concerns of development economists and other interested social scientists. From the perspective of what may be termed "development realism," the conditions of development may be far removed from the majority of authoritative pronouncements and corresponding consciousness about such affairs. The point of emphasis is that while an array of ideological and socio-cultural factors may influence our thinking, it does not necessarily follow that reality is nothing but the product of such influences.

As in most intellectual disagreements, the answer lies somewhere in between. While all statements about the world may be relative to our perspectives, this does not necessarily mean that academic representations do not refer to things that exist independently of our portrayals of them, such as people's daily lives in the developing world. It is at this point that critical interpretive analysis must come into play. The hermeneutic task always takes on added significance when it is perceived that the meaning of a particular phenomenon is unclear, confused, or contradictory, thereby requiring further clarification, explanation, and understanding. The process of attributing significance or meaning differs as much within cultures as between them. It also undergoes changes from one historical epoch to another and may even differ from person to person.

The problem posed for interpretive activity across cultures is that the true meanings of events, situations, or phenomena may not be as they seem to "us" as observers from outside. For example, the dust has not yet settled on the debate whether the behavior of small farmers or rural dwellers in the developing world is motivated more by cultural and community norms of cooperation than by the rational maximizing and individualistic calculus of the economist. Bets on a cockfight in Haiti, Afghanistan, or Bali are not just games but what Clifford Geertz calls "deep play," a dramatic form of status or social commentary. In the Balinese case, he has interpreted the cockfight in terms of a distinction between what appears to be going on "for us" and what is taking place "for them." As he remarks, "for it is only apparently cocks that are fighting there. Actually it is men" (Geertz 1973: 417).

The perspectival nature of interpretation suggests that all understanding is situation-bound, that is, from a given background or context. The implication is that the degree of understanding is inherently linked to the analyst's purposes, motivations, intentions, or what he or she is able to project unto the "text," or object of interpretation. Understanding is not passively neutral, but actively structures what it encounters. This entails a retreat from the totally disengaged stance of pure objectivity or absolutism. Many so-called "objective" measures or criteria are only apparently so. The hermeneutic or interpretive perspective helps to open our eyes to the fact that we are likely to distort our own investigations by assigning "objective" or "universal" criteria a privileged position of validity or truth over insights derived from specific historical and socio-cultural contexts.

The conclusion may be drawn that science and economics are socio-cultural practices whose "objectivity" are politically laden. Accordingly, interpretation is both a social and political practice. "That interpretation takes place within a context or background of beliefs and practices implies that it is social, and hence it is infused with political relations of power and domination" (Hiley, Bohman, and Shusterman 1991: 8). As a result, what Robert Merton terms the "Republic of science" is often superseded by the "psychology," "sociology," or "politics" of truth. This perspective is the starting point for the modern "sociology of knowledge."

In its extreme form, the claim is that all systems of knowledge are ideologies that are shaped by the economic elements of our class position, or well-defined sets of group interests. This worldview, traceable to Karl Marx's material conception of history, has been vigorously disputed by mainstream economists. The larger corpus of economics is grounded in a philosophical idealism that views ideas as the principal force for changing the world. Ideas originate by feeding on others in an endless progression, and knowledge essentially grows through clashes among contending ideas. By contrast, Marx's argument is that the real world is the main source of our ideas. Thus, the motive force for changing it is not provided by ideas but by class struggles or interest conflicts that are associated with society's productive forces. Therefore, economists are thought to favor idealism because it purportedly diverts attention from the real world of class antagonisms and vested interests.

The central but more moderate claim of sociology of knowledge can be stated in the following proposition. Since the social milieu tends to influence and at times even distort, our search for the truth, it becomes necessary to carefully weigh the ideological, moral, and socio-cultural bases of our belief systems and related knowledge claims. As previously indicated, it is impossible to observe segments of social and economic reality without preconceptions. These become a necessary prerequisite for organizing, interpreting, and giving meaning to people's life experiences and the world in which we live. Most disagreements among economists arise because they interpret experience according to certain preconceptions about the real world. The preconceptions may be explicit or implicit, and in the latter case they represent "unexpressed and unexamined assumptions" (Levins and Lewontin 1985: 267).

In this context, Schumpeter reminds us that statements based on ideologies are not "simply lies," but may actually represent truthful accounts of what people perceive as socio-economic reality. Under the circumstances, there is no need to divest ourselves of our ideologies, since they provide a "pre- and extra-scientific vision" of the way we see things. As such, they enter into the "preanalytic cognitive act" by which scientific propositions are formulated. Schumpeter continues that "[a]nalytic work begins with material provided by our *vision of things* and this *vision* is ideological almost by definition. It embodies the picture of things as we see them, and whether there is any possible motive for wishing to see them in a given rather than another light, the way we see things can hardly be distinguished from the way in which we wish to see them" (1954: 42).

Neither can "visions" be objectively tested, nor can their validity be inferred from the success of predictions derived from them. They represent general perspectives that help us to comprehend the world by structuring economic social, political, and germane forms of reality that are the subject matter of interpretation. Statements based on such visions are a classic case of metaphysical propositions. They cannot be tested in an empirical sense and, in principle, cannot be refuted or falsified. As a result, such propositions are usually thought to be meaningless. On the contrary, they are not abstract or meaningless, but usually say something meaningful about the real world. For example, the time-worn proposition that "all men are equal" can be construed as saying that, as moral agents, all human beings should be guaranteed equality of treatment unless some fundamental differences in cases can be rationally shown.

Ideological and evaluative perspectives enable us to attach "significance" to a variety of events, situations, and phenomena. How we attach such significance depends on our interests and therefore involves extra-scientific judgments. The overall conclusion is that progress in the study of economic development, as for all forms of social and economic inquiry, cannot be interpreted solely in terms of an analytical procedure in which the mind of the economist becomes a mere passive and disinterested conduit of so-called scientific and objective truths.

Given the same facts, economists with different beliefs, ontological commitments, epistemological presuppositions, value-orientations, and political motivations may arrive at diametrically opposed conclusions, for example, about the desirability or potential impact of a development program.

The aforementioned factors not only influence our appraisal of the truth, but also tend to shape our views about what is practically possible, the nature of our policy prescriptions, and therefore the form of economic and societal organization deemed desirable. However, this leaves the analyst in the uncomfortable position of total skepticism, in the sense that no particular form of knowledge or truth claim can be accepted as valid. While the problem posed by skepticism cannot be totally overcome, that is, we cannot avoid starting explanation and understanding from a background context of prejudgments, preconceptions, and ideological presuppositions, it is still possible to transcend this context through open-mindedness, or a willingness to appraise perspectives different from ours on their own merits. Indeed, this is the essence of enlightened conversation.

Paradigms and the Growth of Knowledge

The emphasis placed on interpretation helps to highlight the fact that the growth of knowledge about economic development, as for other subject areas, tends to be propagated through paradigms, scientific research programs, or clusters of interconnected theories and generalizations that are shaped by what we term "interpretive communities." The latter are normally bound together by consensual beliefs, research practices, methodological canons, and norms of institutionalized behavior. The philosopher Richard Rorty dubs this the "ethnocentric solidarity of public life," or the fact that certain background judgments or understandings are generally accepted without question within a particular community of scholars or cultural group.

The "insiders" in the group are assumed to have a privileged access to its corpus of theoretical postulates, empirical generalizations, policy prescriptions, and so on. As such, they come to accept as true whatever is the outcome of the normal discourse in the scientific community or culture at any given point in time, including criteria for knowledge and validity. In this context, one noted development economist speaks about "common standards of scholarship," which "assert the universality and the solidarity of any one scholar with the international fraternity of all other scholars." As he continues, "[c]ommitment to the search for knowledge, to scientific objectivity, and to telling the truth as one sees it, know no national frontiers. . . . [T]here cannot be African, Asian, or Latin American criteria for truth and validity. Mining companies can be nationalized, criteria for truth cannot. . . . *There may be an African economics, distinct from European economics; there can be no African truth*" (Streeten 1974: 1293, 1294; emphasis in original).

These sentiments help to explain why the development discourse as we know it originated and matured in North America and Europe where specialists converse with each other in the pages of academic journals, the corridors of academia, government offices, and international lending agencies. Much of the conversation lacks the classic elements of a "dance" and remains an intellectual "game" that is far removed from the daily lives of the people that matter. The dominant discourse has been driven by an "orthodox consensus," which has endured since the early days of British classical political economy. The motive force has been provided by a consensual paradigm that boasts its own pre-ordained logic, ideological presuppositions, and therefore preferred modes of interpreting development and underdevelopment.

It must be admitted that the term "paradigm" still continues to be used rather loosely. We are mindful of Humpty Dumpty's injunction to Alice in Wonderland that "words mean what I want them to mean." Without throwing caution to the wind, the term may be used in an all-inclusive sense to connote the broadest unit of consensus within an academic discipline or subdiscipline. Contextually, a paradigm constitutes the underlying basic idea of what economists and other social scientists are trying to interpret, explain, and understand. It is typically articulated through the language or preferred kinds of cognitive statements practitioners use in writing or talking about things, events, or situations. As such, a paradigm tends to delimit the nature and boundaries of the subject matter, the kinds of questions we are prepared to ask, and the types of answers that are deemed acceptable.

This characterization is akin to the view of Thomas Kuhn (1962) about the "community-fine" structure of science. The idea is that the possibilities for the growth of scientific knowledge are always inextricably linked to the historical, psychological, and socio-cultural practices that influence the belief patterns of economists and other social scientists. This perspective derives from a recognition that in intellectual discourse fundamental ideas tend to guide our perceptions, and they are not simply the results of "facts" we have observed. However, we part company with Kuhn in one important respect. His major concern was with the natural sciences, since he considered the social sciences to be at a "pre-paradigmatic" stage. On the contrary, all social science disciplines, including subfields such as development economics, are "multiple-paradigmatic" rather than pre-paradigmatic. As Masterman states, "far from being no paradigm, there are on the contrary too many" (1976: 74).

Like its parent economics discipline, the development discourse has evolved through the perspectival intermeshing of ideological preconceptions, theoretical postulates, empirical generalizations, and policy prescriptions. As such it consists of rival interpretive communities subscribing to different normative beliefs, conceptions of social and economic reality, and criteria for explanatory adequacy and causation. The ruling corpus of development thought and policy has come to reflect the past successes and failures of mainstream economics, as exemplified by classical, neo-classical, Keynesian, and Marxian paradigms or research programs. As demonstrated in this book, the major theoretical interpretations and policy perspectives of development have roughly followed in the footsteps of general economics. At the same time, development economics has been involved in a constant search for its own autonomy and relevance, on the grounds that different economic principles apply to the more developed vis-à-vis less developed countries. The paradigmatic underpinnings of both the mainstream economics and development conversations help to explain why certain clusters of ideas, sequences of interconnected theories, and policy options have retained their tenacity even in the face of potent challenges from rivals. Nobel Laureate George Stigler (1959) has cited the conservative training economists as a scientific group undergo as one of the main reasons for paradigm tenacity. The process of professional education, he contends, tends to heighten beliefs in the reverence for the timelessness and universality of institutions, values, modes of thought, and techniques for problem solving. Under the circumstances, the practice of economics provides a "psychic balm," in the sense that it merely tries to promote "order," "coherence," and "timelessness" (Shackle 1967).

Thus, dominant paradigms and their supporting research programs tend to provide an emotional need by setting minds at rest. As long as the conceptual structure remains satisfactory, models and theories that put all relevant facts into orderly and schematic "black boxes" tend to absolve analysts from critical thinking and interpretive analysis. Of course, this is not meant to deny that the intellectual activity involved in paradigm articulation typically calls for intense and protracted effort.

Rather, the point of emphasis is that the relative strength of a given paradigm or scientific research program usually lies in the extent to which it permits such an effort, while allowing for hypotheses and theories to be generated within a well-defined conceptual structure, instead of having to be applied to a definition of the structure itself. As Loasby (1976) argues, this permits analysts to concentrate on questions of a short-term import. The task of providing answers to questions of a more long-term significance proves to be much more uncomfortable, since this calls for a re-examination of the nature and scope of the discipline itself.

Like its parent, development economics has undergone a number of "problem" or "paradigm shifts" in its theoretical and policy orientation. During the early days of its modern evolution, development economics became a more or less autonomous subfield of the economics discipline, and was primarily concerned with carving out a well-defined corpus of ideas and supporting conceptual structure purporting to explain causes of underdevelopment and how poor countries can become rich. As emphasized in this book, however, the field never became fully independent, and the boundaries of its discourse were always circumscribed by the paradigmatic structure of its parent. Due to the influence of Marxian, Keynesian, and structuralist perspectives of thought, the development discourse was able to stray off the beaten track here and there. Nevertheless, its recapture and integration into the mainstream economics fold have now been completed.

As a result, the development debate has now turned full circle and is now replete with gory neo-classical, "new" classical, and libertarian perorations about the evils of government failure and "irrational dirigisme." One reason is that the ideas of development economics have more often than not been used as a justification for unworkable, inefficient, and inequitable policies in the developing world. In the large majority of cases, sustained economic growth and possibilities for authentic and broad-based development have been impeded rather than encouraged. Even in those few cases where some modicum of development success has been realized, its configurations have turned out to be different from those articulated by the pioneers of development economics.

Theory, Causation, and Policy

Underlying the dominant intellectual discourse is a value judgment, albeit implicit, that the general aim of science is to construct "good" or valid theories. Nevertheless, the concept of a "theory" remains emotionally laden and elusive. In a very loose and general sense, a theory refers to a hypothesis or sets of hypotheses that are proposed as a means of explaining some phenomena or sets of events. In this general sense, it merely represents a set of ideas or assumptions about something. In other words, it is not a statement offered for scientific testing, nor is it necessarily based on observation. In other cases, a theory can take the form of a hypothesis or sets of hypotheses that can be immediately tested by observation. Even in such cases, it can remain highly speculative or conjectural.

Coming nearer to normal discourse or accepted scientific practice, a theory is thought to represent an empirically grounded generalization, which is purportedly a system of ideas or statements providing explanation of a group of facts or phenomena. In this case, the relevant hypotheses or statements are established, "confirmed," or "corroborated" by observation or experiment, that is, they are propounded and accepted as accounting for the known facts. In this sense, a theory becomes a statement of what are held to be general laws, principles, or *causes* of something known or observed. Contextually, a common expectation is that theories, as intellectual toolkits, would enable economists and other analysts to make sense of events or situations under study, predict the behavior of social phenomena, and ultimately design appropriate guides for policy and action. A related expectation is that the application of these toolkits to diverse situations would lead to a modification or change in old habits as the situation demands.

It is in this sense that theorizing becomes an essential device for interpreting, reinterpreting, and synthesizing established laws, and modifying them to fit circumstances that were unanticipated at the time of their conception. Based on this "reconstituted logic," the intellectual discourse can then be guided toward the discovery of more and more powerful generalizations. Accordingly, Kaplan (1964) reminds us that to engage in theorizing does not just mean to learn from experience, but rather to think more carefully about what there is to be learned. It is only then that economists and other social scientists will be able to devise appropriate policy prescriptions for changing given forms of reality into others.

Such an optimistic goal must remain unfulfilled if theory construction becomes predominantly a heuristic device in which facts are made to fit theories, rather than the other way around. Disagreements about the meaning and appropriate role of theory are related to the fact that our *attitudes to reality*, or ways of viewing the world, tend to vary. They range from perspectives that stress bases external to human beings at one end to the most subjective at the other. As indicated earlier, these attitudes derive their substance from a variety of sources including ontological, ethical, socio-cultural, and epistemological commitments and convictions. In turn, they serve as essential guides for collecting relevant information, hypothesis testing, and theory generation. While no hard and fast methods of classification exist, four broad categories are identified in Table 1.1 for purposes of illustration.

Thus, paradigms are normally articulated through a process of theory construction and validation, which begins with the identification of concepts that purportedly point to features of the environment that are apparently relevant to the phenomena being studied. Examples are concepts such as "income," "economic growth," and "market" in economics and "society," "status," and "class" in sociology. The common practice is to express such concepts in neutral language or mathematical symbols, the objective being one of communicating a uniform or shared meaning to the scientific community. Concepts also typically display varying degrees of abstractness. Some seek to identify phenomena that cannot be concretely located in time and space, while others are meant to depict concrete phenomena at specific times and locations. For example, theoretical concepts do not have exclusive spatio-temporal referents, while empirical concepts tend to display such a quality, that is, they refer to perceivable or discrete events and phenomena.

In the standard practice, the theorist shows a preference for abstract or theoretical concepts because the latter tend to transcend particular events and situations, and purportedly reflect common properties of similar situations and events. Nevertheless, such concepts should be relevant to observable situations, that is, we have to make sense of them. In other words, their usefulness ultimately depends on the extent to which they can be utilized in specific empirical observations. In order to be applicable to the real world, concepts

Table 1.1

Attitudes of Reality: The Bases of Theory

Typology	Description
Immanent	Explains characteristics of the external world based on assumptions about their inherent nature, for example, Platonism.
Teleological	Based on Greek *telos* ("end" or "goal"), explanation that is rooted in notion that structures and processes of nature are fitted together to bring about determinate results, for example, the Aristotelian belief that reality can be properly studied from the perspective of self-justified parts.
Idealist-Essentialist or Functionalist	Dominant belief or "orthodox consensus" that phenomena in the real world can be shown to be instances of recurrent and predictable regularities in which form and function are connected.
Realist-Existentialist	Explanation based on attempt to penetrate behind external appearances or "surface structures" as a means of discovering the real causal mechanisms or "deep structures" that lie behind reality. Belief that no meaningful distinction can be drawn between "facts" and "values," and economic and social laws are not independent of historical structures. External reality does not exist independently of our preferred concepts, perceptions, and interpretations.

have to be supplemented by operational definitions, which describe procedures for identifying particular events and situations to which they are supposed to refer.

A distinction is also sometimes made between two other types of basic concepts - descriptive ones and variables. The former simply label phenomena - for example, the concepts of "economy" and "society" - and do not necessarily reflect the ways in which such phenomena vary in terms of size and growth. By contrast, variables provide some indication of changing properties of phenomena, or the extent to which they differ. Variables are crucial to the explanation, understanding, and prediction of events because they help us to visualize how variations in one set of phenomena are associated with, or can cause or produce, variations in others.

Concepts become theories when they are organized into groups of statements that express close associations or causal connections among variables in the real world or the phenomena under study. Such statements can take either a theoretical or observational form. Theoretical statements employ theoretical concepts whose referents are not actual or conceivable events in the phenomenal world, and are therefore capable of being interpreted independently of such events. By contrast, observational statements refer to perceivable or discrete events and phenomena. It is also possible to derive observational statements from theoretical ones by using operational definitions of concepts.

One class of theoretical statements merely tells us when and where instances of particular concepts exist in the real world. For example, a concept G (economic growth) will exist under conditions C (rapid capital accumulation) and E (export growth). Another class of theoretical statements is usually more complex in the sense of predicting or anticipating how two concepts will occur and vary in some determinate fashion. For example, G (economic growth) and D (authentic development) will become associated through the previous conditions C and E, plus Q (an improvement in living standards) and F(a spread of participatory democracy and freedom). The latter type of theoretical statement is crucial to the theoretical enterprise, since it is only by determining the nature of the relationships among concepts that it becomes possible to understand, explain, and predict events in the real world of complexity.

As mentioned earlier, the underlying relationships among variables can take either of two forms - associational or causal. In the former case, the relationship is simply one in which variations in phenomena take place together, that is, they are associated or correlated. However, it provides no indication whether some measure of causal connection exists. By contrast, a causal relationship tends to show how the variable properties of one set of concepts and their related phenomena *cause* the occurrence of variable properties of other concepts and germane phenomena. One hallmark of causal regularity is that the cause must somehow have the power to produce the effect, that is, it must be logically and intrinsically related to it. While regular association may be taken as evidence that some degree of causal connection exists, this is by no means a sufficient condition. The true meaning of causation somewhat implies that there should be some "generative" or "natural" mechanism linking cause and effect.

Statements about causal relationships are either deterministic or probabilistic. A deterministic statement usually takes the form: "under conditions C, E, Q, and F, if G occurs, D *will* or *must* occur." Such statements are unrealistic, even though they abound in economics and other social sciences. One is on safer grounds with probabilistic statements, which typically take the form: "under conditions C, E, Q, and F, if G occurs, D will occur with a certain probability (PB), where (PB) has a certain probability value of, say, 50 or 80 percent, as the case may be. As shown later in this book, problems raised by deterministic and probabilistic statements help to explain why issues of causality remain a nightmare for economists.

The appropriateness of theories ultimately depends on their ability to provide adequate answers to fundamental questions. Economists typically search for higher and higher levels of generality for their theories by successively testing them against more and more empirical evidence. In this procedure, explanation at the highest level is usually based on a search for the most abstract variables and concepts with the objective of bringing the largest possible number of cases or instances within the scope of the theories in question. However, the search for generality may actually detract from the usefulness of theoretical explanations. The reason is that causes differ, and phenomena or events can be explained at different levels and with varying degrees of specificity and usefulness.

This is particularly true about the study of developing countries where the class of phenomena being investigated may be of a different genre from that encountered in the more developed sector of the world. Nevertheless, like its parent, development economics must rely on certain general rules for appraising the explanatory power or adequacy of its theoretical constructs. The most commonly cited ones refer to the scope, fertility, comprehensiveness, and coherence of theories. The broader the range of phenomena that come under a theory's purview, the more elaborate and useful it is likely to be. For example, a theory based on the hypothesis that investment determines economic growth or development can be elaborated to include causal or explanatory factors such as entrepreneurship, political leadership, good governance, the structure of institutions, and the nature of incentives.

The coherence or internal consistency of a theory implies that the conclusions should follow logically from its stated assumptions and premises. In this context, a burning question remains whether the stated assumptions of a rigorously formulated theory should contradict observations derived from the world of experience. Nobel Laureate Milton Friedman (1953) has posited that economic "science" is primarily concerned with prediction rather than explanation or understanding. From this perspective, any implication of a theory whose validity has not yet been established should be considered a prediction of the theory, even if it is not concerned with the future.

Friedman's argument, therefore, is that as long as economic theory generates falsifiable predictions, there should be no concern about the validity of its assumptions. In particular, where these assumptions refer to people's values and beliefs, no question should be asked about their origin or constitution. This philosophy suggests that economists should tenaciously subscribe to a faith that there exists some independent body of truth in the discipline and that its properties can be discerned independently of value judgments. As previously emphasized, however, all forms of social and economic analysis have moral or ideological dimensions. These result in "distorted communication" (Diesing 1982) and emotional controversies over apparently sterile "facts."

In both mainstream economics and the development discourse opposing interpretations are not only distorted, but also conclusively "refuted" and then largely ignored. More generally, it can be argued that economics and its subfields have been crippled by detachment from moral and political commitment. This is particularly relevant in the practical world, since it is through policies that people's lives can be changed for the better. Under the circumstances, theoretical constructs should enable us to generate coherent policy prescriptions, and to trace and compare their effects on, and consequences for, alternative human futures.

Inherent in the different perspectives of development examined in this book are specific policy scenarios for solving perceived economic problems. These are often consistent with broadly accepted value judgments, or the "unexpressed or hidden assumptions," about human nature and conduct. In the typical case, the policies advocated for desirable human futures are based on description and theoretical interpretation of past and present, with the links between fact, theory, and prescription logically articulated from assumptions to conclusion. In general, each theoretical perspective points to "an area as matching its description, carefully displays the logic of its argument, and arrives at appropriate policy conclusions" (Cole, Cameron, and Edwards 1991: 5).

Ideally, theory should play an instrumental role in generating implications about the real world, and corresponding policy proposals should be grounded on perceptions about the available facts. As demonstrated elsewhere in this book, good policies do not stem merely from theories articulating the relationship between relative prices and optimal allocation of resources, but rather depend on the institutions of society to which they apply. These, in turn, tend to shape the equilibrium positions society reaches and the possibilities for attaining socially optimal or desirable levels of development. Institutional arrangements take on added significance when a balance has to be effectuated between conflicting policy options.

Of particular relevance is the role of economists vis-à-vis political actors in the formulation and execution of policies and strategies. Keynes' oft-quoted remark (1936: 383) can be used as an example. As he states:

> The ideas of economists and political philosophers, both when they are right and when they are wrong, are more powerful than is commonly understood. Indeed the world is ruled by little else. Practical men, who believe themselves to be quite exempt from any intellectual influences, are usually the slaves of some defunct economist. Madmen in authority, who hear voices in the air, are distilling their frenzy from some academic scribbler of a few years back.

Yet, by themselves, economists and other policy scientists rarely decide the development orientations of societies. The effectiveness of their theories and policy prescriptions is always mediated by government and other institutions, and most importantly, by the political conjuncture. While politicians and ruling elites are often prone to rationalize their strategic agendas by quoting from some "academic scribbler," this is not tantamount to a generalized tendency to adopt development ideas or reforms because some famous academics recommended them. The ultimate responsibility usually devolves on the political system, which depends on the amount of power vested in the government machinery and the structural arrangements linking the bureaucratic apparatus to social classes, interest groups, and individuals in society.

The political system is the mechanism through which a consensus can be forged about the ultimate ends of development and the acceptable means for achieving them. It is typically mirrored by the nature of the political regime, dimensions of group competition, and transitory political circumstances, - for example, electoral cycles, that permit changes in political regimes. In this context, it can be said that all societies must face crucial choices about the collective welfare of the people and have to devise rules for making such choices. Even in the face of conflicting interests and values, governments must face the task of accomplishing those goals which ordinary citizens cannot effectively realize on their own. Ideally, what the polity does should reflect the broader set of consensual values, or what is variously termed the "public interest," "general will," or "common good." Such values reflect preferences for specific types of policy choices and therefore reveal the degree of political commitment to the goals of human betterment.

The nature of a society and its development orientation are closely reflected by the sorts of people it permits to hold high offices and the corresponding quality of its political leadership. This very fact throws up a "vicious circle" in the development equation. On the one hand, an appropriate socio-cultural dynamic is a necessary prerequisite for the emergence and nurturing of a development-oriented political leadership. On the other hand, unless the relevant political cadres are imbued with appropriate values, they will not be prone to introduce needed economic changes. It goes without saying that no form of development can take place if the ruling political elite is resolutely opposed to it. Moreover, even if a society produces a development-oriented political leadership willing to introduce good policies, these may not get off the ground or may be poorly implemented because of class, ethnic, and related cleavages.

In conclusion, the success or failure of development efforts, that is, whether goals are achieved and policy instruments are effective, ultimately depends on the political environment or context in which decisions are made, objectives formulated and pursued, and the processes and procedures associated with alternative development agendas. The political processes refer to the mechanisms by which development agendas are generated, including chosen modes of articulating decisions and inducing participation and commitment. The political procedures encapsulate (a) the framework, criteria, and sequences in which various actors are identified and participate; (b) the hierarchical assignment of roles to different layers of leadership; and (c) modalities for participation, or rationales for the inclusion or exclusion of diverse groups in the respective processes.

The interaction between the processes and procedures is ultimately responsible for determining the extent to which the political system will be responsive to the needs of the citizenry. Of particular significance is the amount of information that is made available to the populace at large and its involvement in the selection and articulation of national development goals as well as the means to achieve them. It is the nature of such participation that essentially drives perceptions about the integrity, credibility, and legitimacy of the political process. In the final analysis, alternative theories and perspectives of development and underdevelopment cannot be distanced from such real life concerns.

II

HISTORICAL VOICES AND INTERPRETATIONS

Chapter 2

Classical Political Economy: Origins of the Economic Development Paradigm

In his "Roots of Development Theory," Nobel Laureate Sir Arthur Lewis posited that the "theory of economic development established itself in Britain in the century and a half running from about 1650 to Adam Smith's *The Wealth of Nations* (1776) [and that] much of the development theory of today is already to be found in the writings of the eighteenth century" (1988: 28). This is part of a widespread perception that almost everything which has been said about economic development has its roots in classical political economy. Six of its major stalwarts are identified in Table 2.1 for ease of reference.

Needless to say, their ideological preconceptions and belief systems differed, ranging from the conservative or orthodox at one end of the paradigmatic spectrum to the radical heterodox or revolutionary at the other. Despite their disparate development perspectives, they raised a number of unresolved interpretive problems that remain central to both political economy and the development debate. These include, inter alia, the following: (i) the potential role of individual choice and freely competitive markets vis-à-vis government coercion in transforming societies from poverty to riches; (ii) the interplay between capitalistic forms of organization, growth of human populations, natural resource scarcity, technological progress, and persistent poverty; (iii) the trade-off between economic growth and distribution, or between efficiency and equity or distributive justice; (iv) the role of agriculture vis-à-vis industry and free trade in the economic transformation process; and (v) whether the development process is smooth, linear, and evolutionary, or discontinuous, revolutionary, and dialectical in nature.

In classical political economy, both theoretical hypotheses and empirical generalizations were used as interpretive tools to generate "covering laws" that

Table 2.1

Classical Economists

Major Theorist	Visionary Works
David Hume (1711-1776)	*A Treatise on Human Nature* (1739)
Adam Smith (1723-1790)	*Theory of Moral Sentiments* (1759) *An Inquiry into the Nature and Causes of the Wealth of Nations* (1776)
T. R. Malthus (1766-1834)	*An Essay on the Principle of Population* (1798)
David Ricardo (1772-1823)	*Principles of Political Economy and Taxation* (1817)
J. S. Mill (1806-1873)	*Essays on Some Unsettled Questions on Political Economy* (1844) *Principles of Political Economy* (1909)
Karl Marx (1818-1883)	*Manifesto of the Communist Party* (1848) [with Friedrich Engels] *Capital* (1867)

were supposed to express timeless truths. The main body of thought was concerned with development problems, since the subject matter of development economics was not materially different from that of general economics. In this context, development was interpreted as human progress, so that the task of the overall economic enterprise was conceptualized in terms of its potential contribution to individual human betterment. The overriding concern with progress meant that development was viewed as a moral problem rather than just one of achieving set levels of technical and economic efficiency.

Individual Achievement and Natural Order of Progress

Mainstream or orthodox classical political economy was instrumental in ushering in a liberal tradition in social and economic thought since individual liberty was considered a precondition for the establishment of a just and progressive economic order. The overall vision was grounded in a belief that human progress or development constituted the ruling tendency in all human affairs. The collective development ontology can therefore be construed as a belief in a "natural order of progress." This was based on a presupposition that the world was ordered in terms of certain universal and immutable laws derived from assumptions about human nature.

The worldview was premised on the existence of a unified natural order operating in accordance with the principles underlying the behavior of freely competitive (atomistic) markets and the normative belief that they would produce optimal levels of individual and social progress. This preconception saw the emergence of what has become the dominant paradigmatic thrust of orthodox economics, that is, the idea of economic equilibrium via a self-regulating market mechanism. Application of the equilibrium principle to explain relationships among economic magnitudes inheres in two related tenets: (i) all market transactions are governed by the mutual exchange or interaction of all "values" and prices; and (ii) any goods supplied during the natural course of production activities would be normally matched by a demand corresponding to the exchange values or prices of these goods.

Thus, beginning with classical political economy, alternative economic analyses, including the study of development, have come to be rooted in different theories or understandings of "value." The latter is associated with exchange between consumers and producers. As the starting point for comparing alternative perspectives of economic analysis, value reflects the subjective preference of consumers, the cost of producing goods and services, and the social priority attached to them. A fundamental belief was that the behavior of self-interested individual economic agents is essentially guided by a search for maximum satisfaction or benefits in a relatively free and competitive market environment. It was also assumed that such individualistic behavior would produce maximum benefits for society as a whole.

The modern economist's concept of "economizing," or economic maximizing subject to constraints, is a direct derivative of this perspective. The dominant paradigm in economics consists of a universal application of this principle to all situations and country contexts. This raises a number of "meta-questions" that are significant to the study of both economics and economic development: (i) what does it mean to economize? (ii) across countries and cultures, should the basic postulates of economics be taken on faith? and (iii) do all human beings want more money?

The answer provided by Adam Smith has endured over the centuries. He considered it an incontrovertible law of nature the inherent propensity of all human beings to want to better their own economic circumstances. In his *Wealth of Nations* [hereafter *Wealth*], Smith postulated that the quest for human betterment is reflected in a "desire of bettering our condition, a desire which, although generally calm and dispassionate, comes with us from the womb and never leaves us till we go to the grave. . . . There is scarce perhaps a signal instant in which any man is so perfectly and completely satisfied with his situation, as to be without any wish of alteration or improvement of any kind" (*Wealth*, Bk. 1: 341).

Smith's optimism reflected a confidence in the natural selfishness of people and their willingness to pursue their individual self-interests in accordance with the harmony of interests in society as a whole. In his view, God or nature endowed them with certain instincts, and in particular, "a certain propensity in human nature . . . . to truck, barter, and exchange one thing for another. . . . [which] is common to all men" (*Wealth*: 25). These instincts, combined with the "uniform" and "uninterrupted" attempt to become wealthy, impelled people to work harder, save more money, and produce more goods needed by society, thereby enriching society as a whole. While people were supposed to have these natural inclinations, the caveat was added that the natural order was not necessarily spontaneous. Under the circumstances, people had to behave wisely and sensibly in order to progress.

At the beginning of *Wealth*, the concept of equilibrium is invoked as a means of uncovering the causal laws explaining national wealth and the economic policies that can increase it. The division of labor, or specialization, was identified as the primary mechanism driving the process. Smith imputed to specialization not only improvements in skill, dexterity, and the gains accruing from the saving of time, but virtually all technical progress and the expansion of new investment. A growing economy based on increased specialization was seen as requiring increasing volumes of trade and a market system capable of handling such transactions efficiently. Furthermore, since the division of labor was assumed to be limited by the size of the market, a liberal economic policy was deemed a necessary prerequisite for widening the market, as well as for promoting specialization and augmenting investment. The overall system reached equilibrium through the unfettered play of market forces, with the "invisible hand" providing optimal economic benefits for all members of society. The "invisible hand" is the metaphysical concept used by Smith to indicate the covert intervention of the Deity into human affairs.

His model of the "natural order of progress" was substantially influenced by the philosophies of Sir Isaac Newton and John Locke. The Newtonian perspective of classical mechanics, or the picture of the cosmic universe, provided the basic model for observing social and economic magnitudes. The guiding principle was the existence of a rational and orderly universe whose behavior could be predicted with mathematical certainty. The operation of the Newtonian system was predicated on the idea that all bodies included in it could be regarded as an aggregate of an elementary indivisible unit - the atom. A basic assumption was that no atom is lost in the movement of bodies, and that atomic relationships are determined by the principle of action and reaction.

The Newtonian concept of mutual relationships among physical bodies was the starting point of Smith's belief that a "plan" undergirded nature's operations. Thus, he saw economic systems as resembling machines and searched for a small number of mechanical devices to explain highly complex and diverse phenomena. The Newtonian order was blended with Lockean ideas about natural rights through the concept of an economic system built on atomistic markets, free trade, and the pursuit of individual self-interest. Locke's social contract theory posited that people tend to maintain the social order on the basis of expectations that they would be better able to satisfy their individual needs. His "benefits/utility" calculus rested on the premise that the social order emanates from a value consensus, that is, people are socialized to accept common societal values and ends through their individualistic expectations.

Contextually, Adam Smith expressed the conviction that nature was working through human sentiments to establish a harmonious social order and to ensure a continuous increase in national wealth. The overall philosophy is that people tend to organize social and economic relationships in accordance with their own interests, and that society constitutes no more than a collection of individuals joined together by some form of social contract. Furthermore, the pursuit of self-interest makes individual behavior the goal and standard of moral conduct.

The main empirical laboratory of classical political economy was the historical growth experience of Britain and other European nations. This, in turn, provided the basis for generalizations about the "naturalness" of economic growth. Economists and economic historians sometimes distinguish between "extensive" and "intensive" growth, and characterize world history in terms of long periods of gradual extensive growth and the emergence of short bubbles of intensive growth. Extensive growth is defined as an expansion of aggregate output (GDP), without any corresponding increases in per capita income. This means that any increase in output or an economy's capacity to produce is fully absorbed by population growth. Intensive growth occurs when there is a simultaneous expansion in aggregate output, population, and income per person. This means that a country's GDP or output capacity is rising appreciably faster than its population (Reynolds 1983).

Periods of extensive growth lasted approximately from 1500 to 1800 for countries now considered to be industrialized or developed. On average, such countries displayed the following structural characteristics. First, they were mainly "traditional" or "subsistence" economies in which the majority of the population lived in rural areas. Household production was the dominant form of socio-economic organization, that is, most economic activity was family-oriented. Second, with the expansion of trade routes, there was an increasing movement toward diversification of the production structure and commercialization. Though the industrial era had not yet arrived, the period witnessed a substantial growth in towns, markets, manufacturing by handicraft methods, and the exchange of goods between town and country.

Third, the engine of population growth was driven by an excess of births over deaths. At this stage of the demographic transition, both fertility and mortality rates were relatively high. The former was influenced by uncontrollable reproduction and the latter by war, famines, plagues, and other natural disasters. Nevertheless, the growing population was able to feed itself at a near subsistence level by spreading out its numbers over an extended area of cultivation. Fourth, the growth in agricultural output, industrial production, and population marched in tandem. Correlatively, there was a gradual shift in the locus of manufacturing activity from households to specialized workshops, cottage industries, and later to factory production.

The period after 1800 was marked by a general trend toward intensive economic dynamism. The epoch of intensive growth lasted for about two centuries, with bubbles between 1850-1914 and 1945-1973. The idea of progress was to spread from Britain to other countries in Western Europe, and through European expansion, to new areas of European settlement. As the data in Table 2.2 show, average per capita income in Europe had reached $200 (in 1960 U.S. dollars) by the beginning of the nineteenth century, with that of Britain standing at $343, or 72 percent above the European average. On the comparative basis, the average per capita income in Asian and African countries in 1950 was approximately $150, or about 30 percent below the average level attained by European countries in 1800. By 1860, Britain and the core nations of Western Europe were in the heyday of the industrial revolution, and most of them had more or less doubled their per capita incomes.

Given the empirical reality of economic growth, a major thrust of orthodox classical political economy consisted of an attempt to uncover causal laws that purport to explain how it is generated. As previously emphasized, the economic growth process was considered to be natural and automatic in the sense that it would take care of itself through the free play of market forces and individual human motivation. The dynamics of growth were conceptualized at several levels of aggregation and disaggregation. At the macro-level, the tendency was to examine the economy as a whole as a means of delineating the conditions underlying sustained levels of prosperity. In this process, short-run changes can only be meaningfully understood in the context of changes taking place over the

Table 2.2

Per Capita GNP in Europe, 1800 and 1860
(in 1960 US dollars)

Country	1800	1860
Great Britain	343	558
Earliest industrialized Western Europe	211	454
Scandinavia	193	273
Mediterranean countries	203	309
Eastern Europe	170	180
Austria-Hungary	190	288
European average	199	310

Source: Paul Bairoch, "Europe's Gross National Product, 1800-1975." *Journal of European Economic History*, Vol. 5, No. 2, 1976, p. 279. The figures for 1800 are based on a year average and those for 1860 on a three-year average. *Earliest industrialized Western Europe* includes Germany, France, Switzerland, and Belgium; *Scandinavia* includes Denmark, Finland, Norway, and Sweden; the *Mediterranean* countries include Greece, Italy, Portugal, Spain, and Serbia; *Eastern Europe* refers to data for Bulgarian Russia and Romania.

longer run, and the inherent dynamics of the economic system can only be interpreted from the larger perspective of institutional arrangements that inhere in the social and political system.

Thus, the philosophical orientation was rooted in the broader dimensions of political economy rather than in narrower economic relations. The institutional arrangements, stemming as they do from the more embracing social order, were considered to be intrinsic components of economic dynamics. Accordingly, Baumol (1959) has explained the analytical thrust of classical political economy in terms of a "magnificent dynamics" based on two broad features. It was "magnificent" because it utilized bold and sweeping generalizations to analyze the development of the entire economy over long periods of time. Its "dynamic" nature reflected the emphasis placed on functional dependence of variable quantities in one time period on those of another. For example, economic growth over the long run is dependent on past and present levels of capital accumulation, labor productivity, technological progress, and economic organization.

In this context, the economic growth process is linked conceptually to the properties of a viable and self-sustaining economy. In a technical sense, a necessary condition for viability and sustainability is that the value of inputs or factors of production utilized should at least be equal to the value of output generated by this process. Thus, the nature of the economic growth process depends on the extent to which the economy is able to produce a net output, or surplus of output over inputs, as well as its ability to make the most efficient or best available use of this surplus (Walsh and Gram 1980). On an overall basis, therefore, it was postulated that an economy's capacity to grow required that the technology of production should yield a net output or surplus over the value of the inputs utilized.

The inputs should be interpreted in both a narrow and broad sense. In the former case, they refer to the standard factors of production such as land, labor, and capital. In the latter sense, they reflect the dynamic effects on economic growth produced by a host of interdependent factors: investment, labor specialization, improvements in knowledge and skills, entrepreneurship, protection of private property, free trade, and good governance. In this context, the classical formulation of organic economic growth was to lay the foundations for the development debate which took place over the next two centuries.

Growth, Distribution, and Human Misery

A central theme in classical political economy, as in the modern development debate, revolves around distribution of the overall economic pie and how it can be utilized, either in the form of consumption or saving, to promote economic growth and development in the future. In general, classical economists assumed a mutual interdependence between growth and distribution during the course of economic transformation, and pointed to the relatively weak bargaining strength of workers vis-à-vis other economic classes. An implicit value judgment was made that each factor of production, including labor, was entitled to what it produced. Nevertheless, there were crucial disagreements about the nature of the relationship between economic growth and distributive justice.

Economists typically distinguish between two alternative perspectives of income/assets distribution. One is the "functional" distribution, which refers to the shares of a given country's national income accruing to primary factors of production - land, labor, and capital. The other is the "size" distribution, or the percentage shares of national income (for example, deciles or quintiles) that go to various income recipients. Classical political economy was primarily concerned with the functional distribution of income. Accordingly, different social philosophies were marshalled in order to lay bare the social and class relations undergirding the capitalist mode of production.

Despite major differences in perspectives, many classical economists accepted the capitalist system and its class relations as they found them. Thus, their analyses relied on a number of assumptions about the system's structure and functioning. First, members of the laboring class did (do) not own or control any material resources and therefore had (have) to sell their labor power in the market for subsistence wages. The labor supply was assumed to be infinitely elastic due to the impact of population growth or chronic unemployment. Second, landlords owned property in land, the supply of which was assumed to be fixed. Due to the expansion of agriculture, land rent tended to increase as the economy progressed, thereby enabling landowners to earn a surplus above subsistence. This provided them with the means to accumulate, and to the extent that they did, rent was transferred via accumulation into capital. Third, capitalists possessed the resources by which they could hire the factors of production owned by other classes, and earn profits, that is, the surplus remaining after payments were made for rent to landlords and wages to labor.

Both Adam Smith and David Ricardo saw the functional distribution of factor shares as depending primarily on economic choices with respect to the technology of production, and to some extent on the prevailing socio-cultural milieu. Primary emphasis was placed on the consequences of shifts in the distribution between rent, wages, and profits for capital accumulation and economic growth, with profit expectations playing the pivotal role. In this context, capital accumulation was thought to provide the necessary sustenance to the additional labor needed to permit the growth of wealth, while innovation made it possible for a given quantity of labor to become more productive. The classical emphasis on the interdependence between growth and distribution should be interpreted in this light. While the stage of economic development and supporting processes of economic growth affect the distribution of income and wealth in society, the pattern of distribution, in turn, determines the possibilities for sustained growth and development.

More than Smith and Ricardo, John Stuart Mill recognized that the institutional structure of an economy plays a critical role in determining distributional outcomes. In his view, while the technical conditions of production tend to determine the amount of economic surplus generated, society's institutions are primarily responsible for earmarking the social classes that would receive it. He argued that the outcomes of economic theory and the technology of production could not be meaningfully divorced from social philosophy. In his *Principles of Political Economy* (especially Book 4, Chapter 7), he rejected capitalism as he found it because of its "sufferings and injustices."

Mill's argument, still relevant today, was that where a laboring class depends on another class of employers for work and subsistence, a conflict would inevitably arise between employers and employees, and that this conflict would intensify as workers become more aware of their rights. In the Britain of his day, the overwhelming reason why the poor could not raise the quality of their lives was attributed to the very nature of the asymmetric relationship between employers and employed. On the one hand, employers were prone to squeeze every ounce of effort from workers. On the other hand, workers constantly showed their resistance through conscientious malingering or what nowadays goes under the name of "shirking." This experience not only demeaned both groups but adversely affected productivity and economic prosperity. Since he maintained a strong belief in the competitive market system, Mill did not think that socialism provided an effective remedy, which could possibly be achieved through a judicious combination of private and social action, that is, a mixed economy.

Based on a different set of preconceptions, Karl Marx also rejected the capitalist system as he found it, and interpreted as its central feature the emergence of a ruling class that privately owned the means of production and a corresponding propertyless class whose members were historically separated from it. In explaining the unequal distribution of income, Marx combined the three types of payments to factors of production identified by other classical economists into two - wages and profits. The result is an economy generating two types of income - wages accruing to a laboring class and a surplus in the form of enlarged profits appropriated by non-wage earners. Further, wages are held at a subsistence level, the assumption being that there is a pool of unemployed workers ("the industrial reserve army of the unemployed") from which capitalists can draw.

Thus, Marx found nothing sacrosanct about the market and no Smithian "invisible hand" guiding it toward the greater good of all humankind. For him, the market was simply a social arrangement which the ruling class devised in order to maximize profits. Under the circumstances, the "laws" of economic behavior propounded by other classical economists had to be subsumed under a more fundamental economic relationship existing in every society: the manner in which the worker is linked to his or her product. According to Marx, workers owned what they created, but capitalism constantly denied them their just rewards.

In the above context, Marx departed from mainstream classical political economy by asking new questions about the socio-economic system and how it originated in the first place. He had a different perspective on the role of capital accumulation and its constraining effect on the growth process. The behavior of capital itself was identified as the primary source of social conflict, the cause of uneven development, and successive crises in the capitalist economy. Marx recognized that capitalist-oriented economic growth had wrought unprecedented changes in people's lives, but thought that the system was doomed to failure because of an inexorable historical process. This is explained by his interpretation of the relationship between social class, the inevitability of conflict, and people's struggle to change themselves. In this perspective of human nature, people are not mere passive subjects of their biological inheritance or mindless automatons adapting to economic and socio-cultural forces beyond their control, but actively participate in changing their own lives through social action.

What defines the "species being" of humans and differentiates them from lower animals is their creativity and ability to produce the means of their own subsistence. Marx postulated that in the evolution of society people's consciousness or awareness developed alongside their needs. In the unravelling of this process, people are able to use their creativity to fulfil their potentials, which are constantly changing. People's changing nature and potentials provide the motive force behind the process of dialectical change. As Marx noted, "all history is nothing but a continuous transformation of human nature" ([1847] 1936: 124). The problem is that all individuals strive to realize their potentials through social organization, and they are effectively blocked by a contradictory social structure designed to preserve the status quo.

Macroscopic historical change is therefore predicated on systemic conflict that is a ubiquitous feature of all social systems. The notion of dialectical change implies that states of dynamic disequilibria are endemic to the transformation of conflict-ridden society. Given individual motivations and intentions, such change takes place because the pattern of socio-economic relations and institutional ordering is already established and becomes a "fetter" or external constraint on individual or group pursuit of strategic objectives. Such constraints can only be removed through collective action designed to change the social conditions of production.

Despite its allegedly exploitative nature, Marx viewed the capitalist system as being immensely productive compared to pre-capitalist forms of economic organization. This was explained in terms of the system's unique social and economic structure, which created a tremendous potential for generating technological change. The bourgeoisie was considered unique as a dominant class because its very essence was interpreted as technological dynamism and its very survival depended on an ability to constantly revolutionize production relations. Contextually, Marx saw capitalism as generating a new set of unique incentives for the introduction of cost-reducing and labor-saving technologies. In this process, the quest for survival by profit-seeking entrepreneurs would be accompanied by intense competition of capital, eventually leading to overseas expansion. Thus, a dynamic bourgeoisie was seen as implanting the seeds of development from advanced industrial countries to colonies and other underdeveloped regions.

Marx's prediction that capitalism would spread from Europe to the rest of the world was based on a fundamental belief that the capitalist mode of production contained an inherent need for ever-expanding markets to satisfactorily employ its commodity and money capital. This outward movement was propelled, it was alleged, by the tendency for the rate of profit to fall in advanced capitalist nations. In the process of overseas expansion, the European bourgeoisie would compel all nations, on the pain of extinction, to adopt the bourgeois mode of production. Capitalist expansion was also viewed as necessary and brutal, constructive and destructive, and as incorporating countries which could change only through the shock of European colonial aggression.

Given the disenchantment with Marxism today, a few interesting developments after Marx's death are well worth recounting. From that time to the beginning of the First World War, leading capitalist nations were in the final throes of overseas colonization and eventually dominated most of the globe. The situation then reversed itself, and Marxism came to encompass about one-third of the earth's population. We are now in a third post-Marxian phase, which has been marked by a retreat from Marxian socialism and a concomitant spread of liberal market capitalism to all corners of the world.

It can also be commented that over time expansion of productive forces in mature capitalist societies has witnessed the emergence of a more complex class structure than Marx had predicted. Society is no longer split into two hostile classes, but a variety of new conservative middle classes has emerged on the basis of occupations requiring technical, scientific, and professional training. At the same time, the proletariat has made some significant gains since the nineteenth century, so that the prospects for working class revolutions throughout the world have diminished. It remains true, however, that accelerated improvements in some dimensions of the human condition continue to coexist with the globalization of poverty and human misery.

Population Growth and Sectoral Change in the Development Transition

The apparent persistence of poverty amidst plenty in the world order puts into bold relief two related issues which took a central stage in classical political economy. Then, as now, these concern the implications of rapid population growth in economic development and the nature of changes that take place in production sectors during the process of economic transformation. These two dimensions of the development transition are linked by the fact that the population pressure which occurs in poor countries tends to place severe limits on resource utilization, and through rural-urban migration, generates asymmetrical linkages between rural and urban areas.

Population Dynamics and Living Standards

The point of departure is Thomas Malthus' gloomy predictions about the dangers of increasing population, or the social and economic consequences of humankind's reproductive capacity. A close look at the England of his day had revealed that much of the population was starving and living at the edge of survival. His overriding concern was that an unchecked population would increase geometrically (2, 4, 8, 16), whereas food production and the means of subsistence would lag behind it and could only increase in arithmetic progression (2, 4, 6, 8). Even though the relationship remains in dispute, it has generated an intense debate over the centuries.

As recently as 1994, nearly two centuries after Malthus' pessimistic predictions originally appeared, world leaders gathered in Cairo, Egypt, to discuss rapid population growth and how to control it. The consensus emerged that exponentially increasing numbers of people still represent a mortal threat to the natural environment and indeed to the future of civilization. While politicians and environmentalists share this view, economists and demographers remain somewhat skeptical. In academia, the debate still rages on about the causes of population growth and the extent to which human numbers per se, as opposed to varying societal and institutional arrangements, should bear the brunt of the blame for food and environmental problems.

In the first edition of his famous *Essay on the Principle of Population* (1798), Malthus chided Adam Smith and other philosophers of the Enlightenment for neglecting the fundamental roles played by *food* and *sex* in the development process. On this basis, he was pessimistic about the "naturalness" of economic growth and human progress. The limit to the growth of agricultural production was thought to provide the ultimate constraint to the increase in human population. The slow growth of agricultural output was predicated on the limited supply of land as well as the observation that the state of agricultural technology seemed incapable of offsetting the declining productivity of new lands brought under cultivation. This tendency was explained by the "law of diminishing returns," which suggested that successive improvements in agriculture would become less and less productive as they were exploited over time.

Malthus considered the laws of nature to be inexorable and predicted that the surplus population would die of starvation and violence. This "Dismal Theorem" has been interpreted to mean that "if nothing checks the growth of population except misery and starvation, then the population will grow until it is miserable and starves" (Boulding 1952: 3). Hence, a viable and sustainable economy is not possible unless there is a limitation on population, that is, unless it is checked by methods other than starvation and poverty. In the Malthusian schema, misery could only be checked by more misery, and only a fear of misery would contain the population's biological capacity to reproduce. In other words, the population will grow until it is miserable enough to stop.

In this context, Malthus' "nature-focused" perspective can be contrasted with a "society-focused" one which interprets consonant food and environmental problems in social and political terms. In the latter context, starvation and malnutrition relate ultimately not only to production possibilities, but also to entitlement and rights (Sen 1982).

The majority of the world's population still live close to a Malthusian low-level equilibrium, or at a subsistence level defined by poverty and misery. Countless numbers are constantly being forced below this level because of sheer bad luck, poor harvests, and the fact that imported foodstuffs and technological advances have barely kept up with the population explosion in many parts of Africa, Asia, and Latin America. Furthermore, in the contemporary global environment, a combination of technological advances, rapid economic growth, and population explosion has raised the specter of resource depletion and destruction of the planet's ecological habitat. While the debate rages on, some environmentalists contend that ecological disaster will become a certainty if (i) the exponential growth of population and material production continue for an indefinite time; and (ii) unless the growth of science and technology provided humankind with such revolutionary discoveries as an ample supply of renewable energy, large and cheap supplies of food to sustain life, extensive space travel, and the eventual colonization of other planets.

Like Malthus, David Ricardo also dissented from the classical doctrine about the natural order of progress. However, he started from a different preconception and saw the main obstacle to economic growth as being primarily a result of the "niggardliness of nature." In the Ricardian model, the contribution of capital accumulation to the growth process depends primarily on the productive power of labor, which is considered to be generally greater when there is an abundance of fertile land. The guiding assumption is that such abundance exists in countries at a very early stage of development, so that any apparently excessive population should be interpreted as a *result* rather than a cause of backwardness and poverty. In more mature economies, by contrast, the diminishing returns to agriculture are likely to be more pronounced, so that excess population becomes more a *cause* than an effect of economic deprivation.

In the latter case, the excessive number of people would pose an economic problem because of a lack of productive employment opportunities. In such a situation, "[t]he population increases faster than the funds required for its support. Every exertion of industry, unless accompanied by a diminished rate of increase in the population, will add to the evil, for production cannot keep pace with it" (Ricardo, 1951, 1: 91).

The gist of the argument can be summarized as follows. During the early stages of development, the size of the population tends to be small relative to the availability of fertile land and other natural resources. As a consequence, capital accumulation, profits, and wages would reach relatively high levels. The high rate of investment acts as a catalyst for increasing both production and the demand for labor. This, in turn, leads to a rising population. Since the quantity of land is assumed to be fixed, the result is diminishing average returns to the additional units of labor utilized in the production process. Over time a situation would be reached in which population growth and wages tend to eat up an increasingly larger proportion of the national output, causing a decline in residual profits. Once the size of a working population gets to the point where the net value of total product reaches zero, a "stationary state" would have set in. In this model, population growth per se implies a decline in living standards, which must eventually bring it to an end in the stationary state.

Such a prognosis seemed a realistic one at the time because of a widespread unavailability of virgin land of good quality. However, Ricardo was by no means a pessimist. For him, the most important problem facing Britain at the time was one of organization and efficiency. This problem was conceptualized in terms of the possibility for reorganizing a growing economy facing burgeoning population growth and differential productivity growth rates in the key sectors of agriculture and industry. Thus, he posed a question, still relevant to today's developing countries: given the availability of resources, the state of technology, and the nature of the enabling institutions, what rate of economic growth is possible? In the case of the British economy of his day, Ricardo attempted to demonstrate that a satisfactory rate of economic progress could be guaranteed if the economy was organized efficiently and made the requisite adaptations to its potentialities, including necessary economic reforms.

The orthodox classical model of economic growth implicitly assumed a static technology and therefore ruled out even a modicum of technical progress in agriculture. This assumption has been criticized on the grounds that population growth itself tends to generate salutary changes. As Boserup (1965, 1981) argues, the larger quantities of food required by a growing population can be produced by shifting from an extensive to a more intensive pattern of land use. The underlying premise rests on the general idea of intensification that typically accompanies acreage expansion. In the context of agricultural husbandry, if the length of the fallow period is used as an indicator of such intensification, then a wide spectrum of cultivation systems and techniques can be envisaged.

The historical experience of contemporary developing countries amply demonstrates a wide range - from "slash and burn" through "bush fallow" to "short fallow," annual cropping with no fallow period, and multicropping. In traditional African agriculture, for example, putting land under fallow is viewed as a means of increasing productive capacity or "creating" land, which is itself considered a form of capital. Boserup's argument is that any movement along the spectrum of cultivation techniques should be considered a normal response to exogenous population growth. With the intensification of cultivation, growth in non-agricultural activities may also offset diminishing returns to agriculture.

Sectoral Articulation

This brings us to the issue of "sectoral articulation," or notable shifts in the relative composition of output and employment in agriculture, industry, and services. By the 1860s, most early industrializing countries had gone a far way toward transforming their economic structures. As early as 1841, agriculture contributed as little as 23 percent of GNP and employed only 20 percent of the labor force in Britain. By contrast, industry contributed 34 percent of GNP and accounted for 41 percent of employment (Bairoch 1975). Given this historical experience, the dominant perspective about sectoral change has been substantially influenced by the anti-agricultural doctrines of classical political economy. As previously indicated, there was a widespread belief that agriculture experienced diminishing returns, while industry benefitted from increasing returns.

The decreasing returns to agriculture were considered a justification for exploiting it in order to encourage industrialization. Over the centuries, this belief has been translated into a perspective of economic development that relies on the following interrelated body of propositions: (i) development is coterminous with urban expansion, industrialization, and a concomitant reduction of the role of agriculture in the economy; (ii) the pace of such industrialization depends on extracting a surplus from the agricultural sector through taxation, low producer prices, and similar policies of discrimination at the sectoral and national levels; (iii) as a corollary, it becomes necessary to protect industry through various taxes, prices, and subsidies because exports of industrial products tend to be more profitable than agricultural exports; and (iv) large-scale capitalist farming is superior to small-scale peasant agriculture (Lipton 1977).

The anti-agricultural bias was synergistic with the classical conceptualization of development in terms of a "natural order of progress" taking place through evolutionary growth stages from an agrarian to an industrial society. In his discussion of this progression, Adam Smith pointed out that initially capital employed in agriculture was more productive, followed by capital employed in manufacturing. This implies that if an economy is free of controls investment possibilities in agriculture should be exploited first. As he stated, "most men will choose to employ their capitals rather in the improvement and cultivation of land, than either in manufacture or in foreign trade" (*Wealth*, Bk 111: 357-358).

However, Smith emphasized the necessity of creating optimal intersectoral linkages between agriculture and industry. In this context, he saw industrial progress as being constrained by the nature of the agricultural surplus. In other words, the productivity of farmers whose marketed surplus is exchanged for manufactured goods tends to limit the size of the manufacturing sector and therefore the drive toward industrialization. His argument was that the creation of an agricultural surplus would produce a demand for other goods and services which could be purchased with the excess supply of agricultural products, and that industrial activity would develop as a means of supplying this growing demand. In such a situation of sectoral interdependency, the burgeoning urban population would require food and therefore produce an increasing supply of manufactured goods to pay for its food needs.

The caveat should be added that while Smith saw the possibilities for economic growth in both agriculture and industry, he attributed greater importance to manufacturing as a primary source of accelerating productivity growth. The following three reasons were advanced. The first hinged on the observation that while the richest nations generally surpassed their neighbors in both agricultural and industrial production, they tended to become much more distinguished by virtue of their industrial superiority. Second, the net economic gains are likely to be larger for industry because it offers a greater scope for specialization, division of labor, and increasing returns to scale. Third, the thinking was that the demand for agricultural products would become more quickly satiated than the corresponding demand for industrial commodities, thereby releasing surplus labor which could be more productively employed in industry.

The pro-industrial bias reached a very high water mark in the writings of Marx and Engels. As early as 1848, they made the oft-quoted reference to the "idiocy of rural life" and did not view the peasantry as the principal agents for change in a capitalist economy. Their *Communist Manifesto* was conceived as a blueprint for the disappearance of the peasant class after the expected seizure of power by the proletariat. Contextually, their prescriptions for sectoral articulation included "abolition of property in land, . . . improvement of the soils generally in accordance with a common plan; establishment of industrial armies especially in agriculture, . . . combination of agriculture with manufacturing industries; [and] gradual abolition of the distinction between town and country" (Marx and Engels [1848] 1968: 104-105).

Marx took a less rigid position in his later writings (for example, in Volume 1 of *Capital*) and tried to come to grips with problems which were peculiar to agricultural labor, such as dispersion of the rural labor force and the fact that farming is not just a simple economic activity but involves multi-stage operations. Nevertheless, he continued to insist on the superiority of large-scale over small-scale agriculture. The basis of this claim was that economies of scale were just as readily available in agriculture as in industry and that, in any event, small-scale peasant agriculture must inevitably give way to large-scale capitalist agriculture in the historical process of economic transformation. Marx's idea about the inevitability of large-scale capitalist agriculture and the dissolution of the peasantry were to provide the foundations for subsequent developments not only in Soviet agriculture but also in many parts of the developing world.

The Trade-Growth Nexus and Economic Nationalism

During the classical era, an important debate arose about economic nationalism and the potential role of government in promoting international trade. The earliest period of extensive growth was marked by considerable mercantile expansion. It was one of significant exploration that eventually culminated in the conquest and settlement of new geographical lands by European nations, especially Spain and Portugal. These two countries monopolized the overseas trade in gold, silver, ivory, spices, and slaves as a means of garnering a maximum amount of bullion for the royal treasuries. Spanish and Portuguese hegemony was later disrupted and superseded by the advance of the English Industrial Revolution, the increasing British control over world shipping, the eventual opening up of American ports to international trade, and British suzerainty over large numbers of conquered peoples in tropical lands.

In this context, John Maynard Keynes was to trace the beginnings of the era of material progress to the discovery of gold and silver in the New World and its corresponding impact on the escalation of profits in the colonizing nations. From this point onwards, he argued, the power of compound interest and accumulation was to provide the necessary momentum for the development process for the next 200 years. In support of this thesis, Keynes drew attention to the fact that the plundering of the Spanish treasuries by Sir Francis Drake during the latter part of the sixteenth century played a pivotal role in enabling Queen Elizabeth I to balance the budget, pay off part of England's foreign debt, and invest 40,000 pounds sterling in the Levant Company. The profits from this venture were in turn used to finance the East India Company, which was to become the institutional pillar of England's foreign investment (Keynes 1933: 361-62).

The overall objective of mercantilist policy was to augment the national wealth and power of countries. As a result, foreign trade was viewed as a mechanism to obtain sufficient quantities of specie (gold and silver), raw materials, and other commodities that could be combined with domestically available factors of production to generate maximum growth and employment. The achievement of a favorable balance of trade was considered a necessary prerequisite for promoting economic development. Therefore, it was imperative for the mercantile state to export more goods and services than it imported and utilize the foreign exchange earnings of specie to increase foreign trade and investment.

The period of mercantile expansion was marked by excessive government intervention in economic affairs. This practice was rationalized on the grounds that government had a central role to play in easing the problems afflicting the economy by deliberately interfering with the market mechanism. In the British case, for example, government legal regulation was considered a necessary defense against economic dislocation, and in particular, the fear of massive unemployment in the textile industry, as well as its attendant political implications. Hence, prevailing mercantilist policies placed comprehensive restrictions on international trade and exchange.

This philosophy was based on a very static and one-sided view of the world. It was later superseded by a more dynamic and optimistic milieu based on a belief in progress and the principles of economic liberalism. Industrialization had brought substantial prosperity to Britain, but also created an insatiable appetite for cheap raw materials and larger foreign markets. Thus, trade liberalization was viewed as an essential vehicle that would allow cheap raw material inputs to be imported by manufacturers; also the foreign demand for British products would be increased on account of the incentives given to the resource-abundant external hinterlands to augment their export earnings. In this context, the free trade argument was advanced by a number of British classical economists as a reaction to two primary premises of mercantilist philosophy: (i) a vision of the world in which nation states are wont to pursue their own national interests; and as a corollary, (ii) a policy of making export surpluses the ultimate goal of foreign trade, instead of pursuing a development strategy based on the most efficient use of resources.

For example, Adam Smith viewed foreign trade as the dynamic force in specialization and widening of the market. Smith presented a comprehensive case for free trade based on the principle of "absolute advantage," which states that it never pays a nation to produce goods and services domestically when it is possible to obtain them more cheaply from other countries. In his view, trade widened the market, extended the scope for division of labor, and therefore represented a potent mechanism for stimulating domestic expansion based on economies of scale. The expanded demand associated with increased economies of scale would lead not only to a higher level of domestic output, but also lower prices, and ultimately higher real incomes, savings, capital investment, and self-sustained economic growth.

In reaction to his mercantilist predecessors, Smith posited that various countries should follow one another according to the "natural process" inherent in the development of their industrial activities and their participation in international exchange. On this basis, he contended that the surplus part of the capital stock which could not be employed in domestic production and exchange "naturally disgorges itself" into the "carrying trade" and could be employed "in performing the same office in other countries." Accordingly, a strong emphasis was placed on the advantage that would accrue to a country from importing those commodities that the domestic manufacturing sector could only produce at higher absolute costs. This argument was supposed to counteract the mercantilist claim that industries would migrate to countries with cheap labor unless producers who had to pay high wages domestically were protected by tariffs or could attract skilled labor from abroad.

Smith also viewed free trade as a "vent for surplus" products. Myint (1958) used this argument to analyze the conditions underlying the opening up of the primary producing nations in Southeast Asia during the nineteenth century. His conclusion was that trade enabled their unused or "underdeveloped" resources to be utilized more effectively, since it raised real incomes directly without the need to reallocate resources from import-competing sectors. The implication of this argument is that the domestic resources of a country are not simply "given," but can be "created" in response to the stimulus provided by trade. In general, the "vent for surplus" argument helped to popularize the idea that European suzerainty over conquered peoples and the cultivation of export markets would raise output and employment by permitting a more intensive utilization and efficient allocation of hitherto underdeveloped resources. It was felt that the exploitation of such resources would not only benefit Europe and the world economy at large, but that it would bring tangible political, social, and "civilizing" benefits to the colonies as well.

In Book IV of *Wealth* (especially Chapter 7), however, Smith argued that the colonies, especially in North America, would better flourish if they were left free to pursue their own activities, and that the British monopoly of colonial trade conferred no benefits whatsoever on the colonized nations. On the contrary, he claimed, the monopoly of this trade tended to distort the allocation of capital by raising the profits that could be derived from such trade and deflecting capital into areas and activities where the turnover was comparatively low. The exclusive trade of mother countries with their colonies, it was opined, acted as a depressant on the aggregate level of world real income and tended to reduce its rate of growth. The same could be said for the North American colonies, since both their industrial production and aggregate output were deliberately stifled or curtailed.

The overall result, Smith continued, was that while British merchants earned enormously high profits from colonial trade, the British economy itself did not fare as well. The primary reason was that the monopoly of colonial trade did not in itself create any new trade, but rather diverted trade away from Europe and toward the colonies. Intensive specialization for the colonial market resulted in a lack of commodity and geographical diversification in British manufacturing and commerce. Furthermore, the relatively high profits earned in mercantile trade led to profligate spending and conspicuous consumption, reduced efficiency, a decline in investment incentives (especially in British agriculture), and a drain in the government coffers because of increased expenditures on colonial administration and defense.

Based on a different set of preconceptions, David Ricardo took a more thoroughgoing free trade position. He showed that there could be an advantage to trade even if only one country had an absolute advantage. All that needed to be demonstrated was that one country was relatively more efficient in the production of one commodity, that is, that it had a comparative advantage. As he stated, "it is quite as important to the happiness of mankind, that our enjoyments should be increased by the better distribution of labor, by each country producing those commodities for which by its situation, its climate, and its other natural or artificial advantages, it is adapted, and by their exchanging them for the commodities of other countries, as that they should be augmented by a rise in the rate of profits" (1951, 1: 132).

Thus, the principle of comparative advantage emphasized the mutual benefits accruing from trade when each country exports those goods and services in which it has a relative cost advantage, even if one trading partner has an absolute cost advantage in every production activity. This principle served British interests very well. As the principal trading partner in the majority of markets in which it was involved, Britain found that a unilateral policy of trade liberalization could maximize its gains from trade. However, other European nations such as France and Germany viewed the application of the principle as providing unequal advantages to "leaders" vis-à-vis "followers" in the overall scheme of international trade. Not only were they not prepared to accept this inequality, but also viewed the "wealth of nations" as being intimately intertwined with their "power" and "place" (Landes 1990).

Under the circumstances, they were unwilling to allow cheaper British goods to swamp their domestic markets, and many found it in their own national interests to provide tariff protection for their infant manufacturing industries. In some cases, such as France, trade barriers were accompanied by outright prohibitions of certain goods and services. In the case of the United States, the evidence suggests that forms of trade protection went as far back as 1813 when tariff rates reached levels exceeding 50 percent. Relatively high levels of protection remained intact until the Reciprocal Trade Agreements Act of 1934. After the confederation of 1867, Canada also maintained high tariff barriers as a means of promoting rapid industrialization and limiting competition from foreign imports, especially from the United States .

John Stuart Mill (1909 [1940]) had argued that the theory of international trade based on the comparative advantage principle was more applicable to trade among nations at a more or less comparable level of development as distinct from those who were unequal partners. In this context, he pointed to an important exception to the free trade principle: the case of an "infant industry" for which, in its initial stages, protection against already established foreign competitors may be justified. Even before Mill, the perspective championing industrial protection was given a modern flavor in Alexander Hamilton's *Report on the Subject of Manufactures* (1791), which outlined a dynamic theory of economic development based on the "superiority of manufacturing over agriculture," and a related strategy of industrialization through import substitution. Like his mercantilist forebears, Hamilton identified national power with the development of a manufacturing industry. As he stated, "not only the wealth, but the independence and security of a country, appear to be materially connected with the prosperity of manufactures. Every nation, with a view of these great objectives, ought to endeavor to possess within itself, all of the essentials of national supply" (1929 [1791]: 282).

Hamilton's view was that the necessity of building state power should take precedence over pure economic matters, and that governments should institute the requisite policy reforms to transform their economies and guarantee their position in the international economy. Of some relevance is the fact that Hamilton was one of the prominent economic theorists of the first British colony (the United States) to revolt against European imperialism. Hence, he advocated policies to encourage the transfer of capital and the migration of skilled labor from the more advanced nations of the day as a means of developing particular industries and expediting the process of industrialization. In essence, his prescriptions for the promotion of trade through government intervention can be considered important forerunners of many controversial issues that continue to inform the contemporary debate on international development. As elaborated in later chapters of this book, these include, inter alia, the need for rapid industrialization, industrial protection, and government intervention in the trade regime. Mention should also be made of the great distrust shown for British free trade principles by members of the German Historical School. As noted earlier, those principles were thought to be associated, if not identical, with British national interests and the economic policies of relatively strong nation states. Contextually, it was argued that while free trade was definitely advantageous for a country whose industries dominated the world and benefitted from larger markets, those countries whose industries were relatively weak could never become strong if, unaided, they were left to face the full force of British competition. This was the starting point of Friedrich List's argument for infant industry protection.

In his view, there was nothing natural or immutable about the international division of labor based on the principle of comparative advantage, since it merely reflected the historical outcome of prior uses or abuses of economic and political power. The British, he argued, actually used such power to protect their own infant industries against foreign competition while simultaneously weakening their opponents through the use of military force. Under the circumstances, it was easy to understand why they were to become the foremost advocates of free trade only after they had succeeded in achieving industrial and technological superiority over their competitors. List's argument, articulated in his *National Systems of Political Economy* (1841), was symbolic of the German belief in historical relativity, or the view that economic truth is bound by time and place, and therefore relative. This implied that factors associated with British convenience and national interests were not necessarily applicable to all nations.

The lesson to be drawn from history, he argued, was that free trade would be beneficial to all nations if the conditions of peace prevailed. However, if sufficient account were to be taken of the facts of national rivalry and sovereignty, free trade would only help to enhance British domination of the world economy. However, Britain enjoyed the special advantage of being a manufacturing nation first. Since only manufacturing activity fully released the production and creative powers of the nation, the state could give a further fillip to these by introducing protective tariffs designed to establish infant industries in the face of opposition from other nations that had started earlier.

Thus, compared to other polemicists of his day, List showed that the possibilities for national economic growth tend to be inherently connected with the nature of the interaction between economics and politics. On this basis, he recognized that while free trade may be an instrumental mechanism in achieving efficient allocation of resources at the domestic level, it did not necessarily help to enhance the international competitiveness of relatively weak or under-industrialized nations. The policy prescription, therefore, was that such nations should eschew free trade and rely more heavily on development policies designed to institutionalize protection of domestic industry by the state. This argument persists as a *bête noire* in contemporary development analysis and policy. The developing countries of today continue to view themselves as "unequal partners" in the overall scheme of international trade and investment. As discussed later in this book, the majority perceive free trade as heightening conditions of dependence and peripheralization in the global pattern of unequal exchange.

Chapter 3

Neo-Classical Monoeconomics: Market Fundamentalism and Decentralized Development

The philosophical presuppositions, concepts, and analytical modalities of neo-classical economists now dominate the theory and practice of economic development. Compared to their classical forebears, they have been much more concerned with rational choice and resource allocation than with problems of economic development. Nevertheless, neoclassicism has retained a philosophical commitment to the basic elements of the classical conceptual structure. As such, it subscribes to a worldview that the laws of economics are universal and immutable, and therefore applicable to rich and poor nations alike.

This "monoeconomic" orientation is in the same tradition as classical orthodoxy, especially in terms of the emphasis placed on the benefits of economic liberalism and the ideal role of the market-price mechanism in solving all economic problems. Nevertheless, the neo-classical interpretive mode has been accompanied by a marked shift in the boundaries of the economics discourse. Since the primary concern is with static problems of allocative efficiency, larger problems surrounding societal relations, power, class conflict, and socio-economic change are deemed to lie outside the scope of the technical economics calculus, or theoretical grasp of economics as a hypothetico-deductive and empirical science.

To the extent that there is a neo-classical perspective of development, it is synonymous with "economic" development, or as emphasized in classical political economy, a process of economic growth based on free and efficient markets. Under the circumstances, development becomes a matter of individual initiative, or a process by which individual economic agents constantly weigh the costs and benefits of alternative courses of action through the efficiency rules of a rational cost-benefit calculus. For this reason, some economists claim that the distinction between classical and neo-classical economics is not a useful one. Whether or not this is the case, the dichotomy still carries important analytical and policy implications.

Basic Economic Perspectives

The universalist ontology undergirding the neo-classical paradigm rests on the assumption of a ubiquitous scarcity of resources relative to human wants and needs. Therefore, all societies and individual economic agents must constantly make decisions about the relative degrees of sacrifice that must be borne if resources are to be allocated efficiently among alternative uses. This calls for rational choice in the use of the available resources. The reasoning is that if the alternatives presented to economic agents (private households, business firms, national governments) are not rationally chosen, resource scarcity is likely to increase over time, thereby impairing current living standards and reducing possibilities for future economic growth and improved human welfare.

Economic behavior is interpreted in terms of a model of competitive equilibrium, which assumes that the operation of free markets for commodities and factors of production and the system of relative prices would provide necessary conditions for individual economic agents to achieve maximum economic welfare and personal liberty. A competitive equilibrium simply represents a unique combination of outputs, inputs, and prices for commodities and factors of production. As in the classical case, the corresponding model is grounded in a "methodological individualism," which posits that the individual decision-making units are free and rational actors whose behavior is guided by harmonious equilibrating forces.

The overall economy is assumed to consist of a large number of interacting markets that have a tendency to clear, that is, reach equilibrium, with the latter defined in terms of an equalization of demand, supply, and price. One normative implication is that, given competitive conditions and perfect information, it is possible for self-interested economic agents to receive their fair share of the income and wealth created. Resources will be efficiently allocated and there will be no need to tamper with the way the economic system distributes benefits. Under the circumstances, any attempt to enforce equality in the prevailing pattern of income distribution would be inimical to economic efficiency and growth. Where inequalities exist, they should be considered necessary for guaranteeing optimum production efficiency.

Thus, the rationale for a market system lies in a belief in "independent" individuals and an expectation that it would increase efficiency and maximize economic growth. According to this interpretation, a capitalist economy has the capacity to display a sustained equilibrium of steady or "optimal" growth, with divergences that are "fairly small, casual, and hardly self-actuating" (Solow 1970). Accordingly, development is viewed as a gradual evolutionary process of organic growth. The latter is likely to occur because new resources, knowledge, and technological change are expected to outpace diminishing returns to resources that were previously limited. Furthermore, the process is deemed a harmonious one in which benefits accrue to all major income groups, and are distributed throughout the economic system because of the interdependent nature of the economy.

It should be emphasized that the idea of freely competitive markets, while based on ideology, is not meant to describe any actual economy but merely represents an ideal standard for policy formulation. The ability of an idealized set of markets to reach equilibrium in the allocation of resources is predicated on three fundamental axioms. First, there should always be a sufficient number of markets. This means that if an economic agent wants something that can only be provided through interaction with at least one other economic agent, then a market should exist for the good or service, that is, it should have a price. This "price fundamentalism" is supposed to apply to all goods and services, for example, the consumption of basic necessities such as food (private goods), or the provision of health care and education (public goods).

Second, the behavior of all economic agents should always be motivated by competition. This implies that economic agents must act as if they cannot affect prices and, given the prevailing set of prices, as if they are following optimal decision rules. For example, consumers would maximize their consumption and leisure subject to budget constraints, and producers would maximize profits subject to a technological constraint, but in each case prices would be taken as fixed parameters. This condition will be violated when the actions of economic agents can affect the equilibrium values of prices, thereby gaining undue advantages.

Third, to the extent that an equilibrium exists, then the allocation of resources to which it gives rise should be Pareto optimal. "Pareto optimality" is interpreted as the most efficient configuration or standard against which behavior of the economy as a whole is appraised. Achievement of overall economic equilibrium means that each individual economic agent would have reached an "optimal" position, that is, one that it cannot possibly improve by altering its behavior. In this ideal or utopian state, any attempt to improve a given economic agent's position would have to be at someone else's expense. Implicit in the notion of a Pareto ideal is the existence of a zero-sum society. This ideal configuration of an economy is usually defined as one in which no one could be made better off without making someone else worse off by reallocating the resource endowments of consumers and/or by utilizing the available technology of producers. Thus, a configuration is "optimal" when all other possible alternatives are theoretically inferior or not comparable to it.

The third condition may be violated by the presence of "market failure," or the inefficient allocation of resources due to a paucity of markets, forms of non-competitive behavior, or non-existence problems. For example, insurance and capital markets may not exist. Given these possibilities, neo-classical economists have catalogued a number of ways in which departures from the conditions under which markets *theoretically* deliver optimal outcomes might occur and conceivably call for government intervention.

Thus, neo-classical economists have come to identify a wide array of circumstances in which benevolent governments should intervene in the market system as a means of guiding the economy in the direction of a more efficient or optimal point. The most well known cases involve: (i) the potential ability of a benevolent government to provide public or collective goods that markets do not adequately supply; and (ii) the removal of "distortions" that give rise to "market failure." From this perspective, a market failure is presumed to exist if the conditions for the attainment of Pareto optimality are not satisfied in a way that some benevolent government could correct in a costless manner. In other words, market failure is generally indicated when the prevailing set of prices in various markets are "distorted" in the sense that they diverge from their most "efficient" or "optimal" values. Such failures occur in both developed and developing nations, even though they tend to be more pronounced in the latter cases.

Some types of market distortions are policy-induced, that is, they result from inefficient government policies. These include distorting taxes, subsidies, and government laws or regulations that permit the emergence and persistence of monopolies and other forms of non-competitive behavior. Other distortions tend to be "endogenous," and are unrelated to government policies. These may arise from the presence of externalities in the economic system and structural rigidities in the various factor and commodity markets. Once the distortions have been identified, the standard policy prescription is to "get prices right" through a combination of mechanisms. One is the direct removal of domestic market distortions that might have resulted from previous government interventions or other structural and institutional bottlenecks in the economy. The primary purpose of such an action is to allow domestic markets to operate more freely.

A second type of policy action advocates liberalization of trade and exchange rates through removal of any existing trade barriers and exchange controls. In this case, the objective is to allow the domestic economy to move as close as possible to the requirements of a free trade regime. Following from classical liberalism, international trade is considered one of the most effective mechanisms for ensuring gains in productive efficiency and national income, as well as for enlarging consumption possibilities. The beneficial effects of free trade are predicated on assumptions about the harmony of interests among nation states, the free international flow of resources, patterns of trade based on comparative advantage, and an equitable distribution of the gains from trade. The same normative forces are assumed to operate at both domestic and international levels, with freely competitive markets considered the most effective conduits for allocating and distributing resources in both spheres.

In this regard, neo-classical analysts improved the classical doctrine of free trade by modifying the principle of comparative advantage along the following lines: (i) a greater mobility of factors of production across national boundaries was assumed; (ii) a new emphasis was placed on the importance of increasing returns to scale as a motive force behind trade, and the corresponding dynamic nature of comparative advantage; and (iii) factors other than labor (stressed in the classical labor theory of value), such as transportation costs, were added to the cost of production, resulting in a concept of relative factor endowments as the primary explanation of international trade flows. This more comprehensive interpretation has found a forceful expression in the now famous Heckscher-Ohlin-Samuelson (H-O-S) model, which has dominated the theory of international trade for most of the postwar period. While the Ricardian model of comparative advantage placed primary emphasis on differences of technology among countries as the basis of trade, the H-O-S perspective has focused on variations among countries in their relative factor endowments and differences among commodities in terms of the intensities with which they utilize these factors (see Jones and Kenen 1984).

In this context, a nation's comparative advantage is thought to be determined by the relative abundance and most profitable combination of an array of productive factors such as land resource, labor, capital, technology, and management. The policy implication is that countries should specialize in the production and export of those commodities requiring relatively large injections of those factors of production in which they are relatively well endowed. The overall argument is that, given the conditions of international exchange, specialization according to comparative advantage defined in such terms would lead to increases in national income due to the potentially beneficial effects of production.

In a dynamic sense, therefore, the beneficial effects of specialization are assumed to result from the increased domestic production and export of goods and services based on exploitation of relatively abundant domestic resources, and the importation of others that cannot be produced domestically, either because it is too costly or impossible to do so. These dynamic benefits are also presumed to arise from exploitation of economies of scale, increases in product variety (horizontal specialization), increased production of goods and services at various levels of sophistication (vertical specialization), and technological change. Realization of these gains depends in part on the competitive nature of international markets and their relative size which, as Adam Smith opined, tend to set constraints on the division of labor. Market size is particularly significant because it also helps to define the possibilities for exploiting "comparative advantage by stages" (Balassa 1979).

Contextually, an implicit assumption is that countries at an early development stage tend to gain more by importing those goods and services that can be produced more cheaply and on a larger scale in the more developed world. Thus, trade can be expected to improve the supply of intermediate and capital goods that can provide a needed impetus to the development dynamic. The reasoning is that this would help to reduce domestic bottlenecks and enable countries to overcome diseconomies stemming from the relatively small size of domestic markets. However, while these markets may exist initially for imports, at a later stage they can potentially form the basis of import substitution and industrial development. Over time, countries would therefore be able to exploit overseas markets through expansion.

Thus, given a liberal international economy, countries should follow a linear development sequence based on the initial production and export of resource-based commodities and later light manufactures and capital-intensive products. In some circles, this has been associated with what is known as "staple theory," which developed during the early debate on Canadian economic development (Innis 1915; Watkins 1963). The theory postulated that, given their comparative advantage in natural resources, latecomers in the development process would initially concentrate on the production of export "staples." This prescription rested on the assumption that there were no alternative uses attached to the production of staples or other resource-intensive commodities available for export. Thus, staple production was viewed essentially as a process of domestic capital formation in the economic activities that were linked to the staple commodity. Under the circumstances, the possibilities of further development of the economy would ultimately depend on the characteristics of the staple exports, including dynamic linkages that could be forged between activities linked to export production and other sectors of the economy.

The basic assumption, therefore, was that a relatively balanced and diversified economy could be built even by countries which initiated their development process by concentrating on the production of staples. Historical examples include: Canada (furs, timber, grain, and minerals); the United States (grain, tobacco, and cotton); Denmark (dairy products); Sweden (wood); and to a lesser extent, Argentina (grain, hides, and frozen meat). Reference was also sometimes made to the fact that many "underdeveloped" regions of the world, including colonies, experienced bubbles of intensive growth between 1850 and 1914, based on the production and export of staples.

The stages theory of comparative advantage and staple theory reinforced the belief that less developed regions of the world should initially devote their efforts to primary commodity production and the development of extractive industries, while leaving the production of finished manufactured products to Western Europe and North America. In support of this strategy, it was argued that the average return from the production and export of primary commodities would be significantly greater than the corresponding returns to be realized from alternative investments, and that the supply of foreign investment would be greater for export production. In the context of the previous discussion on mercantilist expansion, most colonies were mandated to produce and export those kinds of goods and services requiring relatively small injections of capital per unit of output and import manufactures, and later intermediate and capital goods that could help to initiate industrialization.

The Sources of Economic Growth

One prominent strand of neo-classical economics has been concerned with attempts to identify and explain the "sources" or "causes" of economic growth. From a development perspective, the pertinent models are important because they rest on a presupposition that rapid economic growth is the best antidote for economic development ills. The problem is that economists disagree about how to foster economic growth. Countries boasting high growth rates usually display many common characteristics. However, there is a lack of consensus about what causes economic growth as distinct from what are simply its byproducts. There is also lack of knowledge about the extent to which successful growth performers can be imitated.

As shown in the previous chapter, the general analytical framework of this "growth accounting" perspective originated in classical political economy, which ascribed the growth of material production or output to various inputs or factors of production. In the neo-classical case, economic growth is attributed to increased factor supplies and improved productivity stemming from long-term effects of technological progress, better resource allocation associated with short-term efficiency gains, and improved efficiency at the level of individual business firms on account of competition. The individual firm has a particular production function which determines the maximum output it can produce through the efficient use of available factors of production. A similar relationship is assumed for the economy as a whole, that is, that there is an aggregate production function which relates aggregate income or output to "aggregate" capital and labor.

Analytically, this is possible only if output, capital, and labor were made up of physically homogeneous elements, and capital and labor can be moved from one firm to another so as to obtain a maximum output for the economy as a whole. Many economists, especially Cambridge capital theorists, contend that neither of these conditions obtain in practice and that an aggregate production function exists only under restrictive and unrealistic assumptions (Harcourt 1972). Nevertheless, the concept of a production function has maintained its tenacity in neo-classical economics. Hence, the properties of national economic growth are modelled by utilizing the concept of an aggregate production function.

The growth relationships are predicated on the free flow of factors of production among individual economic activities, sectors, regions, and countries. It is also presumed that such a free flow of resources will act as a potential catalyst to effect equilibrium and equalization of output, income, and employment growth rates across the different economic spheres. The neo-classical perspective is therefore rooted in the idea of *equilibrium growth*, that is, one that proceeds very slowly, continuously, and on a stable and steady path with minimum disturbances from exogenous forces. Implicit in this mode of interpretation is a "natural" or "biological" conception of economic growth, with progress assumed to depend on the "evolutionary possibilities" facing an economy at any given point in time.

Pioneers of neo-classical growth theory, such as Solow (1956, 1970) and Swan (1956) emphasized the critical role of capital accumulation on the grounds that higher investment and savings rates better allow a country to increase the capital it leaves to its future workers, thereby raising their productivity and, hence, incomes. Ultimately, each country will reach a threshold where the amount it saves is just sufficient to replace the capital it has depleted. Once this point is reached, income per head can grow only as fast as improvements in technology. At the empirical level, the growth of a country's gross domestic product (GDP) is apportioned among distributive shares or earnings of the physical inputs mentioned earlier. The quantitative results have shown that even when this apportionment is made, a large unexplained "residual" still remains. The latter is supposed to capture the influence of causal factors such as increased efficiency and the improved allocation of resources, for example, movement of the labor force from low-productivity agriculture to high-productivity industrial activity, economies of scale, and advances in knowledge and technology.

In a now classic study of this issue, Solow (1957) apportioned the growth in U.S. national output among three causal factors - capital, labor, and a residual change. As much as 87 percent of the growth in output was attributed to residual factors such as knowledge and technical change. In a similar study of U.S. economic growth for the 1929-69 period, Denison (1962) showed that the direct shares of labor and capital accounted for approximately 55 percent of output, leaving the remaining 45 percent to be explained by more technical factors. In an updated study for the 1929-82 period, he found that the growth of knowledge and technological progress accounted for 36 percent of national output.

The share of output growth, which is explained by increases in productivity and efficiency rather than by the direct growth of factor inputs, is commonly referred to as total factor productivity (TFP). Following the Solow-Denison original dichotomy, a number of analysts have developed more elaborate econometric approaches as a means of providing a more exhaustive account of all the possible sources of TFP. While the studies vary in terms of country coverage, time periods, and methods, they generally share the following conclusions. First, and as expected, the share of output growth explained by TFP is generally higher for developed, compared to developing, countries. Second, and on a related basis, growth in developing countries is largely explained more by the accumulation of factor inputs than by the growing efficiency in their deployment. This is borne out in Table 3.1.

Most studies on the sources of growth face a basic problem of causal empiricism. Besides the difficulty of separating primary from secondary causes of economic growth, there is also a lack of knowledge about the precise nature of the interaction between TFP and primary factors of production during the growth process. The attempt to identify causal sequence proves to be even more problematic. The factors that presumably caused Japan's phenomenal rate of economic growth may be taken as an illustration. In a study by Denison and Chung (1976), the main factors were identified as the country's rapid rate of capital accumulation and economies of scale stemming from the growth in domestic demand, which, in turn, enhanced Japanese competitiveness in foreign markets. The high rate of capital accumulation reflected the country's relatively high ratio of savings-investment to national income, while economies of scale can be attributed to the sheer size of a domestic market of over 124 million people.

While such explanations may seem plausible on the surface, they do raise the possibility of circular reasoning and the likelihood that multiple causes may exist for the same phenomenon. In the first place, the relatively high ratio of savings-investment to national income could easily have been a consequence rather than a cause of economic growth, or alternatively, a result of Japanese cultural norms. It can also be argued that growth in the Japanese domestic market was made possible by a more rapid rate of growth in exports, and not the other way around. Furthermore, it is always difficult, if not impossible, to disentangle the multiplicity of feedback mechanisms that are constantly at work in the overall growth process (Currie 1986).

In general, while the neo-classical model provides some useful insights into the relationship between economic growth and savings-investment, it suffers from two basic drawbacks. First, its predictions of specific relationships from basic statistical aggregates do not always fit the facts. For example, income disparities among countries tend to be much greater than savings-investment rates may suggest. Second, while the model concludes that economic growth ultimately depends on the rate of technological progress, no adequate explanation is provided of the factors that determine this rate.

Nevertheless, its staunch defenders still claim that the model is the best way to understand growth. The two primary reasons are that: (i) a goal of growth theory is not so much to explain why countries grow in the first place, but rather why some countries grow faster than others; and (ii) ideas flow freely, and all countries have access to them. From this perspective, poorer countries find themselves in a development fix because they have less capital to work with. If this is true, learning more about technological change cannot explain differences in growth rates among countries.

As noted in Chapter 1, the attempt to fit generalizations or theories to empirical evidence raises a perennial problem about the nature of the relationship between "*causation*" and "*correlation*." The empirical testing of theories relies on a "curve fitting" perspective of science, which attempts to establish some degree of correspondence between predictions and the empirical evidence provided by the real world. In such quantitative research, data are collected, variables are correlated, and the relevant tests of statistical significance are carried out. The implicit assumption is that all statistically significant correlations have the status of causal laws. A "causal law" is a statement which purports to describe the environment in which a change in the values in one or more variables (termed "independent" or "explanatory") is directly associated with a corresponding change in another variable (termed "dependent"). The important point is that the

Table 3.1

Sources of Growth in Sample of World Economies, 1960-87

Region or Group and Period	Capital	Labor	TFP
1960-73			
Africa	59	22	17
East Asia	50	16	35
Europe, Middle East, and North Africa	51	10	38
Latin America	55	20	25
South Asia	81	20	0
Total	56	18	26
1973-87			
Africa	92	37	-27
East Asia	62	17	20
Europe, Middle East, and North Africa	68	19	14
Latin America	94	51	-48
South Asia	55	19	24
Total	76	28	- 6
1960-87			
Africa	73	28	0
East Asia	57	16	28
Europe, Middle East, and North Africa	58	14	28
Latin America	67	30	0
South Asia	67	20	14
Total	65	23	14
Selected industrial countries, 1960-85			
France	27	- 5	78
Germany[1]	23	-10	87
Japan	36	5	59
United Kingdom	27	- 5	78

Source: World Bank (1991)

[1]The Federal Republic of Germany before reunification with the former German Democratic Republic

behavior of the explanatory variables can produce a change in the dependent one without any change in other variables in the environment.

For example, let us hypothesize that a change in exports (X) *causes* economic growth, defined as a country's per capita income (Y). At least three conditions must hold for such a statement to have the status of a causal law. First, the change in X must be associated with a change in Y, in the sense that there is some degree of covariation or correlation between the two variables. When exports increase, the country's economic growth rate must, on average, be much higher than when exports do not increase. Second, while the change in Y can be produced by an increase in X, it should not be possible to increase X by changing Y. Third, there should not have to be changes in other explanatory variables (for example, capital accumulation, entrepreneurship, and government leadership) for export growth to have a direct effect on per capita income growth. This is not meant to deny that the growth of exports may have effects other than the one on per capita income.

The moral of the story is that testing economic theories or generalizations often proves to be as difficult as formulating them in the first place. Despite the ubiquity of the "regression model" that purports to establish causal relationships among variables in quantitative research, the results of many statistical and econometric analyses usually turn out to be inconclusive because of a lack of reliable data or inaccurate interpretation. In modern society, many economic relationships involve expectations that are not observable. Hence they cannot be measured with any degree of accuracy. Furthermore, the sheer complexity of modern economic systems makes it difficult to separate cause from effect, and discrete or linear changes from random ones.

In this context, Hicks (1979) has identified three distinct types of causality: static, contemporaneous, and sequential. Each is defined in terms of some perceptible relationship between cause and effect. Static causality represents a case in which both cause and effect are permanencies. For example, Adam Smith regarded the causes and effects of capital accumulation as being invariant and universally applicable principles governing increases in the wealth of nations. Under contemporaneous causality, both cause and effect relate to the same time period. By contrast, cause precedes effect in sequential causality, that is, temporal sequence is emphasized.

The main body of neo-classical economics is grounded in either static or contemporaneous causality. This ontology is traceable to the tenacious clinging to a Newtonian view of the world. In this perspective, the universe is perceived as a giant machine that is invariant for all time. The implication is that changes taking place at any instant depend only on the state of the world at that point in time. Underlying this presupposition is a notion of "logical time" or instantaneous adjustments. However, as Joan Robinson remarks, "once we admit that an economy exists in time, that history goes one way, from the irrevocable past to the unknown future, the conception of equilibrium based on the mechanical analogy of a pendulum swinging to and fro in space becomes untenable. The whole of traditional economics needs to be thought out afresh" (1974: 8). The concept of sequential causality needs to be interpreted in this light.

"New" Endogenous Growth Theories

One important implication of the neo-classical interpretation of economic growth is that differences in developmental attainment are reflected in gaps in TFP and technical progress between rich and poor countries. These gaps are assumed to become smaller as developing countries move along an equilibrium growth path and "catch up" with their more developed counterparts. Therefore, if countries have access to the same technology, growth rates can be expected to converge across them. While the recent experience of industrial nations offers some measure of support for the convergence hypothesis, the interpretation of development in such terms rests on a number of fundamental propositions of questionable validity.

First, it is implicitly assumed that today's developing countries are more or less exact replicas of the industrial nations when the latter were undergoing their economic transformation. Thus, given the right conditions, the former would in due course move forward and upward along the steady-state equilibrium growth path. A second assumption is that inter-country differences in per capita income attainment can be explained solely in terms of differential rates of expansion in the ratio of capital to labor and the ability of countries to tap the common pool of technologies. Third, and on a related basis, it is assumed that there exists a large and freely accessible pool of production techniques that developing countries can draw on at will. Contrary to the expectations of the convergence thesis, technological change has not been equal nor has it been exogenously transmitted in most developing countries. Moreover, even if all countries have equal access to the same technology, national economic growth rates may diverge on account of differences in the stock of human capital and incentives to adopt new technology.

The so-called "new" growth theories have challenged the neo-classical proposition that most long-term growth can be attributed to exogenous technological change. Rather, they rely on a different theory of *causation* in which technological change is construed as an *endogenous* result of a research and development process that is largely driven by the profit motive. A related proposition is that education and knowledge tend to generate positive externalities or increasing returns. Under the circumstances, investment policies that encourage activities generating externalities, such as improvements in education, or increasing returns (e.g., better infrastructural facilities) can have a salutary effect on economic growth. The same is true of policies that facilitate the spread of knowledge, permit the free entry and exit of business firms, and encourage the free mobility of productive resources such as capital, technology, and people.

While "new" endogenous growth models can certainly be credited with turning the direction of causation around, they bear a close similarity to other perspectives in modern economic thought. These range from the Schumpeterian idea about innovative entrepreneurs, through early Cambridge accounts of dynamic interactions among imperfect competition, increasing returns to scale, and technological change (Kaldor 1957), to the economic significance of learning by doing (Arrow 1962). A number of germane ideas were to resurface in research programs that interpret new knowledge and understanding of the long-term growth process in terms of investment in "knowledge capital" and new technologies.

First, in this perspective, the growth rate is linked to the equilibrium allocation of resources to knowledge-creating activities, with spillover effects playing a critical role in making long-term growth sustainable (Romer 1986, 1992; Lucas 1988). In some variants of the endogenous interpretation, the focus is on the interaction between technology, trade, and economic growth. In this case, technological gaps and international differences in production techniques take center stage in the explanation of development patterns.

As mentioned above, endogenous growth models single out the pivotal role played by the production and utilization of knowledge, ideas, and information flows in the growth process. The usual starting point is to identify distinguishable characteristics of knowledge in comparison to ordinary private consumption and public goods. An ordinary consumption good is "rival" or "excludable," while a public good displays the opposite characteristics of "nonrivalry" and "nonexcludability." Rival goods are those that everyone cannot use at the same time, while excludability, as the name implies, refers to the enforcement of exclusive use. The most important characteristic of knowledge is "nonrivalry" (Romer 1986) and "perfect expansability" (Paul David 1992). This means that different persons can simultaneously use the same information at no extra cost, that is, the use by one party does not preclude its use by others. Unlike public goods, knowledge is also excludable: an agent with a property right can exclude others from its use.

Given these properties, endogenous knowledge typically enters the production system via processes, formulas, designs, and blueprints. Romer (1990a) provides as examples goods such as new chemical processes, chip designs, mechanical drawings, and metallurgical formulas. These are nonrival inputs in production, or reflect the perfect expansability of ideas because they do not wear out or suffer from congestion, and can be used repeatedly. However, their potential role should be interpreted in terms of Paul David's distinction between *codified* and *tacit* (uncodified) knowledge. In most instances, the emphasis is on codified knowledge, which broadly connotes the packaging of information in various forms. This facilitates the process of transmission, verification, storage, and reproduction. Accordingly, it makes information easier to share or exchange and therefore enhances the convenience of transactions. In many cases, the production process is unable to deliver expected output efficiently because of a generalized lack of tacit knowledge, which is a complementary know-how to codified knowledge. It sometimes takes the form of details and material specifications that for one reason or other have been omitted from original blueprints, designs, or formulas. This form of knowledge increases as production processes and product designs become more complex. It is also difficult to acquire and is often expensive.

From a development perspective, the endogenous interpretation rests on the assumption that differential rates of technological progress among countries and regions are embodied in dynamic processes involving private investment in research and development and the acquisition of production experience. The developing countries are presumed to have a smaller stock of knowledge and technology in comparison to their more developed counterparts. Despite the fact that they are non-rival or expansive, these remain excludable goods and more likely to remain in the more developed countries or spill over to firms in countries with an equal level of technological sophistication. Since knowledge and ideas will not flow automatically to developing countries, they stand to gain by deliberately attracting them through private investment and outward-oriented development strategies.

Equilibrium endogenous models that examine the relationships among technology, trade, and long-term economic growth are predicated on the instrumental role of the international environment in determining the incentives motivating particular countries to accumulate stocks of codified knowledge. Since the production of ideas is a function of competitive pressures, the nature of the trade regime takes on added significance, and considerations of comparative advantage are used to explain why certain countries specialize in the creating of knowledge and use new technologies intensively. A germane assumption is that ideas and information will diffuse quickly and easily across international frontiers due to the rapid spread of global communications.

These presuppositions are exemplified in the model by Grossman and Helpman (1990), which is premised on a liberal world economy dichotomized between technology-generating industrial countries of the North and technology-borrowing and imitating countries of the South. In this conceptualization, the economic interests of the North are bound up exclusively with generating innovations through investments in science and invention while the South specializes in technological imitation and diffusion. The transfer of technological innovations generated in the North and their application to the production of tradable goods in the low-wage South will increase specialization between the two country groupings. The entrance of Southern imitators will lead to a contraction of employment in the commodity-producing industries of the North. The displaced workers will be absorbed in research and development activities in the North, ultimately resulting in an increase in the global rate of technological progress.

Needless to say, such theoretical predictions do not necessarily coincide with the facts of experience. Even if it is allowed that technological diffusion is an endogenous factor in long-term growth, there is nothing automatic about the process of transfer and imitation. A few of the more important reasons may be briefly mentioned. Information is costly to obtain and disseminate. Firms in the North are usually wont to claim strategic reasons for withholding their most advanced technology. In any event, local conditions and the imperatives of technological appropriateness require that technology should be carefully adapted to fit particular countries. Most of the technology that is formally transferred to the South takes the form of codified information, which is not always efficiently utilized because of a lack of tacit knowledge or complementary know-how. In the latter context, it cannot be readily assumed that technology would leak automatically to the South in the same way that it typically spreads among competing firms in technologically advanced countries.

Finally, attention has to be paid to the unequalizing mechanisms through which technology is diffused across national borders. These often reveal more areas of conflict rather than harmony of interests between the North and South, with countries in the former sphere increasingly determined to protect their intellectual property rights. The latter claim that the international system of property rights accords monopoly rights to foreign holders of patents and copyrights at the expense of consumers in the South. Under the circumstances, they consistently refuse to ratify international patent and copyright conventions on the grounds that they are inequitable. With the support of the United States and other industrial nations, the prevailing international system has recently been strengthened by the creation of the World Trade Organization. At the same time, countries such as India and Brazil have passed laws restricting the scope of international property rights protection. The dust has not yet settled on the issue about payments, if any, poor countries should make for acquiring knowledge which will ultimately become an integral part of humankind's universal heritage.

Chapter 4

Keynesian Duoeconomics: Turning Stones into Bread

It is widely perceived that John Maynard Keynes introduced a veritable "revolution" in modern economics. His *General Theory of Employment, Interest and Money* (1936) is usually credited with providing a major paradigm shift from the prevailing orthodoxy in economic theory and policy. However, the ideas of Keynes have taken on diverse meanings in textbooks, journals, and policy debates. Thus, a distinction is sometimes made between the "economics of Keynes" and "Keynesian economics." Consequently, "the content of what really is Keynes's own doctrine, Keynes's own version of Keynesian economics, is by no means easy to determine" (Hicks 1974: 5).

Keynes followed a particular current of classical theory, notably the paths trammelled by David Ricardo and Alfred Marshall. Like cost-of-production theorists, he stressed the essential role of production in economic progress. In this context, he defined entrepreneurial activity and people's interests in terms of their technical role in the production process. Nevertheless, the Keynesian challenge raised a basic skepticism about classical and neo-classical preconceptions regarding individual choice and market behavior, as well as their implications for the structure and functioning of the overall economic system.

In particular, Keynes pointed to the irrelevance of market analysis in solving problems of the real world. As he stated, "[o]ur criticism of the accepted classical theory of economics has consisted not so much in finding logical flaws in the analysis as in pointing out that its *tacit assumptions* are seldom or never satisfied, with the result that it cannot solve the economic problems of the *actual world*" (1936: 378; emphasis added). In this context, Hirschman (1981) has drawn a useful analytical distinction between classical and neo-classical former rests on the worldview that the laws of economics are universal and immutable, and therefore applicable to all types of situations and circumstances. Keynes challenged the presuppositions of monoeconomics on the grounds that they did not accord with the "facts of experience."

As he wrote in the opening chapter of the *General Theory* (1936: 3):

> I shall argue that the postulates of the classical theory are applicable to the *special case* only and not to the *general* case, the situation which it assumes being a limiting point of the possible positions of equilibrium. Moreover, the characteristics of the special case assumed by classical theory happen not to be those of the economic society in which we actually live, with the result that its teaching is misleading and disastrous if we attempt to apply it to the *facts of experience* [emphasis added].

Thus, the following "facts of experience" defined the objectives of the *General Theory*. First, Keynes's duoeconomics sought to distinguish between those sets of economic relations, precepts, and policies that are applicable to conditions of full employment (the "special case") vis-à-vis others that are more relevant to situations where resources are unemployed or underutilized (the "general case"). The objective, therefore, was to show how existing orthodoxy was inappropriate for dealing with any economic situation other than the special case of full employment of resources. The reason is that the highly logical system of thought in which orthodoxy was grounded led to the conclusion that the system would tend automatically to equilibrium at full employment.

Second, and on a related basis, Keynes sought to provide a theory of the working of the monetary production economy which would be *general*, that would demonstrate that the system could be in equilibrium at *any* level of employment, and that the special case of full employment would require the components of aggregate demand (consumption plus investment) to stand in a particular relationship with each other. Since he considered this an unlikely occurrence, government intervention would be required. Thus, a fundamental break with existing orthodoxy centered around state intervention, which had been hitherto regarded as an obstacle to the achievement of full employment.

Like many of his classical and neo-classical peers, Keynes was a consummate economic liberal. This meant that he had an abiding faith in the free market capitalist system. Unlike them, however, he was an interventionist and showed a preference for a system of managed capitalism. In such an arrangement, the freedom or ability of private individuals or households to choose between consumption expenditure and savings on the one hand, and the decision by private business firms to invest on the other, would be combined with state coordination of investment activity. Thus, a reformist role for the state is explicitly written into the economic equation.

Economic Development in the Spirit of Keynes

According to one noted economist, "some development economists are Keynesian, others are anti-Keynesian. The split between the Keynesians and anti-Keynesians applies to development economists as well as to those concerned with other aspects of economics" (Singer 1987: 70). Wherever one stands on this intellectual divide, it cannot be denied that Keynesian duoeconomics and its extensions have had a profound and lasting influence on the theory and practice of economic development.

We hasten to add that Keynes did not have any developing countries in mind when he wrote the *General Theory*, and in his advocacy of full employment for the industrial nations. It has also been suggested that the *General Theory* should be interpreted as a special case of "Depression Economics," in the sense that its domain assumptions, key analytical concepts, and policy prescriptions are more relevant to the explanation of characteristics of an industrial economy in depression, such as, Britain during the 1930s. Like some pundits of development theory and practice, Keynes never paid a formal visit to a developing country, even though his first treatise was on *Indian Currency Reform*. His lack of direct concern for poor countries and his English upper-class background might have led him to view development as something that could be easily and quickly achieved through capital accumulation (H. Johnson 1978).

While Keynes may have lacked a direct interest in the problems of developing countries, there is some agreement that the modern evolution of development economics has been significantly influenced by the concepts and analytical themes that he introduced into the lexicon of economics. The paradigmatic shift from "monoeconomics" to "duoeconomics" suggests a high degree of relevance of Keynesian macroanalytic principles and policy prescriptions to the study of development problems (Hirschman 1981). Some pertinent applications include, inter alia, national income accounting and theorizing about economic growth; the role of investment and savings in the development process; the role of the state vis-à-vis the market in economic development; and the macroeconomics of an open economy, that is, the possibilities of achieving internal and external balance through stabilization and adjustment.

Contextually, Keynes laid the foundations for modern national income accounting and the corresponding enthronement of GNP as the primary indicator of economic growth and development. The stimulation of modern national income accounting has been particularly influenced by the emphasis placed in Keynesian macroeconomics on *ex post* aggregates and economic concepts such as consumption, savings, and investment. The United Nations System of National Accounts (SNA), which is now routinely used to estimate the growth performance of countries, is also a descendant of Keynesian macroeconomics.

The Keynesian vision raised the awareness of economists and policymakers to the fact that even a growing economy, or one displaying all the properties of macroeconomic equilibrium, can experience unemployment disequilibrium. In the Keynesian analytical framework, the process of employment creation is treated primarily as a consequence of the general process of national income or output expansion, that is, in terms of a movement from underemployment to full employment equilibrium. The question has arisen, therefore, whether the involuntary unemployment which persisted in Britain during the 1930s bears any similarity to the structural and open forms of unemployment that continue to plague the developing nations of the world. The experience of these countries suggests that rapid growth in national income and output has not been translated into correspondingly high levels of employment and wages. In general, the overall employment situation has proved to be much more intractable compared to the historical experience of industrial nations.

It is commonly argued that the Keynesian notion of underemployed resources seems to have a direct counterpart in notions of surplus labor, underemployment, and disguised unemployment, which have become popular in describing the situation facing developing countries. In particular, the notion of disguised unemployment is thought to have a special intellectual affinity to Keynesian economics, since it was originally developed by Joan Robinson - one of Keynes's illustrious students and collaborators. The original idea was based on the claim that in times of mass underemployment (as was the case during the Great Depression), many of those who were formerly fully employed now had no alternative but to look for work in less appropriate forms of economic activity. As a result, their productive abilities could not be fully utilized, and they received inappropriate levels of compensation. Furthermore, the labor contribution of such people was not normally counted in the official statistics covering the total number of unemployed.

The idea was later used for description and policy analysis of the situation facing poor countries, where there was an apparent superfluity of underemployed people in the rural sector. Large numbers of such people were presumed to make very little or no contribution to agricultural output. Over the years, a considerable amount of intellectual capital has been devoted to providing an operational definition of disguised unemployment in the context of developing countries, and to incorporate the idea into the social cost-benefit analysis of development projects. As indicated in the previous chapter, the common practice is to analyze it from the perspective of labor market distortion, that is, where the market wage rate diverges from the national economic opportunity cost of labor. Early writers on development economics such as Ragnar Nurkse (1953) viewed widespread underemployment as a major factor contributing to the "vicious circle of poverty" and the "low level equilibrium trap." The disequilibrium conditions facing advanced economies with urban unemployment and developing countries with rural underemployment were used as a justification for interventionist public policies that were an anathema to the neo-classical paradigm. As we have emphasized, the latter is predicated on a belief in automatic adjustments toward full employment.

Keynes had advocated expansionary fiscal and monetary policy and an activist role for the state in combating unemployment. In a similar vein, first generation development economists such as Paul Rosenstein-Rodan (1943) prescribed some form of coordinated public investment planning as a means of mobilizing the underemployed for the purpose of industrialization and balanced economic growth. On the other hand, development economists such as Arthur Lewis (1954) and Albert Hirschman (1958) differentiated between Keynesian economics and the situation facing developing countries. In their view, there was underemployment of labor as well as other factors in the Keynesian system, whereas labor was the only redundant factor in developing countries. In his generalized diagnosis of underdevelopment, Hirschman pointed to the fact that these countries had "hidden reserves" not only of labor, but savings, entrepreneurship, and related resources. However, Keynesian remedies would be inadequate to activate them. There was a need instead for "pacing devices" and "pressure mechanisms" within a strategy of unbalanced growth.

Keynesianism has significantly influenced the emphasis that continues to be placed on capital accumulation as a motive force in the development process. Keynes viewed the decision to invest and the corresponding rates of capital accumulation as the primary factors propelling a capitalist-oriented economy toward sustained economic growth. In his schema, capital accumulation is determined by decisions to invest and not by decisions to save, as posited in pre-Keynesian economic theory. Classical political economy had postulated an automatic link between saving and investment. The argument is that when people save, the price (interest rate) charged to borrowers will be reduced. Business firms will borrow more for investment purposes because an increased number of projects will now appear to be more profitable compared to the cost of borrowing. Thus, when consumers reduce consumption (increase savings), business firms will be induced to increase their investment.

A flexible interest rate policy was supposed to guarantee the equality between savings and investment. Keynes argued that households save and business firms invest for entirely different reasons. Households may be motivated to save because of habit, to accumulate an adequate retirement income, in order to buy a house, and so on. By contrast, businesses may decide to change their investment plans based on factors such as expected profitability, confidence, etc. Under the circumstances, there is no reason to expect a flexible interest rate to effect the requisite harmony between savings and investment. If, for example, household savings exceed business investment, gluts will emerge, workers will be laid off, and consumption will be reduced to an even lower level.

The argument turns on the Keynesian notion of aggregate or total demand. The claim is that a depression or recession can occur when the total demand for goods and services is less than total income or inadequate demand by households (consumption) and business firms (investment). If people do not spend enough, businesses will reduce their output and employment levels will fall. In this analytical genre, the significance of investment is explained by its potential to augment aggregate income. As the latter increases, savings will grow not only in absolute terms but also as a percentage of income. The implication is that, as income grows, finding a volume of investment which is sufficiently large to provide an adequate level of aggregate demand poses a more complicated problem.

In the Keynesian system, the marginal propensity to consume (the increment of income spent on consumption goods) is supposed to determine the relation between the increment in investment and the resultant change in income that will induce the increment in saving required to maintain an equality between savings and investment. The multiplier concept is used to describe the relationship between the increment in investment and the corresponding change in income. This means that, as income grows and the marginal propensity to consume declines, increasingly larger increments of investment would be necessary for securing given increments in income.

The belief that investment rather than savings is responsible for increases in national wealth has been explained by the so-called "paradox of thrift." The paradox results because attempts by savers to save more may actually lower current income and aggregate savings by reducing aggregate demand expenditure on consumption goods. A germane idea is also found in the neo-Keynesian differential savings hypothesis (Kaldor 1955). The hypothesis is traceable to the classical view of income distribution, and especially David Ricardo's conceptualization of a dual class structure comprising capitalists and workers.

Among other things, these classes were distinguished by their respective marginal propensities to save. Workers, whose incomes are derived solely from wages, are deemed to have a very low propensity to save. By contrast, capitalists, whose incomes are derived primarily from profits and property ownership, have a relatively high propensity to save. The assumption is that the share of profits in national income is determined by the ratio of investment to income (capitalists are the ones who invest), and the marginal propensity to save of wage earners is near zero. Profits constitute the sum of investment and property income received by capitalists, with wages constituting the residue. With total savings coming almost entirely from profits, the growth of aggregate income or output tends to vary directly with the share of profits in national income. For any rate of economic growth, the share of profits will tend to vary inversely with the propensity of capitalists to save.

The implication of this pattern of reasoning is that the lower savings of capitalists tend to enhance their share of national income. Following from this is the paradoxical conclusion that conspicuous consumption and lower savings on the part of capitalists tend to raise their total profits. This is the parable of the "Widow's Cruse," which is often stated in the dictum: "capitalists earn what they spend, and workers spend what they earn." In this context, Keynes stated that "[t]he outstanding faults of the economic society in which we live are its failure to provide for full employment and its arbitrary and inequitable distribution of wealth and incomes. . . . Thus our argument leads to the conclusion that in contemporary conditions the growth of wealth, so far from being dependent on the abstinence of the rich, as is commonly supposed, is more likely to be impeded by it" (1936: 372, 373).

The next question concerns determinants of the decision to invest. Here Keynes relies on the main corpus of orthodox microeconomic theory, which interprets this decision in terms of the constrained maximization principle. Based on the insights of economists such as Knut Wicksell and Irving Fisher, an investment is considered profitable if the anticipated rate of return is greater than, or at least equal to, the market rate of interest. In Keynesian parlance, the "inducement to invest" reflects the schedule of the "marginal efficiency of capital," or the anticipated rate of return on different volumes of investment. The rate of interest provides some indication of the cost of funds for financing the investments, while the rate of return reflects future yields that can be expected therefrom.

Since the stream of yields normally accrues over a determinate number of future time periods, it follows that the idea of the rate of return involves long-term expectations, and therefore, risk and uncertainty. Contextually, Keynes argued that the level and pace of investment depend crucially on the availability of a sufficient number of dynamic entrepreneurs who are willing to take risks after carefully assessing the long-term future. The lack of certainty means that potential investors have to take chances and rely on the vagaries of what Keynes called "animal spirits." Here, it should be mentioned that Keynes was particularly concerned about the "rentier aspect of capitalism." Accordingly, he called for "the euthanasia of the rentier, of the functionless investor, ...of the cumulative oppressive power of the capitalist to exploit the scarcity-value of capital" through speculative activity (1936: 376).

The idea of an innovative entrepreneur is traceable to Schumpeter (1934), who viewed the entrepreneur as the central agent in the development process. He reasoned that the entrepreneur, as an individual who introduces innovations, is typically responsible for introducing new goods, production methods, markets, and for the reorganization of industry. Since such innovational activities usually involve a relatively high degree of risk and uncertainty, entrepreneurial acts tend to occur in a discontinuous, leap-frogging, or zig-zag manner. Furthermore, entrepreneurial innovation may also reflect superior information which, at the subjective level, enables investors to reduce the risks and uncertainties associated with new investment opportunities.

Given the pivotal role of investment, Singer has remarked that the ideal situation for the application of Keynesian principles is one in which *"there are plenty of stones around to be turned into bread (literally) by the magic of finance"* (1987: 84; emphasis added). In his essay on "The Economic Possibilities of Our Grandchildren" (1931), Keynes laid down four prerequisites for countries to achieve sustained economic development: (i) a high rate of capital accumulation, which is fixed by the margin between production and consumption; (ii) a heavy reliance on the fruits of scientific progress; (iii) a determined effort to control wars and avoid civil strife; and (iv) population control, which, as shown below, was linked to the "natural rate of growth." He also attributed the slow material progress achieved in the world up to the beginning of the eighteenth century to the relatively low levels of capital accumulation and technological development.

As is now well known, the importance attached to capital accumulation found a most celebrated expression in the Harrod-Domar model of economic growth (Harrod 1939; Domar 1946). This model came to serve as the lynchpin for ideas about development policy and planning during the immediate postwar years and after. It is believed that Keynes's essay on "Some Economic Consequences of a Declining Population" (1937) actually anticipated some of the views articulated in Harrod's "An Essay of Dynamic Theory" (1939). Keynes is also credited with inventing the concepts of the "natural" and "warranted" rates of growth. As elaborated below, these concepts were to provide the analytical framework for the design of development policies, such as those targeted at raising the investment ratio, lowering the capital/output ratio, and controlling population.

The Harrod-Domar model basically extrapolates the original Keynesian explanation of short-run unemployment in a capitalist economy into a model of economic growth. As in the case of the *General Theory*, the model highlights the fact that fixed investment is the prime mover of the economy. In general, it postulates that saving and investment not only create capital capacity, but also generate output, incomes, and employment. The entire growth in these aggregates is attributed to investment or the past growth of capital. The relationship between income-output growth and investment is determined by the capital/output ratio, that is, the amount of capital required per unit of output. The model turns on the growth equation $g = s/k$, where g is the output growth rate, s is the average savings ratio, or the proportion of income saved at full employment, and k is the capital/output ratio. The equation therefore states that the growth rate of output is equal to the savings rate divided by the capital/output ratio. It implies that aggregate income or output must grow at a constant rate if full employment of resources is to be assured. At this rate, the growth of fixed capital will generate an amount of increased sales and profits just sufficient to justify the investment made to increase the capital stock. This represents the "warranted rate of growth," which Harrod assumed would satisfy entrepreneurs and motivate them to invest in further growth. On the other hand, there is a "natural rate of growth," which reflects the natural rate of population growth and the rate of technological progress taking place in the economy. Harrod's major concern was with the possibility of guaranteeing an equilibrium between the warranted and natural rates of growth, and on a related basis, with the economic disturbances that could result from a divergence between them. In such an eventuality, macroeconomic equilibrium would become impossible to secure or sustain.

The possibility of disequilibrium can be explained by contrasting two scenarios. On the one hand, if the warranted rate is lower than the natural rate of growth, unemployment is likely to increase. This could arise because the "animal spirits" of entrepreneurs are dimmed, or for other reasons that lead them to underinvest. As a result, capital growth would be less than warranted, and the overall rate of growth of income or output would be even less on account of this underinvestment. On the other hand, if the warranted rate is higher than the natural rate of growth, serious bottlenecks are likely to develop in the supply of labor and other productive resources, leading to a crisis situation. In this case, entrepreneurs are probably overspending because of over-optimistic expectations about the future, among other things. When this happens, capital growth will exceed the warranted level, and the overall rate of growth will be even higher because of the multiplier effects associated with additional investment expenditures.

The logic underlying the Harrod-Domar growth model leads to the following general conclusions. First is that both overinvestment and underinvestment can be major causes of instability in a capitalist-oriented economy. Second, relatively high investment rates and low capital/output ratios can be growth-promoting factors. Third, the prospects for obtaining respectable levels of macroeconomic growth depend on the extent to which such growth is planned. This conclusion derives from the fact that the growth rate that is ultimately attainable depends on the proportion of total production the authorities can extract from the economy in the form of savings, as well as on the volume of additional output that can be obtained per unit of investment, that is, the incremental capital to output ratio.

As mentioned earlier, the concepts of the warranted and natural rates of growth have provided the analytical framework for development policies aimed at raising savings rates, improving techniques to reduce the capital/output ratio, and for controlling population in developing countries. In this context, the typical developing country has come to be characterized as one in which the natural rate of growth exceeds the warranted rate, that is, where the population growth rate is higher than that of physical capital accumulation. This proposition has provided the main guidepost for planning the investment requirements necessary for growth in the majority of developing countries.

The Harrod-Domar growth model has generated an extensive and heated controversy in the development literature. While the key role of capital in the growth and development process is now accepted, considerable skepticism still surrounds the relatively narrow concept of investment on which the model relies. It substitutes an aggregate "k" (capital/output ratio) for the particular forms the capital structure may take. This enables the economist to speak of economic growth as a trajectory following from a specific savings function and capital/output ratio. This assumes a world in which the aggregate capital structure is homogeneous rather than heterogeneous. When an aggregate structure is assumed, any increase in investment merely adds to the capital stock. Therefore, each additional unit of investment tends to diminish its marginal productivity. When the heterogeneous nature of the capital stock is recognized, new capital will not necessarily become a substitute for existing capital.

In a world where all investments are homogeneous, no creativity or innovative behavior on the part of entrepreneurs is called for. By contrast, when a heterogeneous capital structure is assumed, new investments can be complementary to the existing structure. Entrepreneurs will take account of the existing structure and try to discover as yet unrecognized holes in the structure that their investments could fill. Some may even see future possibilities that others could not imagine, thereby propelling the chameleon-like structure into entirely new directions. The point of emphasis is that an aggregate variable cannot possibly account for the many complexities the real capital structure could take, and may therefore misrepresent the actual nature of economic growth. Whether the available artifacts are ploughs, machines, or computers, individual entrepreneurs can use their creativity and imagination in marshalling all the local knowledge of their particular positions in the economy in order to build on what is already there - Hirschman's "hidden reserves." This ability of individuals to interpret the existing structure in new ways and to build on those ideas constitutes an important aspect of economic development.

Thus, the emphasis placed by the Harrod-Domar growth model, and in Keynesianism itself, on aggregates tends to lose sight of certain important questions that are of considerable relevance to the development equation. One of these relates to the form capital investment should take, that is, what should be the nature and composition of such investment? In this regard, there is now widespread agreement that a poor country can ill afford the type of investment designed to "dig holes and fill them up again" merely as a means of breaking the impasse of unemployment equilibrium and setting the Keynesian multiplier to work. As highlighted below, a predominant reason is traceable to supply bottlenecks (physical, technological, and human) and institutional constraints that disable the investment environment.

In both the original Keynesian framework and in the Harrod-Domar model, investment takes the form of additions to physical capital goods, which are distinguished from consumption goods. Since capital goods are assumed to be responsible for augmenting income and creating employment, many sympathetic economists and policymakers have been wont to overstate the importance of physical investment. In this context, it can be argued that investment for sustained economic development also requires enhancement of the stock of human capital and public goods such as health, nutrition, and education. This is not to deny that most forms of investment in human development have a physical component, such as textbook production, and the construction of schools, hospitals, and clinics. The point of emphasis, however, is that the relevant mixes of physical and human investment should always be fully demarcated.

A second, but germane, question relates to the sources from which the increases in savings and investment should emanate. This requires a careful assessment of the "structural rigidities" that typically prevent investment in developing countries from rising in tandem with, or as a predictable response to, increased aggregate demand or profitability. The most widely mentioned ones include: (i) the lack of technological capacity to produce investment goods; (ii) stringent balance of payment difficulties or foreign exchange constraints that preclude the alternative of importing such goods; (iii) the lack of complementary inputs in the form of skills, intermediate products, and market institutions; (iv) pressure on wage goods, especially food, that prevents the expansion of investment; (v) the difficulty of financing increases in investment through additional savings and taxation; and (vi) the presence of cumulative and circular causation (Myrdal 1957).

The overall effect of these bottlenecks is to make the Keynesian and Harrod-Domar prescriptions for increasing the rate of physical investment of little practical value. The solution lies in pursuing several interdependent courses of action. One concerns endogenous change through improvements in capital productivity, education and knowledge, the fostering of an entrepreneurial spirit, introduction of appropriate technology, and reform of government policies and institutions. Another is a process of exogenous change through improved export earnings, foreign investment and aid, and less burdensome sources of external finance. As discussed in the final section of this chapter, the latter path was suggested by the "international" Keynes in his proposals for the establishment of the Bretton Woods system and a liberal international economic order.

Public Expenditure and the Activist State

A focal point in Keynes's analysis inheres in his advocacy of expansionary government expenditure to stimulate investment in new capital formation, and via the investment-consumption multiplier, consumption expenditure as well. In this context, a basic idea behind the dynamics of full employment policy revolved around the possibility of generating a volume of expenditure that would secure sustained economic growth and a maximum utilization of resources. This requires a concept of total expenditure or aggregate demand that is extended to include not only private spending on consumer and investment goods, but also government expenditure on consumption and investment. Where an economy is operating below its full potential, private expenditure may be insufficient to generate a level of aggregate income corresponding to full employment. In most cases, consumer spending cannot be easily increased because it is constrained by an inflexible distribution of income that cannot be altered, at least in the short run. It may also be difficult to increase private investment because of a lack of investment opportunities, a weak urge to accumulate, or because "animal spirits are dimmed."

Where levels of private consumption and investment are inadequate, recourse to public expenditure may be needed to fill the gap between the level of income generated by the automatic operation of market forces and the requirements of a full employment level of income. Where public expenditure becomes an important determinant of national income and employment, government activity must be considered an endogenous force in the overall economic system. As in the case of private investment expenditure, the Keynesian multiplier plays a crucial role in determining the level of public expenditure required to achieve a level of aggregate income or output corresponding to the full employment of productive resources. The general idea behind the multiplier is that it highlights the potential effect of any type of investment expenditure in augmenting income and reducing or eliminating unemployment.

Thus, any type of expenditure, be it private or public, tends to induce additional spending. The operation of the multiplier implies that any increment in the level of public expenditure will tend to increase aggregate demand by more than it has increased public demand for goods and services. As Keynes argued, the aggregate level of such expenditures matters more than their composition. A primary example is public works designed to "dig holes only to fill them up again." The focal point is on the increments of government expenditure required to create an additional demand that fully utilizes the underemployed productive capacity.

A germane and contentious issue concerns the method by which such increased government expenditure will be financed. It is evident that public expenditure aimed at increasing national income and employment can be effective only if it constitutes an addition to, rather than a substitute for, the volume of expenditure that would have been generated in the absence of such government intervention. In cases where the additional public expenditure is a substitute for private expenditure, the total level of expenditure is likely to remain at the same level, with no perceptible effect on national income and employment. In any event, how the additional expenditure is financed ultimately determines whether it adds to total spending, or is merely substitutive.

For example, where the increment in public expenditure is financed through additional taxation, it partly becomes a substitute for private forms of expenditure, and is therefore not an effective means for increasing national income and employment. For this reason, Keynes favored a type of fiscal policy based on deficit financing, or the creation of public debt. The overall rationale is that when a government borrows from the public (for example, by issuing bonds and other financial securities), it is making use of private savings. Public expenditure financed in this manner is much less likely to become a substitute for private spending than if it is financed through increased taxation. Contextually, Keynesian-type fiscal policy has historically emphasized at least three ways of guaranteeing full employment: (i) increased government purchases of goods and services, with an attendant budget deficit; (ii) a reduction in taxes, thereby requiring a large budget deficit; and (iii) an increase in government expenditure and taxes by more or less equal amounts, with a balanced budget.

All three alternatives envisaged a larger role for the state in economic management. As Keynes stated, "I expect to see the State, which is in a position to calculate the marginal efficiency of capital goods on the long views and on the basis of the general social advantage, taking an ever greater responsibility for directly organizing investment. . . . The State will have to exercise a guiding influence on the propensity to consume, partly through its scheme of taxation, partly by fixing the rate of interest, and partly, perhaps, in other ways" (1936: 378). This philosophy represented a distinct change from the pre-Keynesian paradigmatic schema in which state intervention was considered an exogenous intrusion into the economic process.

By assigning a larger and endogenous role for the state or public sector in the economy, Keynes prepared the way for the interpretation of development policy in terms of a discretionary type of economic management at the national level. Thus, planning came to be viewed as an effective mechanism for overcoming the deficiencies of the market-price system, and for enlisting public support to achieve national objectives related to economic growth, employment creation, and poverty alleviation. It was against this background that the pioneers of modern development economics utilized Keynesian and Pigovian critiques of the market-price mechanism to advocate the necessity for planned development.

Since development could not be left entirely to market forces, government investment was thought to be needed to create "social overhead capital" as a means of laying the foundations for the developing countries to "take off" on the flight toward self-sustained economic growth. From the perspective of Pigovian externalities, the private sector could not be expected to invest at sufficiently high levels in the creation of such forms of capital because of increasing returns to scale, technological externalities, and the fact that such investments tend to display the characteristics of public goods. Since neo-classical-type adjustment or marginal changes could not adequately address the problem at hand, planning was conceived as a necessary means of devising macroeconomic targets and providing the coordinating efforts and consistency required for the preferences of society to be realized.

In the economic management of both the more developed and less developed countries, a great deal of controversy has surrounded Keynes's advocacy of more state intervention. As he wrote in his *Essays in Persuasion*, "I think that capitalism, wisely managed, can probably be made more efficient for attaining economic ends than any alternative system yet in sight, but that in itself, it is in many ways extremely objectionable. Our problem is to work out a social organization which shall be as efficient as possible without offending our notions of a satisfactory way of life."

Contextually, Keynes' rejection of laissez-faire cannot be interpreted as an endorsement of the bureaucratic type of planning that was once popular in erstwhile socialist countries and the developing world. The issue had surfaced during the celebrated Socialist Calculation debate of the interwar years as a means of showing why a decentralized market economy is likely to provide a greater degree of socio-economic coordination than a centralized one. In particular, Nobel Laureate Friedrich Hayek (1935) had argued that increasing political involvement in the economic system would eventually lead to totalitarian dictatorship. Hayekian anti-Keynesianism was to usher in the idea of a "dirigiste dogma," or the potential dangers inherent in government solutions to economic and social problems.

Yet, it can be countered that the "dogma" was perhaps more applicable to his disciples than to Keynes himself. As we had emphasized, his analysis of the British economy during the 1930s was based on assumptions about reasonably functioning markets. The case for planning was limited to the establishment of a macroeconomic framework in which microeconomic choices could be rationally orchestrated. The guiding philosophy was that in the absence of an appropriate macroeconomic "enabling" environment, markets will generate the type of stagnation implicit in "underemployment equilibrium."

Open Economy Macroeconomics: Maintaining Internal and External Balance

Turning to the "international" Keynes, a fundamental expectation was that independent governments would become increasingly responsible for maintaining both internal and external balance. An explanation of this requirement requires a shift of the analytical focus from the components of domestic aggregate demand for goods and services to an open economic setting involving international transactions. A country's aggregate demand consists not only of domestic private and government expenditure on consumption and investment goods, but also includes the net demand of foreigners for its exports. This means that imports have to be subtracted from exports because the former constitute a demand for goods produced outside the country.

In other words, any surplus or deficit in the balance of merchandise trade must be added to the internal component of aggregate demand, that is, domestic private and public consumption, and investment expenditure. On this basis, earnings from a country's trade surplus can be considered as the foreign exchange counterpart for domestic savings, and tend to play a role analogous to investment. Given the level of domestic savings, the net earnings from foreign trade represent the additional amount of foreign exchange needed to meet a country's investment requirements and to preserve its economic growth momentum.

Within the Keynesian macroeconomic framework, a country's external balance can be construed as the difference between its aggregate expenditure and aggregate income, with the latter comprising consumption, saving, and the amount absorbed by taxation. The portion of this income which is saved can lead to increased expenditure if one or more of the following conditions hold: (i) if it is channelled into private investment; (ii) if it is used to finance that part of public expenditure not covered by tax revenue; and/or (iii) if it is absorbed by a deficit in merchandise trade. Thus, if all other elements of aggregate expenditure remain constant, a balance of trade surplus will tend to augment aggregate demand or income, while a deficit is likely to produce the reverse effect.

The mechanism is supposed to work as follows. A country with a trade surplus will initially experience a rise in aggregate demand and therefore income. The increase in aggregate income will in turn generate additional savings which, by definition, must be equal to the surplus in the balance of trade. It can also be expected that the increase in income will induce additional spending on imports, thereby reducing the initial trade surplus. The size of the reduction will depend on the marginal propensity to import, which is defined as the proportion of additional income spent on imports. Conversely, where a country faces a trade deficit, aggregate demand and income will fall, and savings will be reduced by the amount of the deficit. In this case, however, the fall in income will reduce import expenditure, and therefore the size of the overall trade deficit. The point of emphasis is that in cases of both surplus and deficit, Keynes's equilibrating mechanism relies on variations in the levels of aggregate demand and income. This is in contrast to the pre-Keynesian perspective in which the balance between exports and imports is achieved primarily through movements in prices.

One implication of the above analytical framework is that the economic growth potential of any country tends to be constrained by its balance of payments performance - a phenomenon termed "the balance of payments equilibrium growth rate" (Harrod 1933). As a general rule, no country can grow faster than its balance of payments equilibrium growth rate, unless it can find funds to finance the deficit created by an import growth rate exceeding that of exports. This is explained by Harrod's "foreign trade multiplier," which, in an open economy, is considered the primary mechanism for keeping the balance of payments in equilibrium.

The concept can be explained by extending the Keynesian income-saving relationship to the case of an open economy. Given elements of domestic private and government expenditure, the foreign trade multiplier shows the effect of a trade surplus or deficit on income. Conceptually, the effect of introducing foreign trade into the analysis of a closed economy is to reduce the value of the Keynesian multiplier. The reason is that imports, like savings, constitute a leakage from the income stream. This means that a given level of income generates less domestic expenditure than it would in a closed economy.

In the case of an open economy, the situation can be further explained in terms of the following simple assumptions: (i) a given country produces two types of output - goods for home consumption and exports; (ii) all domestic income is disposed of by purchasing goods produced for home consumption and imports; and (iii) any autonomous changes in imports, that is, imports not induced by any increase in domestic income, can be expected to change income sufficiently, so that the import changes will adjust to the level of exports. Thus, given the marginal propensity to import, any increase in exports can be expected to induce a high enough upward change in income. This, in turn, will lead to an increase in imports to match the new level of exports. The reasoning behind the balance of payments equilibrium growth rate thesis, therefore, is that, given certain conditions (e.g., that there are no income leakages in the form of savings and taxation, or induced expenditures due to government transfers and investment), income will adjust to preserve the balance of trade. The overall implication is that any plans to import in excess of exports will depress income, and vice-versa.

The conclusion for open economies is that export demand plays a critical role in determining economic growth, especially when the propensity to import is substantial. However, the overall effect on domestic income depends on the extent to which any shortfalls resulting from disequilibrium in the trade sector can be made up by other compensating expenditures, such as government income transfers designed to maintain domestic consumption and investment levels. This conclusion is also synergistic with the "export-led" growth model of economic transformation, which stresses that it is only through export expansion that the economic growth rate can be raised without a simultaneous deterioration in the balance of payments. But, the overall impact of any export expansion will ultimately depend on the relative size of import spending that it is likely to induce. This explains why the stabilization and adjustment programs of the multilateral lending agencies typically rely on a combination of policy initiatives designed to promote both export expansion and import restraint.

In the above context, Keynes can be credited for his seminal analysis of the ideal conditions necessary for countries to achieve internal balance (full employment, economic growth) and external balance (a viable balance of payments position over the medium term) simultaneously. The implication is that when a country accepts economic growth and full employment as national priorities, it will always have to face the problem of having to pursue progressive domestic economic policies that are free of a balance of payments constraint. In general, monetary and fiscal policies are now relied upon as the main instruments for achieving internal equilibrium, while exchange rate adjustment is typically used as the primary policy tool for correcting balance of payments disequilibrium, especially in small open developing economies. Of some significance is the fact that the evolution of views about the exchange rate is a direct outcome of Keynes's proposals for reform of the international monetary system and the corresponding establishment of a liberal international economic order, with the Bretton Woods institutions playing a pivotal role in this arrangement.

Keynes was a major player at the International Monetary and Financial Conference held at Bretton Woods, New Hampshire, in July 1944. The Bretton Woods Conference was called primarily to establish the International Monetary Fund (IMF), with the International Bank for Reconstruction and Development (IBRD or World Bank) coming as an afterthought. The new international monetary system was expected to provide sufficient liquidity to finance trade, facilitate balance of payments adjustment, and provide enough financial reserves. As the foundation pillar of the new system, the central task of the IMF centered around the balance of payments positions of its members, and its establishment was inherently linked to an entirely new framework of balance of payments adjustment. In particular, it was supposed to assist members to avoid the excessive cyclical swings in their domestic economies that were caused by the need to maintain external stability during the days of the gold standard. Therefore, alternatives to domestic deflation had to be found in order to counteract balance of payments deficits.

In retrospect, the new international monetary and financial system came to represent only a pale shadow of what Keynes originally proposed. He had called for a new system of global demand management based on the creation of a world central bank, a world currency, automatic liquidity, stable commodity prices, and a more symmetric system of global adjustment in which more pressure would be put on the balance of payments of surplus countries and not unilaterally on deficit ones. What ruled the day was the more modest proposal of Harry Dexter White and the U.S. Treasury for a stabilization fund (see Williamson 1983).

The hypothetical question can be raised whether the world as a whole, and developing countries in particular, would have been better off had Keynes's plan prevailed at Bretton Woods rather than the less ambitious White Plan. While a satisfactory scientific answer cannot be provided, it can be speculated that the Keynesian alternative would have provided a superior global environment for developing countries (Williamson 1987). For example, the balance of payments surpluses of Japan, Germany, and oil-exporting nations would have supplied the finance needed to reduce the persistent unemployment in developed countries and restart economic growth in a developing world still struggling to adjust unilaterally under balance of payments deficits and heavy debt burden.

Of some relevance to this situation is Keynes's views about German reparations. In his *Economic Consequences for the Peace* (1919) [*Collected Writings*, Vol. 2], Keynes expressed a concern about the proposal to make Germany pay reparations on the grounds that sufficient attention was not paid to the country's ability to pay. In his view, Germany could not pay the amounts expected from its potential production without a substantial change in its terms of trade, or the relationship between its export earnings and import costs. Any attempt to enforce payment would require creditors to accept German imports (the "transfer problem"), which in turn would damage the competitive nature of firms in payee countries.

A similar situation faced contemporary developing nations after the oil shocks of 1973-74 and 1979-80. Their outstanding foreign debt could only be serviced and amortized through increased exports to creditor countries. This meant that the latter had to increase their import spending relative to domestic production. Correlatively, debtor countries had to reduce their spending on imports relative to production. In other words, a smooth process of international adjustment required specific patterns of spending relative to production in both creditor and debtor nations. Alas, this has yet to be!

Despite the failure to implement Keynesian proposals for global adjustment, the lending policies of the IMF and World Bank still rely in part on an extended

Keynesian analytical framework in the interpretation of the macroeconomic disequilibrium facing debtor countries. Their stabilization and structural adjustment programs are predicated on the need to achieve internal and external balance through policies based on expenditure "reduction" and "switching." Internal balance refers to the highest levels of aggregate demand and domestic employment that are consistent with the achievement of non-inflationary growth. External balance depicts a situation in which the balance of payments would be in equilibrium over the medium term.

Expenditure reduction involves the use of Keynesian-type aggregate demand management, or changes in domestic spending via monetary and fiscal policies that directly affect the level of economic activity. Contrary to Keynesian preconceptions, however, the policies advocated for developing countries tend to be contractionary. Expenditure switching policies are designed to change the composition of domestic and foreign expenditure through changes in relative prices, or devaluation of the domestic currency. Even in this case, Keynesian analytical tools became instrumental in determining the theoretical and practical effects of exchange rate adjustment on the balance of payments and other economic aggregates.

In this context, neo-classical and Keynesian perspectives of devaluation reach different conclusions because they are predicated on different beliefs and preconceptions about how the economy works. The former relies on an *elasticities approach* to ascertain the effects of a devaluation on countries with different trade structures. The typical case is a small open economy which cannot influence world prices of its exports or imports. In such a case, devaluation is expected to improve the balance of trade while leaving the terms of trade unchanged. The primary focus is on the *partial effects* (elasticities of supply and demand) on the balance of trade, that is, all other variables are held constant.

Needless to say, the effects of a devaluation depend on the behavior of the entire economic system, that is, on *total effects*. This reflects the analytical thrust of the Keynesian-type *absorption approach*, which rests on a belief that devaluation affects not only the relative prices of domestic and traded goods, but also aggregate income and expenditure, or "absorption." The argument is that the nature and degree of alteration in the trade balance will be reflected in the difference between the change in aggregate income and income-induced changes in absorption that result from the process. Over the years, both perspectives have been integrated into the *monetary approach* that now undergirds IMF and World Bank philosophy. Consequently, the effects of devaluation are analyzed in terms of monetary movements associated with balance of payments surpluses and deficits.

III

THE REVOLUTION

Chapter 5

Birth of Development Economics: Pioneering Interpretations

Development economics emerged during the 1940s and 1950s as a more or less self-contained branch of the economics discipline. It was essentially concerned with explaining and interpreting why some countries are poor and others rich, and prescribing policies to effect a meaningful transformation from poverty to riches. Its very birth reflected the tension between orthodox monoeconomics and duoeconomics. The Keynesian revolution had put on firm footing the belief that there were two kinds of economics: a monoeconomics grounded in the classical and neo-classical tradition, which purportedly applied to the "special case" in which resources are fully employed; and a duoeconomics of Keynesian vintage, which relied on a different set of beliefs, preconceptions, theories, and policies designed to interpret a situation characterized by substantial idle capacity and unemployment.

This raised a question whether the same or different economic principles applied to developed and developing countries. The new development economics was rooted in the stance of duoeconomics. Evolution of its subject matter has reflected the search for a distinct mode of interpretation based on preconceptions and interests (ideological presuppositions), theoretical propositions (explanation), causal empiricism (historical extrapolations), and policy (prescriptions). As in the case of Keynesian duoeconomics, a veritable "revolution" was to take place in the theory and practice of economic development. As we approach the end of the twentieth century, however, the field's unmistakable demise is apparently at hand.

While the discourse on the development-underdevelopment antinomy is alive and well, there is now a widespread perception that what used to be called development economics has returned to the fold of mainstream or general economics. With the "neo-classical resurgence" in economics, the study of development has been transformed into the application of orthodox economic principles to the interpretation of the deep development cathexia facing the majority of countries in Africa, Asia, Latin America, and the Caribbean. The subject is now interpreted from the perspectives of various subfields: macro- and microeconomics, trade, growth, agriculture, and the like. While specialists in these areas hardly communicate with each other, the majority share a common belief in the basic tenets of monoeconomics.

This chapter highlights the major preconceptions, normative beliefs, and theoretical interpretations undergirding the birth and early life of development economics. It adds some measure of credibility to a central thesis of the book that the growth of knowledge is the product of a cumulative interplay between ideas and interests. According to Meier (1984), development economics did not arise so much as a formal theoretical discipline, but was rather fashioned as a practical subject in response to the needs of policymakers in the more developed sector of the world to advise governments of emergent nations on the steps to be taken in effecting the transformation from poverty to riches.

Formative Influences: The Interplay of Interests

In the above context, Hirschman (1981) proffered the view that the emergence of development economics was based in part on the assertion of the "mutual benefits" thesis, or the claim that the relations between rich and poor countries could be handled in ways that were beneficial to both. This optimistic belief hinged on the expectation that the rich countries were capable of making a lasting contribution to the sustained development of their poorer counterparts through adequate financial transfers, expanded trade, and technical assistance. Economic development and foreign assistance were linked to the expected emergence of stable political democracies in the tropics.

In the eyes of many influential analysts in North America, the establishment of the good society in the newly emergent nation states required the creation of preconditions for instituting American-style democracy through rapid economic growth. In this context, the interests of the richer countries were rationalized as "an effort to maximize the attractiveness and feasibility of the third choice: to help make the evolution to modernization successful enough that major groups will not struggle either to repress change entirely or promote it by ruthless and extreme measures" (Millikan and Blackmer 1961: 98). It would be remembered that this ideology gained ascendancy during the heyday of Cold War politics when the superiority of a "First World" of capitalism and freedom was being constantly juxtaposed against the decadence of "Second World" communism. Since the majority of the newly emerging "Third World" countries were already under the Western sphere of influence, it was incumbent upon the West to ensure that they did not fall prey to communism.

From a different perspective, a pervasive feeling among Third World countries was that their *de jure* political decolonization was replaced by *de facto* economic dependence and underdevelopment. Under the circumstances, a primary concern centered around the necessity of intermeshing political freedom with the prerequisites of economic self-determination. Thus the new idea of "thirdness" came to depict the essence and authenticity of a Third World with its own uniqueness and economic identity. Despite its original links to First World interests, development economics added intellectual rigor to the interpretation of this philosophy. The struggle for an autonomous development order was eloquently expressed by Jawaharlal Nehru, the first Prime Minister of independent India, in the following terms (1949: 91):

> It is not a question of theory; or communism or socialism or capitalism. . . . The method which delivers the goods and brings about the necessary changes and gives satisfaction to the masses will justify itself . . . . Our problem today is to raise the standard of the masses, supply them with their needs, give them the wherewithal to lead a decent life, and help them to progress and advance in life not only in regard to material things, but in regard to cultural and spiritual things as well.

Nehru's sentiments reflected the willingness of the newly independent states to make deliberate economic choices and experiment with policy options that were outside the pale of the historical experience of the more developed capitalist and communist nations. As further discussed below, the desire for rapid economic and social transformation was translated into ambitious national development plans and programs that envisaged a quick repetition (though in a different form) of the growth momentum experienced in North America and Europe. The overall mood was one in which the pursuit of broad-based economic and social goals was deemed critical not only for the nation-building efforts of the Third World, but also to the process of forging relations of equity and equality with the rest of the world.

However, these optimistic objectives could only be realized within the parameters of the extant liberal international economic order. Its establishment was predicated on a strong belief that financial transfers could give the needed fillip to the development process in two interdependent ways. Since domestic investible resources were insufficient in countries at low per capita income levels, private foreign investment and official aid were considered as necessary catalysts to increased domestic capital formation. At the same time, such resource flows would relieve the foreign exchange bottleneck, which was interpreted as an additional and separate constraint. In this context, the emergence of development economics was rooted in the traditional belief that capital accumulation tends to play a critical role in initiating and nurturing the development process. As shown earlier, this was a central tenet in classical political economy through to the Keynesian Harrod-Domar model.

From the latter perspective, the central problem of development was construed as simply one of increasing resources devoted to fixed capital investment. This model of investment-led growth gained primacy in the determination of policy with respect to domestic savings and foreign aid. For example, if a country wanted to achieve an aggregate growth rate of 5 percent, and if the average capital-output ratio was, say, 4:1, the net investment rate would have to be targeted at 20 percent. Hence, a developing country with a relatively low savings rate of, say, 5 to 10 percent would be in no position to initially attain the required rate of investment. Under the circumstances, two related courses of action would have to be followed: (i) it would have to set a manageable target for raising the rate of domestic savings gradually; and (ii) while the savings rate was being pushed to the desired target level, the gap between planned investment and available domestic savings would have to be financed through foreign capital inflows.

Other things being equal, the need for such transfers would progressively diminish as the domestic savings rate rose. In the above example, such a need would no longer exist when the planned "self-sufficiency" savings rate of 20 percent is achieved. Based on considerations of comparative advantage, the underlying assumption was that poor countries could not produce certain goods efficiently, and therefore had to import them. This was particularly true of specialized intermediate and capital goods needed to fuel the initial stages of industrialization. The reasoning was that such countries had an inflexible and undiversified production structure that required a special complementary factor - foreign exchange. The bottlenecks caused by shortages in domestic savings and foreign exchange were conceptualized in terms of "two gap" models of economic growth, which became essential tools for projecting capital needs and justifying international aid (see, for example, Chenery and Bruno 1962; Chenery and Strout 1966).

Linked to the requirements of international cooperation and the mutual benefits thesis was an ideology of development based on the "modernization" ethic. From this perspective, the process of change was interpreted in global evolutionary terms, or the belief that all human societies should follow a unilinear and continuous development path. This meant steering of a single or uniform course through a series of stages between two types of societies considered as polar opposites - from simple, traditional, or pre-capitalist to more complex, modern, and capitalist. Contextually, modernization was viewed as a unique process of structural change toward those types of economic, political, and socio-cultural systems that accompanied the historical transition of North America and Europe.

Accordingly, the following types of development strategies were advocated: (i) massive capital investments in industry: (ii) infusion of modern technology, skills, and managerial techniques; (iii) promotion of an entrepreneurial and competitive spirit; (iv) upgrading traditional institutions; and (v) in general, internalization of Western values of economic rationality, individualism, achievement motivation, and political democracy. The basic idea was that, to the extent that pressures for modernization did not develop within the poor countries themselves, they could be helped along the development road through a constant diffusion of Western values, knowledge, technology, and skills.

A germane idea was that underdevelopment was primarily the result of internal deficiencies in the poor countries themselves due to maladaptive motivational, institutional, and social structures. While the diffusion process could go a far way toward removing these inhibiting factors, the implication was that the success of the process depended ultimately on the receptivity of countries to these external influences. Thus, it was argued, the extent and degree of modernization depended on the recipient countries' own potential "absorptive capacity" for various forms of foreign assistance inherent in the diffusion process.

The ideology of modernization rested on the assumption that there would be an inevitable diffusion between economic dimensions of transformation and concomitant changes in the socio-cultural and political spheres. The justification for political change was (is) inherent in the fact that cohesiveness of various groups in society can be considered a necessary prerequisite for modernization. Where such cohesiveness is present, the political system would be better equipped to cope with the diverse demands of different groups for change, as well as to absorb these changes into the system. The absence of such a coping mechanism means that group conflicts cannot be resolved easily or amicably, resulting in a breakdown of the modernization process.

Besides the influence of the modernization ethic, changes in the European intellectual milieu during the interwar years were also instrumental in shaping the philosophical orientation of the new development economics. First, the peace settlement carved out after the First World War ushered in the equivalent in Europe of contemporary developing nations based on the principle of self-determination. This was strongly influenced by the German economic model and its implications for developing the Balkan states. The model was responsible for infusing the debate on development with a strong nationalistic bias. The ruling corpus of ideas centered around the need for industrialization and the potency of economic planning and protectionism in achieving it. The migration of European economists to Britain and the United States was particularly instrumental in the dissemination of these ideas. The central concepts were synergistic with the psychological attitudes of the emerging developing nations and their conception of development.

A second set of influences emanated from the apparent success of Russian five-year planning for economic growth and full employment in contrast to the collapse and attendant misery which marked the experience of capitalist countries. The economic breakdown of capitalism implanted in the minds of many non-communist socialists that an inherent defect in capitalism itself was the main stumbling block in the way of achieving a just, equitable, and prosperous society. From this perspective, what seemed to be needed was an intelligent Fabian-type arrangement based on an intelligent socialist management of the economy through nationalization of industry and the adoption of sweeping policies for income redistribution. The socialist-oriented emphasis on centralized planning, nationalization of industry, and redistributive policies was to exercise a lasting influence on development priorities at the onset of the "revolution" in development economics.

Retreat from Monoeconomics: The Search for a New Interpretive Mode

The general interpretation of development ideas emanating from the experience of the 1930s was that defects in the capitalist system were the root causes of underdevelopment in the tropics. This was linked to a belief that any country could enter the development path once it was willing to adopt economic planning, accumulate capital, and invest in order to industrialize and eliminate its dependence on primary commodity production. As Sir Arthur Lewis, a major pioneer in development economics, reminded the economics profession, a question arose "whether there was a need for a separate economics - Development Economics - for countries with less than 1980 US$2,000 per head. . . . This adds up to asking whether such countries differ in structure or behavior from the richer, in ways that require different concepts or tools to understand their functioning" (1984: 1).

A general question was raised about the appropriateness of Western-oriented concepts, models, and theories to the interpretation and understanding of the quite different reality facing poor countries in Asia, Africa, Latin America and the Caribbean. A common belief was that while these countries shared a specific set of economic characteristics, as a group they were set apart from the more advanced industrial nations. A lack of realism was attributed to the tendency of Western economists to generalize from the "special case" of these countries to their poorer counterparts. Such generalizations were considered to be inappropriate because of differences in historical, social, and institutional settings (Seers 1963; Myrdal 1968; Myint 1971).

At one level, some of the early pioneers of development economics raised questions about the relevance of the market-price system undergirding the neo-classical paradigm to developing countries where markets tended to be fragmented and localized, market imperfections were prevalent, and there was little opportunity for the sophisticated exercise of the logic of choice. It was felt that the market-price mechanism could not achieve optimal outcomes either in individual countries or among them because of its heavy reliance on unrealistic assumptions such as a linear homogeneous production function and no increasing returns or economies of scale. Here it should be commented that market-based analysis was never meant to be realistic. If it is presumed that the assumptions about human nature are veridical, then the market framework can be interpreted as depicting an "ideal world" and as providing a standard for policy formulation designed to make the real world move closer to the ideal.

Be that as it may, the feeling also emerged that neo-classical economics could not adequately address the much larger issues of structural transformation facing poor countries. The reason is that it rests on different assumptions about the nature of the economic transformation process, that is, marginal or incremental adjustments. The application of static neo-classical principles of efficient resource allocation, while relevant to all economies, would miss the mark in a situation that seemed to require a comprehensive transformation of economic structures and a widening of the economy rather than simply tightening it up. In this context, one of the pioneers in development economics has characterized his thoughts on development as reflecting a philosophy based on the motto: "natura facit saltum" ("nature does make a jump") as opposed to Alfred Marshall's "natura non facit saltum" (Rosenstein-Rodan 1984: 207). From this perspective, analysis of the *disequilibrium* growth process rather than neo-classical *equilibrium theory* is more appropriate for understanding problems of economic development.

At another level, Keynesian economics was also found wanting because its primary concern was with unemployment of labor and the underutilization of capital in advanced countries during the Great Depression. In the first place, Sir Arthur Lewis differentiated the Keynesian system from that existing in an underdeveloped economy because the former emphasized underemployed labor as well as other factors, whereas labor was the redundant factor in the latter. Many of the underemployed would be willing to work long hours if jobs were available. Some faced a situation of "disguised" unemployment, that is, they appeared to be employed, but were actually adding little to total output. Others were among the "working poor," in the sense that they toiled for long hours in low productivity tasks that yielded incomes below poverty levels.

In the second place, the Keynesian diagnosis of an advanced capitalist economy experiencing short-run cyclical depression attributed unemployment of labor and underutilization of capital to oversaving. By contrast, the unemployment problem facing the developing countries was thought to be related not to too much savings, but to a deficiency of capital. This meant that the Keynesian remedy of increasing aggregate demand would miss the mark in a developing world where the primary task was to mobilize more savings and increase investment. The poor countries were not deficient in investment and related opportunities but rather in savings, or the availability of real resources. Therefore, it was argued, attention should be directed toward the ability or capacity to save on the part of poor countries.

This meant that policy should focus on enhancing the capacity of those who can save, that is, members of the capitalist class, since they were presumed to represent the primary savers in society. As Lewis states, "the central problem in the theory of economic development is to understand the process by which a community which was previously saving and investing 4 or 5 percent of its national income or less, converts into an economy where voluntary savings is running at about 12 to 15 percent of national income or more. . . . The central fact of economic development is that the distribution of incomes be altered in favor of the savings class" (1984: 155, 156).

Both Lewis's model of economic dualism and the Cambridge capital theory of distribution which emerged during the 1950s were based on neo-Ricardian or classical assumptions. They postulated that savings by the capitalist class should be encouraged since they were presumed to be the people who invest capital productively. Thus, the ability or capacity to save was linked to the strategic role of profit accumulation in the development process. On the assumption that capitalists have a relatively high propensity to save and reinvest, the reasoning was that increased profits would automatically lead to the transformation of savings into additional productive capacity. It was also expected that the growth of reproducible capital would lead to an induced demand for human capital formation. This followed from the argument that the general availability of capital for development would lead capitalists and government authorities to provide the facilities needed for training more skilled labor, as well as to create an enabling environment for the nurturing of other growth-promoting mechanisms such as technological change.

The ability or capacity to save was also linked to the opportunity or willingness to save. The latter depends on decisions individual economic agents are prepared to make about the desirability of present vis-à-vis future consumption. This is essentially an assertion about the future incomes people expect to receive from saving rather than spending most of their incomes now. The requisite decisions are typically influenced by two related factors. One is the degree of monetization or the proportion of total transactions in the economy that is carried out through the monetary medium. The other is the availability of an appropriate set of financial assets in which savings can be held, that is, the level of development of the financial system and the nature of the supporting financial intermediation process.

A relatively large nonmonetized sector was predominant in the majority of developing countries during the early stages of their development, and it still continues to play a significant role in some countries. Examples of nonmonetized activities include: (i) the growing of food for family subsistence and consumption; (ii) the unpaid labor of women and children, especially in those countries where women play complex roles as housewives in terms of child care, fetching water and firewood, and providing labor on farms; (iii) self-help or do-it-yourself activities such as the collective building of roads, erection of buildings, and land reclamation; and (iv) forms of payment in kind, such as wages in kind, commodity loans, and sharecropping.

The degree of monetization has been traditionally measured by the monetization ratio, or the proportion of the total value of goods and services that is paid for by money. Increases in this ratio, and the corresponding path of monetization, typically reflect changes in a country's financial structure that are supposed to accompany development. Early studies of this phenomenon revealed that it displayed at least three characteristic features. First, it is an evolutionary process. Second, it is discontinuous, and tends to vary across countries and regions over time. Third, it is closely correlated with patterns of economic growth, that is, low monetization ratios are usually associated with low per capita incomes, and vice-versa (Goldsmith 1969). Observation of these broad patterns has led to the empirical generalization that the possibilities for development are closely bound up with the degree and speed of the monetary transformation process. The requisite monetary and financial changes are facilitated by the creation of an appropriate institutional structure for mobilizing savings and rechanneling to borrowers in order to finance real investment.

The differential effects of monetization were also stressed in the early debates between "formalists" and "substantivists" in anthropology. In this context, mainstream economics was put on trial by what Polly Hill (1986) dubs the "anthropological case for a prosecution." Formalists, like their counterparts in economics, maintain that the universal rules of maximization and choice that are assumed to motivate people in modern economic situations can also help to explain behavioral patterns in a variety of choice-making situations, for example, the rational maximizing behavior of small farmers in developing countries. People the world over are seen as having similar natures and motivations, and hence the same market analysis is relevant everywhere. Economic life under industrial capitalism is perceived to be different only in degree and not in kind from that obtained in poorer countries, when the two are compared.

This "abstract empiricism" (Godelier 1972) posits that a theory of economic behavior can be derived from an aggregation of rational individual propensities. Contextually, formalists take what are interpreted as universally applicable concepts and generalizations of economic theory (scarcity, economizing, maximizing, supply, demand, price, etc.) and analyze the empirical data of "primitive," "peasant," or "less developed" societies in these terms. The argument is that the basic similarities between the latter and industrial capitalism are so close that some notion of a universal economic theory seems to be warranted. In particular, the tenets of conventional economic theory were thought to be relevant to the commercial sectors of peasant economic organization, that is, where purchased inputs, wage labor, and other market arrangements were quantitatively significant. Conventional economics was also considered to be important in the empirical measurement of economic performance in such societies, for example, in determining the amount of composition of marketed output (Dalton 1971).

By contrast, substantivists or contextualists argued that if economic behavior is embedded in patterns of life that are not primarily economic, then such behavior will be dominated by criteria other than the pure market and abstract economic principles of rational choice. In other words, economic life should be interpreted as an integral part of the total cultural fabric, or as a subset of some specific cultural practices that are pursued in terms of a more embracing system of values and preferences. This is related to Godelier's concept of "functional empiricism" which, unlike "abstract empiricism," posits that a theory of economic behavior should be functionally deduced from the patterns of conduct observed in a given society. Such societal patterns, it is argued, are responsible for creating a variety of organizational systems and value orientations. From this perspective, the ethical neutrality underlying the formalist approach was construed as a cloak for inertia and intellectual detachment from the conditions of poverty facing the developing nations of the day.

On the above basis, some anthropologists claimed that the differences between industrial societies and poorer ones were so extensive that a completely different set of concepts was considered necessary because dimensions of social organization tend to have a direct bearing on economic organization and performance. Substantivists believed that production and exchange relationships in traditional societies were governed less by economic considerations of income maximization and more by noneconomic ones, such as satisficing, ritual laws based on kinship and authority status, and the "moral economy of the peasant." Under the circumstances, only a socio-economic or holistic approach that explicitly addressed the relationship between economy and society could produce meaningful generalizations and policy prescriptions. For example, in his analysis of the "transformation" of societies from traditional to market economies, Polanyi (1944) pointed out that production was only one facet, albeit important, of a more embracing socio-cultural relationship. Accordingly, the economy should be viewed as a set of rules of social organization rather than in terms of quantitative performance measures such as levels of output, productivity, and profits. In Polanyi's view, the concepts of conventional economic theory were more applicable to industrial market economies because the institutionalized rules of market exchange and the reliance on relatively advanced monetary systems and sophisticated technology tend to induce "economizing" and "maximizing" forms of behavior. However, such concepts tend to produce distorting perspectives and results when they are used to analyze traditional economies or the non-market sectors of developing nations. In the latter case, variants of reciprocity and redistribution tend to act as integrating organizational principles in what are commonly perceived to be economic arrangements, such as the disposition of produce, land and labor allocation, work organization, trade, and the use of money.

The Growth-Oriented Development Perspective

From the very inception, economic development was interpreted in terms of a categorical imperative of material economic growth which would enhance the ability of poor countries to provide requisite bundles of goods and services needed to foster an improved standard of living. This philosophy was rooted in both the Western perspective and the radical heterodox alternative undergirding socialist economic development. At least in Western thinking, an economically developed society was construed as a materially wealthy one based on wealth-seeking values and the thralldom of money. By contrast, a less developed or developing country was viewed as one entering the wealth-seeking or modernizing path. Therefore, a consensus emerged that growth in the stock of wealth and corresponding flows in income and production constituted inevitable preconditions for sustained human progress. The normative implication was that rapid economic growth should be preferable to slow, stagnant, and negative growth, or growth that was too tardy to meet the material needs of the population.

The material in Table 5.1 highlights some presuppositions underlying both the orthodox and radical heterodox variants of the growth-oriented development perspective. To reiterate, the main aim of economic development is achievement of sustainable levels of GNP per person through capital accumulation and efficient resource allocation. The ideological pillar or value standard rests on a set of implicit assumptions about beneficial effects of economic growth. First, it is presumed to expand human choice by enabling people to better control their environment, thereby enlarging the potential for freedom. This includes positive freedoms related to the expansion of human choice as well as negative ones such as freedom from want, poverty, joblessness, and excessive government control. Second, a milieu of freedom better enables people to pursue leisure and related human amenities.

Third, economic growth may forestall inordinate social and political upheavals when resources and other constraints militate against an economy's ability to meet the aspirations and demands that are thrown up by the political and social system. Fourth, by offering better avenues for the satisfaction of human wants and needs, economic growth enables people to escape unbearable material deprivation and servitude. The competition for economic survival, and hence the incidence of political and social tensions, is likely to be much more acute at low growth and per capita income levels compared to higher thresholds. The obvious reason is that the majority of people are typically locked into the basic strving to escape from the negative conditions of human existence. As the experience shows, the mere struggle for survival that takes place at low levels of development typically results not only in social and economic divisiveness, but also in various forms of militarism and political dissension (Lewis 1955).

In the early dénouement of the development debate, a variety of hypotheses were to surface about the conditions necessary for the attainment of economic growth and material success. A perennial one has centered around the extent to which people are allowed to seek and seize opportunities for material gain, for example, by subscribing to a competitive ethos. This requires an understanding of the new "rules of the game" based on a dogged promotion of individual self-interests rather than the wider set of social and cultural obligations. On a related basis, it was also hypothesized that people's ability to initiate and maintain the growth momentum required a differential incentive structure that encourages hard and conscientious work and the acquisition of relatively scarce skills. Such an incentive system would compensate people according to "hard work, conscientious work, for skill, for responsibility, and initiative" (Lewis 1955: 39).

In the orthodox growth-oriented development perspective, the principal instruments of economic growth are interpreted from an extrapolation of classical, neo-classical, and Keynesian-type models of economic transformation.

Table 5.1

Growth-Oriented Development Styles

	Orthodox	Radical Heterodox
Primary Objectives	• GNP per capita growth • High degree of structural coherence	• GNP per capita growth • Growth in areas of national priority • Radical redistribution of productive resources
Development Values	• Utilitarian social goals • Individual self-interest	• To each according to his or her need
Performance Criteria	• Market-rational growth • Removal of economic distortions	• Plan-rational growth • Industrial growth
Policy Instruments	• Balanced capital accumulation • Efficient resource allocation • Trade & financial liberalization	• Planned investment • Centralized planning
Principal Mechanisms	• Modernization • Structural transformation • Technical innovation • International economic integration	• Control of commanding heights of economy • Capital-intensive industrialization • Autarky
Agents of Change	• Individual economic agents • Private entrepreneurs • Benevolent or "nightwatchman" state	• Vanguard party • Government bureaucracy • Liberated proletariat

As previously indicated, a pivotal role is assigned to capital accumulation through increased domestic savings and capital inflows from abroad. At the domestic level, the possibility of increased savings is linked to a process whereby some resources are withheld from consumption through more efficient husbandry and output efficiency, leading to higher profits. Incentives to increased flows of foreign capital are provided through improvements in the domestic investment climate, or by the government creating the wherewithal of an "enabling environment."

Given a balanced structure of capital accumulation, the key mechanisms correspond to those identified in neo-classical "sources of growth" and "endogenous growth" models, including: (i) improved factor accumulation in both quantitative and qualitative terms as a means of fostering higher levels of production and total factor productivity; (ii) technological change and corresponding improvements in knowledge and information flows needed for the scientific transformation of society; (iii) enlarged investments in human capital; and (iv) export-led growth based on an outward-orientation and the principles of comparative advantage. The overall process is assumed to be cumulative, or as taking place in an expanding virtuous circle in which economic growth induces more savings and investment, technological change, and further growth.

Employment is increased through the augmented demand for finished goods and factors of production. Given the adoption of an appropriate technological set (defined by a country's resource endowments and factor proportions), more jobs will be created as innovative Schumpeterian entrepreneurs, whose "animal spirits" are uplifted, invest to produce more goods, thereby increasing spending power and effective demand à la Keynes. The model of change is essentially rooted in the neo-classical vision of individual development, as reflected in the rational behavior of private economic agents in freely competitive markets. As noted in Chapter 3, the government is expected to play a secondary role by correcting market failure, maintaining the quality of markets, and guaranteeing a system of property rights and price incentives.

This development perspective rests on the implicit assumption that a policy mix can be designed to ensure the integrity of the growth process, defined in terms of viability and sustainability. It also assumes that there are certain strategic economic foundations of viable economies. Comparative studies of viable economies, it is argued, have consistently demonstrated that the molding of a specific structure and dynamic process of capital formation is a necessary prerequisite for successful social and economic development. The history of viable economies has revealed the pivotal role played by differentiated forms of development and the interlinking of production sectors, an orientation that has produced a relatively high degree of structural cohesiveness in its wake.

Thus, based on an extrapolation of the historical experience of viable economies in the more developed sector of the world, protagonists of a development style based on a growth-oriented approach contend that it is logically complete because it emanates from the rationality and dynamics inherent in the growth process itself. This development experience suggests that viable economies are typically marked by a congruence or organic interplay between balanced capital formation, a heterogenous production structure, high employment levels, and symbiotically related consumption and income distribution profiles. From this perspective, the masses of people tend to be integrated productively in the economy, find gainful employment, and become valued consumers on the basis of their earnings. Consequently, their needs can be met in varying degrees, depending on the level of societal development. Endogenous developmental outcomes become reflected by a long-term process of socio-economic change in which the structure of consumption is matched by the complexity of production and technological relations, with continuous feedback between the level of productive capacity and the growth of real earnings.

For analytical purposes, the orthodox growth-oriented perspective of development bears comparison with its radical heterodox counterpart, which is rooted in Marxist-Leninist dimensions of political economy. In this approach, the primary goal of development is not only the attainment of aggregate income growth, but also the radical redistribution of resources. Like other classical thinkers, Marx had viewed the growth process as being driven by capital accumulation, entrepreneurship, and the efficient management of resources. In fact, he considered the capitalist class to be highly motivated in this regard. As previously noted, however, he saw this very class as denying workers participation in the benefits of the socio-economic surplus which was the product of their own labor. In the Marxian schema, the structural and institutional system underlying production relations bears the primary responsibility for the systematic generation of poverty and underdevelopment. Radical structural and institutional change therefore becomes a main instrument of viable and sustained development. Since class struggle forms the bedrock of this approach, the possibility of such development is predicated on a revolutionary class struggle which culminates in the oppressed classes seizing power with the help of a vanguard party. The main catalysts of development are supposed to be reflected in collective forms of organization based on directives from the vanguard party, political and economic plans, and the overall management of the supply and demand process. In passing, it can be commented that the implementation of this approach in developing countries has not met with very much success. It has invariably resulted in an over-centralized system of planning and an alienation of the poor and oppressed from the "vanguard party" which was supposed to champion their causes and facilitate the process of liberation.

Chapter 6

Perspectives of Investment-led Growth

The nascent development economics was imbued with a measure of self-assurance stemming from at least three sources. As noted earlier, one was the apparent discrediting of orthodox monoeconomics during the 1930s. A second revolved around extolment of economic planning as a primary means of achieving national development goals. Third, the mutual benefits thesis and corresponding need for financial transfers from rich to poor countries fitted neatly into the prevailing ideology about macroeconomic management and planning.

Despite the widely proclaimed adherence of donor nations to free enterprise and an abhorrence of socialist planning, policymakers in the West played an instrumental role in implanting ideas about planning into foreign countries. As an example, the United States government eagerly advocated and gave tangible support to the preparation of Ten-Year Social and Economic Development Plans as a precondition for aid under the Alliance for Progress in Latin America. In general, existence of a national development plan was seen as a paramount measure of the seriousness that could be attached to a country's development purpose. Without such a plan, the aid donor could not be assured that its assistance was deserved or merited.

Under the circumstances, a common practice was for countries to formulate ambitious development plans that required considerable inflows of foreign aid for their implementation. The availability of such plans was in turn used as an argument for the donor countries to provide the required aid. This practice was euphemistically called the "Indian rope trick" because it allegedly became an effective means whereby Indian planners were able to "rope" aid donors into providing needed development assistance. This tactic was commonly practiced in the developing world as a whole. "New nations desirous of aid were under strong pressure to practice economic planning - as a means of extracting economic aid, if nothing else" (Johnson 1972: 38).

Using India's First Five-Year Plan (1952-56) as an example, the logic of comprehensive development planning was expressed through a rational determination of desired national objectives, related quantitative targets, and specification of the means to achieve them. Given the capital-output ratio, a certain volume of investment was needed to achieve a specific target GNP growth rate. Sources of domestic savings and foreign capital to finance the planned investment had to be identified, but priority was accorded to the potential for raising desired levels of national savings to meet investment targets. The next step was to allocate investible resources among various sectors of the economy and projects within such sectors. Given the desired private/public investment mix, a variety of calculations were then made to trace the relationships among inputs and outputs, imports and exports, the income to be generated, and the sectoral distribution of consumption and investment.

In essence, such comprehensive plans sought to establish optimal balances at several levels of aggregate and disaggregation: between conditions of demand and supply; consistency between resource availability and financing, income generation and utilization, sectoral programs and the aggregate plan; and feasibility in both physical and financial terms. However, most countries favored a Keynesian type of indicative planning, that is, one grounded in a philosophy of a mixed economy. This implied government coordination in setting macroeconomic targets but allowing the market to work at the microeconomic level. This ideology and style of planning was predicated on the idea that the developing nations were less interested in controlling the "commanding heights" of the economy, but more in making investments in social and physical infrastructure required as an incentive to attract domestic and foreign investors.

Balanced Versus Unbalanced Growth

Implementation of this planning model raised a question about the type of growth path necessary to achieve sustained economic development. The limited size of internal markets posed an obstacle to the attraction of viable forms of industrial investment. Given this environment, Nurkse (1953) argued that only a rapid rise in productivity could meaningfully generate the requisite market expansion. In his view, foreign capital rather than domestic savings provided the best mechanism for increasing per capita productivity and for breaking the "vicious circle of poverty" characterizing developing nations. On the other hand, it was recognized that the attendant monetary flows could have inflationary effects, and that their concentration in raising the level of exports from modern sector enclaves could actually exacerbate the vicious circle rather than break it.

What seemed to be needed, therefore, was not an isolated rise in productivity but rather a wave of increased capital investment in an array of industries, that is, a type of economic planning and industrialization strategy focusing on "balanced growth." The chain reactions produced by such waves of new investment were expected to provide the necessary impetus to the creation of a "virtuous circle" of sustained growth. The strategy calling for a balanced distribution of investment was popularized by Rosenstein-Rodan (1943) who proposed a development sequence based on large-scale multi-sectoral planning and supported by substantial foreign loans and investment.

In retrospect, it should be noted that Rosenstein-Rodan's now classic paper was intended as a quantitative outline of a Ten-Year postwar development plan designed to push the growth rate of Eastern and Southeastern Europe from virtual stagnation to over 4 percent per annum through a combination of increased domestic savings, capital investment from abroad, German reparations in kind, emigration, and massive industrialization. The latter was considered an essential prerequisite for fully employing a labor force initially characterized by substantial open unemployment and underemployment.

The building blocks of the strategy relied heavily on Keynesian-type concepts such as the marginal propensity to save and the capital-output ratio to make calculations for shifting rural unemployed labor to more productive pursuits. In addition, Keynesian and Pigovian critiques of the market and price mechanism provided the basis for an argument that development could not be left exclusively to the market, but had to be planned. Government intervention was thought to be needed in order the create the large-scale investments necessary for sustained economic growth. The private sector could not be expected to undertake such investments because of increasing returns to scale, the presence of technological externalities, and because they displayed the characteristics of public goods.

Thus, the presence of a variety of "market failures" constituted Rosenstein-Rodan's case for planning the kind of "Big Push" necessary to propel a relatively stagnant economy on to a path of self-sustained economic growth. His proposed strategy turned on the identification and interpretation of interrelated sets of indivisibilities that are inherent in the development process. For example, there are production indivisibilities that are linked to the supply of social overhead capital, that is, investment in public utilities such as power, transport, and communications. While such investments have a long gestation period, they tend to create opportunities for investment in more directly productive and quick-yielding industrial activities. Guaranteeing of such benefits for the economy as a whole requires a large minimum size of investment in social overhead capital.

Production indivisibilities are inevitably associated with others that show strong complementaries on the demand side. The existence of an indivisibility or complementarity in demand means that various investment decisions in the real world are interdependent. In the case of a single investment project, some degree of risk may result from the uncertainty over finding a ready market for the goods and services produced. However, the degree of risk is significantly reduced when investments are made on a wide front. Where there are many investment projects, the new producers will become each other's customers, and this complementarity will tend to reduce the risk of not finding markets, thereby providing a natural incentive to invest.

It remains true, however, that a potential difficulty in achieving complementarity between supply and demand may arise because of relatively low demand elasticities that typically face low-income countries. The incidence of such an obstacle tends to vary with the size of the market, with smaller markets posing higher risks compared to large and dynamic ones. According to Rosenstein-Rodan, there is probably some minimum threshold level of investments required before any complementarity between demand and supply can arise. In order to reach this threshold, a minimum level of investment may be required to produce the additional basic commodities on which newly employed workers are likely to spend their incomes. Thus, assuming that an economy's capacity to generate investment funds improves as aggregate income starts to grow, a clear implication for development policy is that the planning authorities should mount a massive investment program based on complementarities between supply and demand. Such a strategy, it was claimed, would enable the industrialization process in developing countries to absorb the rural population, thereby stemming the flow of rural-urban migration.

Finally, Rosenstein-Rodan considered the indivisibility in the supply of savings to be one of the most crucial problems facing countries operating at a low level of equilibrium. Under the circumstances, a necessary condition for the attainment of a high minimum level of complementary investments was a policy aimed at pushing the marginal rate of savings above the average rate. Thus, the development problem was identified as simply one in which investment had failed to materialize. Therefore, the task of the planner or policymaker was construed as one of identifying the causal factors and removing them. In Rosenstein-Rodan's schema, the problem arose because of what economists call the Prisoner's Dilemma. Some investors were wary of taking a chance since none of them in isolation had the assurance that others would invest simultaneously and create a demand for the goods and services produced by the originators. It was on this basis that he prescribed a coordinated plan for investment by the government in order to break the impasse.

While other economists agreed that savings and capital formation should be increased, they disagreed with the "balanced growth" policy prescription. For example, Albert Hirschman (1958) viewed the development task as one of creating an inducement to investment. For him, the situation did not call for well-coordinated plans for government investment, but rather for decisions that would help create a suitable climate for private investment. His proposal for a strategy of "unbalanced growth" was based on the premise that a chain of technological requirements in some "leading sectors" in the economy might induce investments in lagging ones. The preconception was that sectoral imbalances can produce corrective reactions through investment linkages.

Hirschman's specific interpretation of imbalance was based on his experience in Colombia during the 1950s. As he states, the search was for "hidden rationalities" or "elements and processes of the Colombian realities that *did* work, perhaps in a roundabout and unappreciated fashion" (1984: 99). In dissenting from the received view, he perceived that what might be regarded as irrationality, distortion, or imbalance in a developing economy might itself set up powerful incentives to solve problems, thereby contributing elements of rationality to the growth process. Examples of Hirschman's own version of the "invisible hand" or "seemingly reprehensible social behavior" include: (i) shortages, bottlenecks, and other unbalanced growth sequences in the course of economic development; (ii) capital-intensive industrial processes in an apparently labor-surplus economy; and (iii) pressures on decision makers induced by inflation and balance of payments deficits.

These and other processes observed in Colombia and elsewhere in the developing world had revealed a number of "sequential" solutions that were contrary to the "balanced" or "Big Push" path of economic growth, which required a carefully planned large-scale effort on many fronts simultaneously. Thus, development was interpreted as a record of "how one thing leads to another," with the *linkage* concept providing an exemplar of that record from a specific point of view. The significance attached to linkages reflected a paradigm shift from the dominant aggregate income growth model of the day, and the relative influence of income vis-à-vis production in the overall development process. The ruling paradigm emphasized the once-for-all effects of investment on national income and did not pay sufficient attention to the specific multiplier effects of such investment on future income levels. Adequate account was not taken of what happens to the final products that partly determine both the investment rate and income in the future.

One strand of the criticism focused on the distribution of income, or the idea was that a more egalitarian distribution of income would generate rapid economic growth because it would then be much easier for domestic markets to grow to the size necessary for the establishment and profitable operation of consumer goods industries (Baldwin 1956). A germane claim was that it might be more desirable to employ fiscal policy as a means of attaining an income distribution profile that promised to yield sufficient savings, rather than rely on planned investment based on some reinvestment quotient. Linked to this was the idea that "endless growth for its own sake does not make much sense," and there might be circumstances where the value of current consumption to the community should be accorded a higher priority.

While such challenges looked askance at the excessive aggregation underlying the ruling paradigm, they continued to emphasize the income side of the economy. The Hirschmanian linkage concept formed part of a more radical departure from the aggregate income perspective of economic growth because it viewed the determining influence as emanating from the production side of the economy. It saw insufficiency of entrepreneurial motivation as posing the major constraint, and was based on a systemic search for "constellations of productive forces" that would induce public and private decision making to "do something" through *special pressures* "that are more compelling than those that are expected to move the rational decision maker of received economic theory." Accordingly, it is argued that "entrepreneurial decision making in both private and public sectors is not uniquely determined by the pull of incomes and demand, but is responsive to special *push factors*, such as linkages, emanating from the production side" (1977: 70; emphasis added). While the idea of linkages is now part of the lexicon of development economics, it was intimately tied to input-output analysis, which formed part of the extant corpus of technical economic knowledge.

By its very nature, however, input-output analysis is synchronic. This implies that it depicts the economy and its constituent parts as they exist at a given point in time. By contrast, linkage effects are more diachronic in nature, i.e., they need time to unfold. As such, they are connected to specific historical sequences of development. Hirschman's "generalized linkage approach" is articulated in terms of the following linkage sequences: production, consumption, fiscal, and technological. These are in turn subdivided into two broad categories - termed "insider" and "outsider" linkages.

First, the existence of production linkages is meant to highlight the fact, alluded to earlier, that entrepreneurial decisions in both private and public sectors are not uniquely determined by the pull of incomes and demand, but are responsive to push factors emanating from the production side of an economy. In this case, the linkage effects represent an array of investment-generating forces that are typically set in motion when productive facilities utilize the outputs of others as inputs (backward linkage) or supply inputs to other lines of activity (forward linkage). Backward linkages lead to new investments in input-supplying facilities and forward linkages to investments in output-using ones.

Second, and in contrast to the more direct impact of the production linkages, there are consumption linkages that typically come into play through a roundabout process, for instance, where certain import-substitution industries develop from the production of an export staple commodity. The presence or absence of such linkages is perhaps best exemplified by the situation that faced most primary commodity exporters during the immediate post-colonial era and after. The evidence suggests that the first phase of export expansion in many developing countries did not witness the creation of new industries to satisfy rising consumer demand, but was accompanied by the destruction of handicraft and artisan activities. The main reason was that labor was withdrawn from staple production, and new imports of consumer goods became their primary competitors due to a lack of domestic industries producing mass consumption goods. Not only were the linkages weak or nonexistent in most post-colonial societies, but in many cases their effects have been downright negative.

Third, fiscal linkages can emerge where a government is in a position to tap the income stream generated by the production activity, especially mining and plantation agriculture. The development prospects for many countries with resource-based productive activities became transformed because of the new ability of national governments to tax or participate in the incomes generated from such sources. Some foreign-owned enterprises were even nationalized, with substantial revenues channelled directly into government coffers. In general, the overall effects of such fiscal linkages depend on whether the proceeds find their way into productive vis-à-vis wasteful investments. In some developing countries, they were spent on an enlarged bureaucracy, armaments, and increased imports of conspicuous consumption goods. Moreover, the evidence suggests that such practices have not been self-correcting, but expanded for a considerable period of time until some measure of fiscal discipline was introduced by the "international public sector" - the IMF and World Bank.

Finally, there are technological linkages which affect the differential speeds with which new investments emerge. While the nature of the relationship between market size and the scale of a production activity may help to induce new investments with backward and forward linkages, a crucial factor lies in the degree of technological "strangeness" or "alienness" of the new activities in relation to ongoing ones (Hirschman 1968). In the latter case, the linkage effects would be weak if the required inputs have to come from an industry whose processes and techniques are totally unfamiliar to operators in the ongoing activity. The nature of the linkage dynamic depends on the size of the requisite technological leap, which varies with industry and across countries. It becomes particularly problematic when the development of new processes requires a massive injection of foreign technology and/or substantial allocations of time and money in learning-by-doing and technological adaptation.

Hirschman's overall perspective, therefore, rests on the presupposition that it is possible to conceptualize development in terms of the advantages and disadvantages associated with each type of linkage described above. Some are termed "insider" linkages, in the sense that economic operators who are already engaged in ongoing activities may be impelled to undertake additional ones. Insider linkages have the advantage that they can be instrumental in facilitating local entrepreneurial development and permit existing agents to become involved in Schumpeterian-like pursuits. Other, or outsider linkages, may come into play when new activities are undertaken by foreign parties. Such linkages may facilitate the introduction of new technology, managerial techniques, and related ways of doing things. Hence, they can serve as effective catalysts for mobilizing new economic agents. In the contemporary developing world, the balance between the advantages and disadvantages associated with different mixes of insider vis-à-vis outsider linkages tells an interesting story about alternative country profiles and development orientations.

In conclusion, there are no hard and fast rules that can be used to settle the issue of whether it is preferable for countries to follow a balanced growth path based on a set of "simultaneous" investments as suggested by Rosenstein-Rodan or an unbalanced trajectory that relies on "sequential" investments à la Hirschman. Its resolution is outside the scope of technical economics and stands firmly in the court of politics. Both alternatives suggest the need for a development will and the corresponding willingness and ability of the relevant development authorities to formulate coherent investment strategies and follow through on their plans. Few developing countries, if any, have been able to make the kinds of complementary investments required for balanced growth. Those with the potential for resource-based industrialization have been equally tardy in exploiting the dynamic linkage sequences inherent in the strategy of unbalanced growth, or have been prevented by force of circumstances from doing so. As detailed in subsequent chapters, a combination of both external environmental factors and internal structural rigidities must share the blame.

Some comments may also be made about the investment-led growth perspective itself. In the first place, what seems to be lacking in these fundamentalist accounts of economic growth is any explicit interpretive analysis of the strategic endogenous factors that not only lie at the heart of the development challenge, but which may also enable or disable the investment effort. Like economic theory itself, while the models highlight some of the economic conditions necessary for initiating and maintaining the growth process, it is forgotten that these conditions are by no means sufficient. A full statement and analysis of the necessary and sufficient conditions must include not only material economic resources and technological possibilities, but more importantly, the wider spectrum of psychological, political, institutional, and socio-cultural dynamics in which the growth potential is embedded.

Second, while applied economic theory can state the necessary conditions for self-sustained economic growth to be realized, it cannot predict with any degree of certainty that such growth will actually take place. In this context, the investment-led growth models could not predict the difficulties inherent in absorbing the reservoir of unemployed and underemployed, the growing inequality between rural and urban sectors, and what is now an endemic problem of persistent poverty in the developing world. This is also true about the array of structural forces in the global political economy that tends to restrict the ability of developing countries to formulate and execute autonomous and self-reliant development strategies.

Economic Dualists versus Price Mechanists

In the evolution of modern development theory, a major bone of contention has surrounded the critical nature of "structural transformation," that is, concerted alterations in the economic structure that typically accompany aggregate economic growth during particular historical epochs and in specific country contexts. This has given rise to alternative interpretations of the role of agriculture vis-à-vis industry in the development process. Agriculture still remains the largest single "industry" in terms of absolute size even in many rich countries. In poorer countries, it continues to generate over 50 percent of national output and employs over 80 percent of the labor force.

The dominant interpretation of agriculture's role has been significantly influenced by the notion of dualism. The modern development debate is replete with definitions and interpretations of dualism - for example, socio-cultural (Boeke 1953), technological (Eckhaus 1955; Higgins 1968), and international (Myrdal 1968; Singer 1970). Our main focus is on economic dualism, which has been traditionally defined in terms of production and organizational asymmetries between two sectors: traditional - subsistence - agricultural vis-à-vis modern - urban - industrial.

As is extensively reported in the literature, the modern discourse on the subject originated with Arthur Lewis's model of the dual labor surplus economy (Lewis 1954, 1958). To put the matter in its proper theoretical and policy perspective, the model turns on the following assumptions: (i) the urban or modern sector wage is fixed at a premium over the subsistence agricultural wage, thereby providing an inducement to rural-urban migration; (ii) there are unlimited supplies of surplus labor in the agricultural sector, and such supplies are perfectly elastic at the fixed urban wage rate; (iii) the marginal productivity of agricultural labor is zero, implying that the transfer of people out of agriculture would not depress output significantly since output levels in agriculture might be maintained by the fact that those remaining might work harder; (iv) capital investment in the modern sector is derived from reinvestment of capitalist profits and, given constant wage rates, the share of profits in national income would rise with technological progress and further industrial capital formation; and (v) the modern sector would continue to grow until the supply of rural surplus labor is exhausted, at which point wage rates would begin to rise.

In general, the picture painted by Lewis is in many respects similar to some variants of the classical growth model. Among other features, the latter turns on the following types of assumptions: (i) the critical role of a capitalist class that accumulates by automatically transforming savings into fixed investment; (ii) the motive force provided by the choice of techniques or technological progress; and (iii) pervasive unemployment, or the existence of a "reserve army" (Marx) from which surplus labor can be drawn as necessary. As the economy grows, employment increases and real wages are bid up from their institutionally fixed levels. As the process unravels, capitalists undertake more innovations and begin to substitute machines for labor. A part of wages becomes frozen into fixed capital, putting a downward pressure on the rate of increase in labor incomes.

The Lewis model envisages a gradual transition from a classical to a neo-classical growth path. The "reserve army" becomes coterminous with the "traditional" or "subsistence" sector from which surplus labor is drawn at the institutionally determined wage until unemployment begins to abate. At the same time, accumulation proceeds apace, the share of savings in national income rises along with profits, and more labor is employed. After a certain point is reached, the conditions of demand and supply in the labor market become the primary determinants of wage rates, and the world turns into a neo-classical mode.

Given his classical orientation, Lewis writes in the same tradition as the large number of market theorists who constantly stress the pivotal role of individual motivation, and therefore the necessity for delineating the conditions necessary to generate the appropriate individual behavior for development. His model turns on the implicit belief that large-scale entrepreneurs and informed capitalists in the modern sector are capable of making rational decisions directed toward organizing the process of modernization. The philosophical premise is that these cadres hold the promise for bringing developing countries into the modern world by taking them out of what was thought to be their traditional backwardness and incapacity to produce efficiently via relative prices and individual motivation. Individuals in the traditional or subsistence sector were deemed incapable of generating the increase in reproducible capital or production, or of responding to the incentives offered for making a profit. As a result, their fate was supposed to lie in a painless and gradual extinction, which would be produced by the pull of a modernization process defined by capitalist production, savings, and investment.

Therefore, economic policy should be primarily and ruthlessly geared toward the possibility of a capitalist-driven modern sector pulling the traditional sector out of its backwardness and decadence. The implication is that all policies (for example, those related to investment, credit, and technology) were to be directed toward promoting modern sector development. Moreover, it was recognized that some modicum of sectoral and class inequality might be necessary in the short run in order to promote the requisite levels of capital accumulation and growth over the longer run. In other words, because of the length of the transition period, the environment for income distribution in the traditional sector and the economy as a whole might become worse rather than better in the short run. There was no reason, however, to believe that such short-term consequences would be acceptable in political and human terms.

The Lewis two-sector model was later formalized and developed by Gustav Ranis and John Fei who further explored the effects of growth in the dual economy on the subsistence sector, and in particular, changes in the marginal productivity of labor as more and more workers moved to the modern sector. The conclusion was that, initially, as workers with a zero marginal productivity were transferred, agricultural output would register no visible change. At a subsequent stage, there would be some decline in agricultural output, as workers whose marginal productivity was greater than zero but less than the subsistence wage migrated. Finally, the marginal productivity of migrating workers would rise above the subsistence wage. The agricultural surplus available for consumption in the nonfarm sector would fall during this process, worsening the terms of trade for industry and putting an upward pressure on wage rates (see Ranis and Fei 1961, 1963; Fei and Ranis 1964).

The Lewis-Ranis-Fei interpretations of the dual economy have been termed "classical" because of their focus on capital accumulation, the effects of technological change on population growth, and their characterization of the agricultural sector as a source of industrial labor and wage goods. By contrast, the "neo-classical" model of Jorgenson (1961, 1967), while similar in many respects, assumed that the marginal productivity of labor in agriculture was positive rather than zero, the real wage rate variable rather than fixed, or that the market wage rate was free to reflect the social opportunity cost of additional employment instead of being institutionally determined, as in the classical interpretation. His model delineated a critical point toward which average agricultural output would have to grow in order to create the conditions for a viable modern industrial sector. Beyond this point, a food surplus would be generated and employed growth in the modern sector would become possible.

While there have been many extensions of the dual economy models, an area of greatest controversy has surrounded the question whether or not surplus labor really exists in the agricultural sector of developing countries. The optimistic view was that rapid industrialization would be made possible through mobilization of the large pool of surplus agricultural labor that was presumed to exist in poor countries. In this context, dual economy models can be interpreted as being concerned not so much with whether surplus labor existed, but that there should be labor willing to transfer to industrial employment at the going urban wage rate. The simple reality remains that burgeoning rural population growth rates and the sheer size of the subsistence sector in the majority of developing countries have continued to build up a substantial pressure for migration from the countryside. The models of Harris and Todaro explained the migration from rural to urban areas in terms of the expected rural-urban wage differential and probability of finding a job (see Harris and Todaro 1970; Todaro 1981). The paradox remains that rural-urban migration persists even in the face of constantly increasing urban unemployment.

Nonetheless, wage differentials between rural and urban areas have been maintained, and might have even increased in some cases. The migration factor, far from effecting the expected equilibrium between the two sectors, has added more fuel to the process of cumulative disequilibrium. Such migratory flows have had at least two noticeable effects on the prospects for employment and growth. On the one hand, the employment of migrants in the urban sector has led to a marginalization of previously employed workers, thereby heightening the forces of polarization already existing in the sector. On the other hand, the departure of migrants from the rural sector has tended to rob the agricultural sector of potentially valuable human capital, thereby accentuating the decline of the rural sector and widening the development gap between the agriculture and industrial sectors.

Thus, dualistic economic theory has not been able to provide a satisfactory explanation of some of the major structural problems that continue to plague developing countries. A continuously pressing one concerns measures that should be taken to transform the generally poor absorptive capacity of the industrial sector where employment growth has not lived up to expectations. To some extent, the problem revolves around the way in which the labor market functions and the factors that determine absolute and relative wage rates in both agricultural and industrial sectors. The other side of the coin pertains to the persistent poverty of the agricultural and rural sectors and their lack of meaningful transformation.

Contextually, the dual economy models were thought to have ignored the factors needed to modernize traditional agriculture so that it would make a positive contribution to the overall development process. An early salvo in the debate was fired by Theodore Schultz (1964), who denied the existence of surplus labor and claimed that the agricultural sector could be transformed through the provision of adequate price incentives. In his view, rural income remained very low relative to urban income because of discrimination against agriculture due to low producer prices and the effects of industrialization strategies. His policy prescription, now implemented by the multilateral lending agencies, was that better incentive should be provided to rural producers by raising agricultural prices to their world market levels. On a related basis, Schultz advanced the thesis that responses to price and profit incentives tend to be universal and do not differ across countries or regions of a country. The idea is that traditional farmers act rationally and tend to allocate resources efficiently in order to maximize output gains and profits.

Schultzian price fundamentalism provided the springboard for the critiques of a new generation of "price mechanists" whose diagnosis of agricultural stagnation rests on the premise that agricultural prices have been kept too low in comparison to world prices. Their prescription of higher agricultural development is premised on the need to improve the internal terms of trade between agriculture and industry. Under the circumstances, the Lewis and other dual economy models become irrelevant since their primary focus was on the effect of the terms of trade on industrial accumulation. The remedies proposed by Schultz and price mechanists have been criticized on the grounds that they do not pay sufficient attention to the class structure and related institutional conditions that are pervasive in developing countries.

A More Balanced Interpretation of Structural Transformation

As previously indicated, the debate on the role of the agricultural sector in the development process has gone through many historical twists and turns. From the inception, delineation of this role seemed to rest on a perceptible paradox. On the one hand, it was recognized that a dynamic agriculture could provide food, labor, and even capital that were essential to economic modernization. On the other hand, since historical observations revealed a natural decline in the sector's share of national output and the labor force, no favorable policy environment seemed necessary to ensure its endogenous development.

The dominant development paradigm of the 1950s seemed to suggest that agriculture should be squeezed in favor of more "dynamic" sectors of the economy. For example, Hirschman's model of unbalanced growth stressed linkages to manufacturing activities and paid little attention to the possibility of investing in modernizing agriculture. As he remarked, "agriculture certainly stands convicted in the count of the lack of direct stimulus to the setting up of new activities through linkage effects - the superiority of manufacturing in this respect is crushing" (1958: 109-10). As we have also indicated, the focus placed by the Lewis and other dual economy models on labor transfer and industrialization seemed to imply a relegation of agriculture to a totally subsidiary role.

In Lewis's view, however, critics have misunderstood the orientation of such models. As he states, "[a]s it happened most Governments neglected agriculture for reasons of their own, but this was in spite of and not in accordance with economists' advice" (1979: 219). A further defense of his position is provided in the World Bank's *Pioneers* volume (Meier and Seers 1984) where he reemphasizes the need for an agricultural policy that would have equal priority with industrialization. Contextually, there are two agricultural options: to export or produce for the domestic market. Hence, three strategies are available for supporting industrialization: (i) to export more agricultural commodities or resource-based products: (ii) to develop a self-sufficient economy, emphasizing the home market; and (iii) to export manufactured goods. The argument is that all three strategies imply vigorous industrial and agricultural policies, and differ only in terms of their foreign exchange requirements and potential earnings.

During the 1960s, and 1970s, the thrust of theoretical and empirical analysis of agricultural development was predicated on the need for "balanced growth" between agriculture and industry. First, a prominent view was that agriculture should supply the food output needed to meet domestic consumption requirements, especially since the shortage of foreign exchange placed a constraint on the alternative of importing food. Second, while the role of agriculture as a potential supplier of industrial labor was still mentioned, this option was downplayed. Greater emphasis was placed on its significance as a source of domestic savings to finance capital formation both within agriculture itself and in non-agricultural sectors of the economy. Third, rising agricultural incomes were also viewed as a potential source of demand for manufactured goods produced domestically, with the requisite balance assumed to be determined by the marginal propensities of the rural population to consume and save. Fourth, it was also recognized that agricultural exports could provide the foreign exchange needed to finance imports of essential intermediate and capital goods needed for industrial expansion (David 1979; David and Scandizzo 1982).

Achievement of the latter goal depended on the extent to which the agricultural sector could generate a surplus over domestic consumption requirements and the nature of specialization in export production. As alluded to in Chapter 3, this expectation was also inherent in "staple theory," which suggested that resource-based production activities could become the leading sectors in economic development. It is also synergistic with what Balassa (1979) terms the "stages approach to comparative advantage." The latter refers to certain sequential stages in domestic and export production. To reiterate, the idea is that countries would begin the development process by exporting primary commodities and then graduate to the export of light manufactures, except for simple processed goods based on natural resources. At a much later stage, exports of heavy industrial products might become feasible. Over time, therefore, the structure of production and exports would change with the accumulation of physical and human capital.

In the above context, there have emerged several alternative interpretations of agriculture's potential role based on models depicting the transformation of the sector from a large and stagnant subsistence arena with a low capital/output ratio and little technical change to a much smaller, but more efficient, commercialized sector based on innovation and rational decision making. These models share the same dynamic as Rostovian stages by delineating specific sequences inherent in the growth of the agricultural sector - ranging from a traditional stage when the pre-conditions for growth had to be established, through a "take-off" or growth stage, to a more mature capital-intensive stage. Timmer (1988) has conceptualized these evolutionary stages in terms of "environments," which reflect the dominant interpretive modes that guided the debate during specific historical epochs.

The first, or Mosher interpretive environment, was concerned with "getting agriculture moving" (Mosher 1966). This phase is initiated by a rise in productivity per worker in agriculture and is fuelled by public investments in infrastructure and research, favorable price incentives to farmers, and the adoption of new technology. As productivity increases, a surplus is generated and agriculture is in a position to make a positive contribution to the balanced growth of the economy. This initiates a second stage, or Johnston-Mellor interpretive environment, in which the surplus can be tapped to develop the non-agricultural sector. During this phase, which has been the primary focus of dual economy models, the agricultural surplus is tapped directly through taxation or resource flows, or indirectly through government intervention in the rural-urban terms of trade.

The presupposition was that agriculture can make a positive contribution to broad-based economic development if an "unimodal" development strategy is followed, that is, one based on large numbers of smallholders, as distinct from a dualistic or "bimodal" strategy in which production is concentrated in a few large farms. The perspective suggested an agricultural development strategy involving expansion in agricultural production based on labor-intensive or capital-saving techniques with a strong emphasis on technical innovations. The overall picture was one of a technologically dynamic, small-scale agriculture generating sustained increases in output, employment, and incomes (Johnston and Kilby 1975; Mellor 1976; Mellor and Johnston 1984).

Considerable emphasis was placed on the need for supportive institutional development as a means of improving the generation and dissemination of appropriate innovations, including investment in agricultural research, extension services, marketing and distribution arrangements, and general educational facilities. This orientation was given a dramatic impetus with the introduction of high-yielding varieties of wheat and rice (Green Revolution technology) in Asia during the 1960s and after. While a number of technical, economic, and social problems subsequently tempered the original optimism surrounding the introduction of this new technology, the dominant belief was that, given the right conditions, a positive impact could be produced on output, employment, and productivity levels in smallholder agriculture.

The third interpretive environment of Schultzian price mechanists was based on the premise that improved price incentives were necessary to facilitate the optimal flow of resources out of agriculture. As previously indicated, the corresponding models of agricultural transformation were rooted in the assumption that small farmers are responsive to economic incentives in determining input-output mixes and investment priorities. This challenged the conventional stereotype of the small farmer in the developing world as someone who is tradition-bounded and not at all influenced by market price signals or the economic environment. It was even suggested that price incentives influenced farmer behavior to such an extent that they were a significant determinant of the success or otherwise of non-price measures designed to influence the level of farm output or the promotion of structural change. In particular, it was argued that the system of relative prices tends to exert a significant influence on both the direction and intensity of technological progress (Hayami and Ruttan [1971] 1985).

Thus, the third interpretive phase called for a progressive integration of agriculture into the macroeconomy through more efficient product and factor markets linking urban and rural sectors. It was envisaged that the proper functioning of such markets would induce capital and labor to move from activities where returns were low to those with a higher productivity, thereby offering new opportunities for those previously trapped in low-income occupations. What was overlooked, however, was that as agriculture became more integrated into the macroeconomy, it would become much more vulnerable to fluctuations in aggregate economic activity, macroeconomic prices, and trade.

Finally, the foregoing models of agricultural transformation did not sufficiently address the question concerning the distribution of benefits from agricultural growth. Growth stage theories and dynamic dual economy models posit that the incorporation of peasants and smalllholders into the market would lead to a disappearance of dualism. This conclusion has been challenged by dependency theorists. As elaborated in Chapter 8, interpretations based on dependency attribute the lack of agricultural transformation in the majority of developing countries to the endemic structure of center-periphery relations and the economic policies of urban-based governments that favor a small urban elite and large landowners at the expense of powerless and dispersed smallholders (Griffin 1974; de Janvry 1981). From this perspective, the attempt to modernize agriculture by integrating rural areas into the system of market-equilibrium relationships tends to perpetuate rather than erode marginalization and traditional forms of dualistic development.

Chapter 7

Historical and Empirical Generalizations: The Search for Causation

The ongoing process of interpretation and reinterpretation in the development discourse has involved the search for historical, theoretical, and empirical generalizations purporting to explain the causes of development and the factors underlying the transition from poverty to riches. The dominant research practice has constituted attempts to fit observed events and phenomena into a paradigm-based interpretive mode. This orientation is exemplified by the neo-classical and endogenous growth perspectives discussed in Chapter 3. As we have indicated, an important issue surrounding such models is whether economies at different per capita income levels can "converge" to the same income level, or the circumstances surrounding the capacity of poor countries to catch up with their richer counterparts.

While the consensual view has emerged that the former can realize a smooth transition by accelerating the pace of investment in physical and human capital, there are divergent interpretations of the potential for economic growth that is not associated with the accumulation process. In particular, this is reflected in a number of research programs that have tried to unlock both uniform and variable patterns of historical growth across countries at different levels of economic development. This chapter focuses on alternative interpretations of empirical regularities and uniform historical features of development. These "historical laws" or "stylized facts" are supposed to "be observed in a sufficient number of cases to call for an explanation that would account for them ... independently of whether they fit into the general framework of theory or not" (Kaldor 1985: 8-9).

Economic Growth Stages and Historical Variations

The process of natural economic evolution has been explored in macrohistorical growth models that first identify the economic, political, and social factors traditionally linked to economic development in the West and then extrapolating these to the situation facing developing countries. The most prominent has been Rostow's "Stages of Economic Growth" or "Non-Communist Manifesto" (Rostow 1960). While it has remained highly controversial, Rostow's interpretation of economic modernization still remains a paradigm case of an approach that links ideological preconceptions, technical economic assumptions, theoretical postulates, and policy prescriptions into a comprehensive model of development and change.

The overall analytical thrust is based on an attempt to apply economic theory to history by examining the economic and non-economic characteristics of entire societies. The complexities of history suggest that no simple theory of economic causation is sufficiently robust to capture all the ramifications of what is essentially a multifaceted development process. Starting from this presupposition, Rostow interprets development from the perspective of the "Marshallian long period," or the idea of a complex intermeshing of people and societal processes. Alfred Marshall is credited with the idea that if economic analysis is to move beyond the postulates of static short-period equilibrium encountered in neo-classical theory, it must be prepared to come to grips with "real life," the "high theme of economic progress," and "society as an organism." (1920: 461).

One implication is that the study of economic and social reality should utilize an "organic" or "biological" framework of interpretation rather than continue its heavy reliance on the more entrenched linear or neo-Newtonian methodological stance. If it is believed that people and societies are inescapably complex, then it follows that the assumptions of maximizing behavior underlying neo-classical economics can only tell part of the development story. In the evolution of change, there can be no certainty about the consequences emanating from the complex interaction of economic and non-economic motives. The interactive process may be mutually reinforcing or contradictory, in which case attainment of the ideals of modernization may be totally frustrated.

Under the circumstances, more emphasis should be placed on understanding the *process* rather than the *theory* of economic growth. As Rostow states, "economic growth is the result of an interacting process involving economic, social, and political sectors of society, including the emergence of a core of entrepreneurs who are psychologically motivated and technically prepared regularly to lead the way in introducing new production functions" (1984: 236). As elaborated below, Rostow believed in individual motivation, which is a necessary prerequisite for development of the advanced technology needed for modernization. Hence, a free market environment in which the profit motive is encouraged is assumed to provide the requisite incentives for individual producers to apply technology to production.

Given such presuppositions, Rostow analyzes the process of economic growth in terms of an interweaving of economic and non-economic factors that are endemic to the evolution of societies in the more developed sector of the world. The complex admixture of these components is effected through an array of "propensities" that reflect how society responds to the various challenges and possibilities facing it. As such, they transcend the pure profit motive of entrepreneurs. Explicit assumptions about the strength and position of the propensities are needed in order to make informed judgments and statements about the population, labor force, investment, production functions, and so on.

The propensities are akin to the Keynesian notion of "animal spirits" or the "temptation to take a chance" alluded to in Chapter 4. In this context, modern economic growth is interpreted as a unique process of complex linkages among basic science, invention, and innovation that generate a flow of new production functions, including a sequence of "leading" sectors. It involves a slowly emerging societal framework (the propensities) that is defined by a set of dynamic and optimal sectoral paths to which an economy approximates over time. At the economic level, Rostow's assumption is that the modernization process cannot be usefully analyzed in aggregate terms, but requires examination of dynamic production sectors absorbing technology and tracing out their development trajectories.

As in the case of Hirschman, a disproportionate role is assigned to rapidly expanding leading production sectors in directly reinvesting profits in plants and equipment, and indirectly influencing the aggregate growth rate and therefore investments in other sectors. The analysis extrapolates from the behavior of traditional leading sectors that have characterized major industrial and technological revolutions of the past two centuries, as well as supporting sectors that have emerged through backward, forward, and other linkages. The various sectors grow at differential rates, and the aggregation of their individual expansion provides the historical picture of economic modernization. A primary example is Britain, which, according to Rostow (1978), developed in the sequence shown below.

In general, Rostow's perspective of the economy consists of a notion of a dynamic moving equilibrium embracing *endogenous* changes in population, the labor force, technology, and the supply of basic commodities such as food and energy. The dynamics of the system generate optimal sectoral capacity levels, aggregate growth rates, and investment designed to keep all sectors on their equilibrium paths. In the later context, the sectoral bias of the analysis draws support from a perception that high and steady aggregate growth rates require adequate flows of investment to supporting sectors such as agriculture, infrastructure, and education.

However, the investment process is by no means smooth, and systematic errors are likely to occur because: (i) investors are typically inclined to base their decisions on current indicators of productivity without paying sufficient attention to the total volume of investment that would be induced by the current situation;

Time Span	Leading Sectors
1. 1780s - 1830s	Cotton textiles, Watt's steam engine, iron and coke
2. 1840s - 1900s	Railroads, steel
3. 1900s - 1960s	Automobiles, electricity, chemicals
4. 1970s -	Microelectronics, biotechnology, new industrial materials, lasers

and (ii) the tendency for investment instability to be exacerbated by inevitable time-lags that are built into the investment process. As a consequence, inordinately high levels of investment can continue until investors come to realize that their net returns have begun to fall. From this perspective, economic growth follows a cyclical path of varying lengths and depends on the type of duration of investment undertaken. "And so economies made their way through history, overshooting and undershooting their optimum sectoral paths, like a drunk going home from the local pub on Saturday night" (Rostow 1984: 238).

At this point, it is necessary to emphasize some of the more critical assumptions underlying Rostow's disaggregated model of economic growth and production. In general, he relies on some of the broad assumptions underlying the neo-classical model of economic growth. These include the availability of natural resources, a flow of technology, and the behavior of the labor force when real wages change. However, his interpretation of the process of economic growth diverges substantially from the neo-classical paradigm in terms of (i) investment; (ii) technology and the entrepreneurial adoption of innovations; (iii) business cycles as a factor in the development process; and (iv) the role of non-economic factors, especially politics.

First, investment expenditure, or capital formation, depends on the level and rate of change of profits rather than on the level of GNP, as assumed in neo-classical growth theory. This carries the important implication that any propulsion in the economy through, say, a technological invention, will itself raise the rate of saving and investment for some time in the future. The reinvestment of profits by businesses is assumed to be a major source of investment funds. The positive association between profit levels and rates of expansion is explained by two factors: (i) a high rate of growth of profits provides a signal to business firms of enhanced opportunities for earning future profits, and, therefore an effective inducement of investment in the Keynesian sense; and (ii) where such firms are accustomed to distribute relatively fixed levels of profits, they can retain a high proportion of returns during periods of accelerated economic growth.

A second assumption is that technical change is endogenous, that is, it depends on the proportion of resources that a society is prepared to expend on its production. Thus, the concept of a dynamic economy and the related stages of economic growth are explained by the extent to which particular productive sectors progressively absorb a sequence of sophisticated technologies currently in the world, and/or which may be available to latecomers as a backlog. For any production activity, it can be assumed that the most advanced countries would have progressively absorbed all the available technology, whereas the less developed ones would have a larger backlog on which to draw.

The possibilities for technical change are therefore linked to an overarching research and development (R & D) process which constitutes the entire gamut of activities necessary for new technology to be developed as well as its efficient adoption by productive sectors. Two related types of activities are involved: the production of inventions themselves; and the buildup of "absorptive capacity" for their incorporation into the economy as efficient innovations. Across societies, the determinants of entrepreneurial capacity to absorb potentially profitable innovations tend to be complex, but include, among other things, previous investment in education and training; society's institutions, incentive structure, and public policy environment; and, therefore, the propensity of managers to innovate and take risks.

Third, Rostow criticizes conventional economic theory for providing no credible linkage of business cycles to the growth process. Such cycles, he argues, have constituted the historic form of economic growth from the eighteenth century to the late 1930s. Under the circumstances, fluctuations, whether cyclical or not, should not be separated from the growth path of modern economies (Rostow 1990). In this context, emphasis is placed on relative price trends between basic commodities and manufactures in inducing corrective changes in investment, generating "Kondratieff cycles," with consequences for the price level, interest rates, income distribution, aggregate and sectoral growth rates. D.N. Kondratieff was the main proponent of the notion that capitalist economies are subject to cycles of fifty years in length. In Rostow's analysis, the cycles are related to the interplay between economic aggregates and sectors, and in particular, the severely lagged process of adjusting supplies of food, raw materials, and energy to the requirements of a growing world economy.

Fourth, the assumptions of conventional economic theory are questioned on the grounds that no credible mechanisms are provided for introducing non-economic factors into the systemic analysis of economic growth. While subscribing to the same set of modernization ideals identified in the previous chapter, Rostow places special emphasis on the crucial role played by politics during the early phases of modernization. As he recognizes, the transition to modern society is inherently painful, volatile, and accompanied by disruptive instability in varying degrees. In his eyes, the effects of such potentially negative forces would be damped if developing countries were to concentrate their reactive nationalist impulses on the task of economic modernization itself rather than on other possible sentiments of nationalism.

Given the analytical framework outlined above, the modernization or development sequence is first interpreted in terms of three periods or stages: a long period when the "preconditions" for "take-off" are established; the take-off itself (two to three decades); and a long period when growth becomes normal and relatively automatic. Two further substages are presumed to emerge within this latter period of self-sustained economic growth: "the drive to technological maturity" and "the age of high mass consumption." Rostow's conclusion, therefore, is that two centuries of growth have yielded five stages in the evolution of modern societies: traditional society; the preconditions for take-off; the take-off itself; the drive to technological maturity; and the age of high mass consumption.

The stages are analyzed in terms of complex interactions among economic and non-economic variables, but represent definable patterns and recurrent processes. Though certain relationships manifest themselves at each stage, each country may display its own unique configurations. Thus, definition of the stages diverges from the practice encountered in mainstream economics, which relies on the per capita income yardstick. Rather, the predominant emphasis is on the capacity of countries to absorb modern technology efficiently. This technological fundamentalism, with its linkages to large and powerful leading sectors in the economy, also cuts across the traditional Keynesian savings-investment relationship.

As indicated above, Rostow viewed forces at work in the developing world as lending themselves to tensions and instability. In particular, his "non-communist manifesto" can be interpreted as a blueprint for stemming the ideological competition between communists and non-communists. Therefore, his prescriptions for development policy and foreign aid hinged on the premise that it was in the interest of the United States for the developing countries of the day to evolve with a minimum of violence and instability through development assistance. The concept of the take-off was linked to the possibility of providing soft loans which would no longer be required when recipient countries moved on to the path of self-sustained growth. As noted in Chapter 5, the basic justification for foreign aid was political. It was based on the expectation that stable political democracies would emerge in the developing world through the orchestration of the "mutual benefits" thesis. This ideology played a prominent role in shaping the vision of advisers mobilized at MIT's Center for International Studies (CENIS) in the 1950s.

Rostow's disaggregated theory of economic growth and the attendant policy prescriptions have been the subject of a long and heated debate. While all the details cannot be addressed here, a few critical areas deserve further comment. In the case of the growth model itself, there is a lack of sufficient clarity about the interpretation of "equilibrium" vis-à-vis "disequilibrium." To reiterate, the Rostovian thesis of the Marshallian long period is articulated in terms of nations displaying what are termed "optimal" sectoral capacities related to labor force growth, technical change, and the supply of basic commodities. In this process, the system generates optimal aggregate growth and distribution of investment in particular sectors. Hence, the historical growth process is viewed as one in which the world hobbles along "like a drunk," alternatively overshooting and undershooting its optimal paths. There is lack of clarity about how the sectoral "optima" are to be ascertained and the corresponding rules for determining targets. On a related basis, a question arises whether the engine of economic growth is best fuelled by countries persistently following prescribed equilibrium paths, or through the kinds of disequilibria and imbalances suggested by Hirschman and others.

In Rostow's analysis, the explanation of such phenomena is embedded in an interpretation of Kondratieff long swings in which prices of basic commodities play a prominent role. The experience of the 1950s and 1960s is located in the downswing phase of the fourth Kondratieff cycle depicted by cheap energy prices and the favorable terms of trade for industrial countries. It was a period of high growth, and its diffusion to the developing countries seemed to work through increased foreign aid. The world entered the fifth upswing phase of the cycle in the 1970s, which witnessed protracted increases in the prices of food, energy, and other basic commodities. Growth rates declined in the industrial nations, which were now faced with a combination of domestic inflation and deteriorating terms of trade. The upswing brought harder times for developing countries, foreign aid was drastically reduced, non-oil exporters faced burgeoning balance of payments deficits and were forced to contract debt at relatively high real interest rates. The majority of developing countries have not yet recovered from the structural consequences of this experience.

Yet Rostow has derived an optimistic prognostication from this train of events. In the World Bank's *Pioneers* volume, he saw it as important for the world economy "to assure that the sectors supporting *continuity of industrial civilization* are expanded and sustained: energy, agriculture, raw materials, water, and other environmental sectors" (1984: 255; emphasis added). Since the requisite investments could not be left to the "magic of the marketplace," functional cooperation aimed at bolstering these critical sectors was seen as constituting the heart of North-South cooperation. "If a sense of communal interest and communal purpose can be reestablished by enterprises in these critical sectors, I am confident that progress can be made in other areas of mutual North-South interest," Rostow continues (1984: 256).

It can be commented that both North and South probably agree that global welfare and that of its constituent parts would be enhanced through higher investments in and supplies of food, energy, and strategic raw materials. However, the correctness of this view does not hinge on the validity of long-term development theory. Moreover, Southern perspectives on food and energy are definitely non-Rostovian in orientation and have nothing to do with "the continuity of industrial civilization." Investments in such sectors are predicated on survival needs. As such, the relevant measuring rod is not so much production, but the prerequisites of fair distribution, poverty alleviation, and guaranteeing of ownership rights and exchange entitlements.

Contextually, a question arises whether developing countries can be expected to evolve along the lines suggested by the historical experience of the industrial West. It can be asked even if relevant institutional barriers to development were to be removed. The Industrial Revolution and the rest of what Rostow views are necessary economic stages came as a part of particular historical epochs, which may not be replicated, or in the same way. The uncritical acceptance of a supposedly objective, non-culturally bound, standard of developmental evolution can have quite real effects when inadequate theory translates into dangerous policy. If an economy does not spontaneously follow the Rostovian growth path, then the implication may be that it should be "forced" on to the "take-off" or industrial stage. We must add that this may not have been what Rostow intended. The point of emphasis, however, is that his model was developed within the framework of a particular cultural, structural, and historical context. Without this particular context, the imposition of what may be mistaken as a universal standard is likely to thwart rather than enhance economic growth and societal development.

A related argument is that the concern should be more than "historical variations," that is, with diversity in the historical patterns of growth. From this perspective, not only do contemporary developing countries face a greater difficulty in reaching "takeoff," but their industrialization process has differed considerably from that of their more developed counterparts both in terms of the speed of development as well as in the productive and organizational structures that have been established. Such considerations are emphasized in what is known as "late industrialization theory," which hypothesizes that development outcomes within and among any given set of countries are affected by the character of the world economy, technological changes (timing), the nature of competition among nation states, and the tenor of state-society interactions at the time countries enter the industrialization race. These variables tend to change over time such that late industrializers often deal with changed sets of circumstances compared to the case for early developers.

Alexander Gerschenkron (1962), the foremost exponent of this perspective, states the thesis as follows. The economic and political requirements of early industrializers have been different in the sense that they have had to face few competitors and a simple, low-capital technology compared to countries that industrialize when competition already exists and industry has become highly complex and expensive. The more advanced the world economy and the less developed a country, the more likely that it would face higher entry costs. Meeting these costs requires a greater degree of collective mobilization and therefore more central coordination. The process is facilitated by the existence of a strong state bureaucracy that is capable of containing the divergent interests of various conflict coalitions and directing their energies toward achievement of a common national objective.

The claim is that societies which were able to develop strong central institutions prior to industrialization will find them useful if they attempt to catch up with the early industrializers. According to Huntington (1968), these institutions are the antecedents of industrialization that involves a relatively slow process. The latter allows more time for the different strata of the population to adjust to change and reduces the shock of a sudden transformation that is more typical when industrialization occurs very rapidly and sometimes in the course of a single generation.

Gerschenkron cites Britain and Germany in the eighteenth and the late nineteenth centuries, respectively, as examples of countries that followed the path of early industrialization. The British case was marked by a congruence between the liberal character of the society and the relatively simple nature of economic development during the first stage of the industrial revolution. Given the relatively strong and centralized nature of the state, the guilds were unable to prevent the introduction of new practices. In the German case, a corporatist societal ethos in which the state was pulled in different directions by various conflict coalitions gave way when the industrialization process moved from a concentration on textiles to iron, steel, and chemicals. The increasingly massive capital investments needed at this stage of the industrialization process called for a high degree of centralized organization and coordination.

Barrington Moore (1966) and Albert Hirschman (1971) have also utilized this thesis to demonstrate how the policy process was significantly influenced by the nature of societal development and the structure of the national economy obtained when each of the countries they studied entered the path of industrialization. In particular, Hirschman found interesting similarities and differences between the German-Japanese model and Latin America's "late development." Other studies of the rapid industrialization of East Asian countries have also attributed their spectacular success to the autonomy of the bureaucratic state in imposing its will on a more or less compliant civil society (see Amsden 1989; Wade 1990).

Historical and Statistical "Stylized Facts"

The point of departure is a series of seminal papers (1956-67) by Nobel Laureate Simon Kuznets who attempted to establish "stylized facts" about structural transformation through a systematic study of the average behavior of growing economies with different per capita income levels. He did not rely explicitly on any development theory, but his empirical research program was guided by implicit empirical generalizations based on the historical growth and transformation experience of industrial nations. The long-run processes are distilled in a comparative framework that seeks to establish "common features and patterns" among countries varying in "size, location, and historical heritage" as well as to identify "divergences from such patterns." The overall rationale for the comparative study of growth and economic structure "is conditioned on the existence of common, transnational factors, and a mechanism of interaction among nations that will produce some systematic order in the way modern economic growth can be expected to spread around the world" (Kuznets 1959: 170).

Using long time series and national income data, Kuznets advanced the thesis that the growth of total product tended to accelerate as countries entered the epoch of "modern economic growth." This idea is in line with the phenomena of extensive and intensive growth that were discussed in Chapter 2 of this book. The new epoch was thought to have begun in Britain in the late eighteenth century, and to have spread to other industrializing nations, especially in Europe. The developing countries were left out of this process because of low initial levels and rates of growth of GDP per capita as they entered the era of modern economic growth.

In Kuznets's schema, some of the principal transnational factors, that is, "those common to the world," included the industrial system, or a system of industrial production based on the application of science and technology. In turn, the enlarged pool of science and technology led to increased productivity, and therefore an acceleration in GDP per capita. Some fundamental requirements undergirded the industrial or production system: a minimum level of literacy; non-familial and impersonal types of organization; saving and capital formation; sectoral transformation and urbanization; and changes in the pattern of income distribution.

As emphasized in the classical model of sectoral articulation (see Chapter 2) and by Colin Clark (1940), Kuznets found that the modern economic growth process has been accompanied by an accelerated rate of urbanization and a corresponding shift in the labor force from agriculture to industry. In this process, the agricultural sector declines both in terms of its relative contribution to GDP and labor force participation. Correlatively, the share of the industrial sector rises, and while the share of the services sector rises less consistently, on average, it nevertheless demonstrates a conspicuous escalation in product share in certain relatively rich countries. Moreover, the average lower productivity in services compared to industry yields a marked increase in the proportion of the labor force employed in the services sector at high per capita income and product levels.

Second, transformation in the industry/production system is accompanied by universal changes on the demand side, as exemplified by the structure of human wants and aspirations. In the economics arena, this is normally explained by the ubiquity of Engels' law, which is considered to be the most pervasive force in a growing economy. It states that the proportion of income spent on basic food items tends to decline as per capita income increases, or in the parlance of economics, the income elasticity of demand for food is less than unity. Goods and services with a higher income elasticity of demand become increasingly more important in final demand and consumption as per capita income rises. This shift in demand patterns is attributed to: (i) the decline in agriculture, with a gradual transition in the mix of commodities produced and a concomitant growth in processing, marketing, and distribution activities; and (ii) the widespread desire of all people for a better life based on higher standards of economic performance and levels of living. A third universal process involves the organization of the world into nation states.

Finally, perhaps the most celebrated of Kuznets's findings concerns the way in which the size distribution of income changes as per capita income rises. Based on fragmentary historical data for now developed countries, he hypothesized that the process of economic development was likely to be accompanied by a substantial increase in inequality, which would reverse itself only at a relatively advanced stage of development. More specifically, countries were thought to pass through three stages: a pre-industrial stage of relative income equality, an industrialization stage of relative income inequality, and a modern developed stage of reduced income inequality.

This "inverted S-curve" relation is explained in the following terms. During the early phases of development, the income distribution profile is relatively equal because most of the population derives its income from its own labor. Average income is low and the absolute minimum income for subsistence provides the basis for equalization among lower income groups. Increased income concentration can be expected during the industrialization phase because of the differential effects of capital accumulation, education, and the increasing division of labor. There is a higher level of savings by the capitalist class and the educated elite, and the corresponding widening of the income gap between these groups and unskilled workers. Income concentration is expected to lessen during the modern or developed phase for the following reasons: (i) a decrease in population growth; (ii) reduced savings among higher income groups due to waste; (iii) concentration of new enterprises due to the failure of existing ones to adjust sufficiently to changing economic conditions and times; and (iv) state intervention in the system of distribution.

In the above context, the low inequality profile observed for contemporary developed nations was attributed not only to their level of development but also to the impact of specific historical and political factors. Of special significance was the strengthening of organized labor after the First World War and the political role it came to play in the creation of a welfare state. However, it is highly unlikely that such institutional changes will be replicated in countries on the modern development path. Moreover, these changes represented an integral part of the economic transformation in labor relationships stemming from labor scarcity and the greater emphasis placed on human skills in the production process. The tremendous economic, social, and political changes taking place in the development sector of the world would seem to suggest that tendencies toward greater inequality are being strengthened. The main causal factors include: (i) the election of more conservative governments and a concomitant reduction in the influence of organized labor; (ii) the influence of immigration, which has swollen the pool of low-wage unskilled labor; and (iii) the impact of technological change, de-industrialization, and failure to retrain the labor force.

Like that of Kuznets, the research program of Hollis Chenery and his associates attempted to distinguish between universal vis-à-vis particular (national) factors in the growth process. Kuznets did not use formal statistical techniques and, as previously mentioned, his comparisons were based on long historical time series. By contrast, Chenery used statistical techniques and cross-sectional analyses to develop empirical generalizations about the average behavior of countries at different per capita income levels during the 1950s and 1960s. The results obtained from the cross-sectional method diverged from Kuznets's comparisons in several important respects.

First, there was more disaggregation of economic categories. For example, Chenery and Taylor (1968) developed more "typologies" of countries based on population size and relative specialization in exports of primary and manufactured goods. This led to a four-way classification - large primary-oriented, small primary-oriented, large manufacture-oriented, and small manufacture-oriented. Industries were also disaggregated into "early, middle, and late." Second, Chenery and Syrquin (1975) used correlation analysis to establish average patterns of "stylized facts" in the growth process. Third, and perhaps most important, the cross-sectional analyses, country typologies, and stylized facts were intended as a guide to development policy. The objective was to help economic planners and policymakers by identifying the typologies to which their countries belonged, isolating their deviations from average behavior, and deciding whether or not they wished to stay with the existing development pattern, move closer toward the average, or pursue an entirely different course. The overall idea was to emphasize the structural character of planning vis-à-vis less policy-oriented growth models.

Some of the specific findings or uniform changes observed by Chenery and his associates include the following. In the case of final demand, the most uniform changes are a decline in the share of food consumption and a corresponding rise in the share of resources allocated to investment, implying a shift in demand away from agricultural to industrial goods. Like Kuznets, therefore, the universality of Engels' law was also observed. Using a sample of 93 countries for the 1950-70 period, the study by Chenery and Syrquin found that as per capita income rises from \$100 to \$1,500 there is a major change in the composition of demand, with a decline in food consumption from 36 to 15 percent of GDP. Primary production activities make up about 45 percent of a country's value-added at the \$100 per capita income level and decline to about 14 percent at the \$1,000 level. Over the same income range, primary employment falls from 68 to 25 percent. Industry has sector shares in value-added and employment rising from about 15 to 35 percent and from 9 to 32 percent, respectively, over the same income range.

During the process of development, total use of intermediate goods relative to national output tends to rise, while varying in composition. This increased use is not due to changes in the composition of output, but rather reflects the evolution of a more complex system defined by a higher degree of fabrication and shifts from handicrafts to factory production. There is also a parallel expansion of the services sector. The effects of these and related changes in the structural composition of the economy were also deciphered through sorting out countries by size and export orientation. Large countries transform their economic structures at an earlier point in their development. In the $200 to $800 per capita income range, for example, the share of industry is 5 to 6 percent higher for large countries compared to small ones. The exports of large countries are also more biased toward industrial rather than primary products.

Across countries, the extent of a country's participation in international trade is only weakly correlated with its level of development. This is contrary to the empirical prediction of standard trade models to the effect that the size of the economy is a principal determinant of trade. The shares of trade and capital imports in GDP are relatively high, domestic markets are relatively small, and the production structure is much more specialized in small countries compared to large ones. The commodity composition of trade and the pattern of specialization are largely determined by the availability of natural resources, traditional factor proportions, and a country's policy orientation. Small countries that lacked a broad natural resource base had to develop exports of manufactured goods at an earlier stage than their resource-rich counterparts. Large countries also tend to shift away from specialization in primary production through import substitution policies, and are more likely to adopt inward-looking development strategies.

It can be commented that it is meaningless to measure the average behavior of certain large countries, for example, India and China, since they account for roughly one half of the behavior of developing countries and are rooted in different cultural traditions. Furthermore, a large number of factors determining the growth performance of developing countries have been conveniently excluded from Chenery's cross-sectional studies. These "missing variables" include, inter alia, the critical role of government and institutions. According to one sympathetic critic, "the studies pay little attention to the cultural, political, and administrative elements that also affect development. They are useful, indeed essential, in bringing economic policy alternatives to light, but they provide an incomplete picture of the sources of the limitations of growth" (Mason 1984: 7).

The relative importance of these non-economic variables has been emphasized in the studies of Irma Adelman and Cynthia Taft Morris (1961, 1973), who have applied statistical methods to test the association between economic growth and a wide array of socio-cultural and political variables that do not normally lend themselves to time-series analysis. While this kind of associational study has skillfully identified the main uniformities of social and political life that accompany the modernization process, it nevertheless shares the basic weakness of the comparative statistical analysis of economic growth. This inheres in a failure to sufficiently come to grips with the dynamics of change. In other words, despite the recognition of conditions which must be satisfied at a point in equilibrium, it masks the dynamic path to be pursued toward this equilibrium.

Correlation between "Outward-Orientation" and Economic Growth

As previously indicated, free trade has been considered an "engine" or "handmaiden" of growth ever since the days of the classical economists, in the sense that it is associated with entrepreneurship, technological progress, productivity, and thrift. During the 1960s and 1970s, a number of comparative studies of developing countries demonstrated that export growth or "outward-orientation" is apparently positively associated with faster aggregate economic growth and greater equity. The dominant perspective has been that tariff protection in developing countries, by channelling production toward limited domestic markets, leads to low capacity utilization, a loss of economies of scale, a lack of specialization, and few incentives for technical change.

Theoretical support was provided by neo-classical trade theory, even though it is now accepted that a number of anomalies and asymmetries militate against the rules of mutually beneficial exchange. The neo-classical case was bolstered by the experience of the newly industrializing countries (NICs), which achieved remarkable growth in output and exports of manufactures. Furthermore, the apparent "failure" of the import-substitution strategy strengthened the case for adoption of more outward-oriented policies and strategies. By providing similar incentives for sales in domestic and foreign markets, such policies were expected to enhance growth performance through resource allocation according to comparative advantage, exploitation of scale economies, and technological improvements.

At the empirical level, a number of comparative studies have attempted to establish a correlation between export growth and overall economic performance. An early study by Michaelopolous and Jay (1973) was based on estimation of an aggregate neo-classical production function for thirty-nine countries. Not only was export growth found to be a highly significant factor in the development process, but GNP growth was also highly correlated with the export growth rate. In similar vein, Michaely (1977) found a significant relationship between exports (measured by the change in the share of exports in GNP) and GNP itself (measured by the rate of change in per capita income).

An interesting result of the latter study is that while a strong positive association exists between export shares and aggregate growth performance for the more developed countries, the relationship becomes negative for the least developed economies. This suggests that economic growth is influenced by export performance only after countries have reached a minimum threshold of development. This is particularly true of low-income countries in Africa, where there is little evidence to support the proposition that the degree of export orientation is associated with growth performance (Helleiner 1986).

Studies by Heller and Porter (1978), Tyler (1981), and Feder (1983) also provided evidence that outward-oriented policies enabled countries to allocate resources optimally and enhance productivity. Studies by Balassa (1978, 1982) confirmed a positive association between exports and economic growth as well as a greater ability of outward-oriented economies to adjust to external shocks compared to their more inward-oriented counterparts. In particular, the 1982 study found that outward-oriented developing economies experienced average gains of 14 percent and inward-oriented ones an average loss of 8 percent in their export market shares during the 1974-78 period.

However, doubts can be raised about Balassa's statistical methodology, for instance, the choice of base year and form of decomposition, since it tends to bias the results against inward-looking countries in his survey. As Fishlow states, he tends to confirm the "advantage of more inward-oriented development in limiting susceptibility to adverse external shocks, at a potential cost in average performance. The results might have been better still had the inward-oriented NICs not succumbed to the temptations of cheap and abundant foreign loans. Their problem was not inwardness alone, but rather an asymmetric openness built partially upon the exaggeration of their export potential" (1984: 389-90). In this context, one survey of the literature up to the mid-1980s concludes that "almost all empirical work seems to have concluded that exports are probably good for growth" (Ram 1987: 51). By contrast, a nearly contemporaneous review found the results "remarkable for the lack of support that they provide for the export promotion hypothesis" (Jung and Marshall 1985: 10).

The analysis by Bradford (1987) of transitional economies found no statistically significant differences between outward- and inward-oriented countries, indicating that general policy conclusions should be drawn with extreme care. Others argue that the thesis of the World Bank and IMF that outward-oriented policies are closer to the free market ideal and consequently better able to reap the gains of free markets than traditional import-substitution alternatives has little foundation in theory and contemporary reality. Successful export-led growth economies have export sectors where the government has played a highly interventionist role, for example, South Korea and Taiwan in Asia, or Argentina and Brazil during the 1970s. Thus, the empirical evidence clearly suggests that successful export promotion tends to be associated not so much with free markets, but with "careful government intervention" (Chichilinsky and Heal 1986: 44).

In general, it can be commented that while empirical investigations of the export-growth nexus display what is tantamount to "stylized facts," no firm conclusions can be drawn about causal relationships. This raises the more fundamental question, introduced in Chapter 3, about research programs based on formal and informal statistical analyses of the structure of economic growth. As we have emphasized, statistical correlations that rely on time-series or cross-sectional measurement cannot always answer questions about what is cause or consequence, and can only provide an imprecise or conditional approximation to causation. One reason is that specific or unique variations in historical conditions are particularly relevant to the study of the dynamic effects of factors of production and other variables such as exports that are presumed to make a positive contribution to the growth process. The study of dynamic historical processes is intimately bound up with Hicks's notion of "sequential causality," which cannot be adequately captured by using the standard techniques of statistical inference.

IV

STRUCTURALIST AND PEOPLE-CENTERED REINTERPRETATIONS

Chapter 8

Development of the Underdevelopment

A significant challenge to the theoretical, empirical, and policy foundations of the orthodox development paradigm was mounted by scholars from the developing world itself, and in particular by Latin American structuralists. The consensual view was that the postwar theory of economic growth, grounded as it was in neo-classical and Keynesian economics, depended on the nature of an implicit production function and was therefore largely inapplicable to the conditions facing the developing world. Underdevelopment, by its very nature, could not be explained by growth theories but required a diachronic mode of interpretation, or forms of explanation based on a comprehensive analysis of historical, structural, and institutional mechanisms.

Epistemological Presuppositions

The brand of Latin American structuralism which emerged during the 1950s was grounded in "realist-existentialist" traditions of thought as distinct from the "idealist-essentialist" stance of orthodoxy. The latter is based on a belief that real world phenomena reflect instances of recurrent and predictable regularities. From this perspective, economic theories provide explanation and prediction based on observed regular relationships. As noted in Chapter 1 (see Table 1.1), the dominant research practice rests on the implicit assumption that progress in knowledge takes place through a continuous search for causal regularities or correlational properties of the real world through direct observation or statistical evidence. The epistemological anchor is provided by what is termed the "logico-empirical" or "hypothetico-deductive" model of explanation, which tries to achieve prediction based on empirical regularities or "covering laws."

In this interpretive mode, the phenomenon to be explained is logically deduced from a set of general laws combined with statements of antecedent conditions that are supposed to describe relevant facts about the real world. This *Covering*

Law model basically states that the occurrence of a phenomenon or event is explained when it can be subsumed under, or covered by, a general law, that is, when it can be shown to have occurred in accordance with some generality. The model rests on the claim that every explanation is made up of two parts--termed an explanans and an explanandum. As shown in Table 8.1, the explanans has two components: (i) statements of general laws ($L^1L^2L^3 \ldots L^m$), which pertain to the particular deductive science under consideration, such as the laws of supply and demand in economics; and (ii) statements of antecedent conditions ($C^1C^2C^3 \ldots C^m$), which describe facts about the real world. The explanandum (E) is a statement describing the phenomenon or event that has been explained. Thus, one implication of the model is that explanation takes a deductive form, which is based on a logical connection between the explanans and the explanandum. The Cs or initial conditions can be interpreted as "causes" and E as the "effect," which is connected by a general law. In the standard form of deductive explanation, the lawlike statement is the major premise, the causes the minor premise, and the effect is the conclusion. The general implication is that any legitimate form of explanation must take the form of a deductive argument in which the explanandum follows as a logical consequence of, or can be deduced from, the explanans. In other words, if the antecedent conditions and general law(s) hold, the phenomenon described by the explanandum *must* occur as a matter of logical necessity. This follows from the requirement that only universal laws or lawlike generalizations are allowable in scientific explanation.

As a general rule, the adequacy of a deductive explanation depends on the truth value of its premise (initial conditions and statements of general laws) and the reliability or validity of the arguments marshalled in the explanation. Under the circumstances, the explanation becomes unsound or inadequate if the premises on which it relies are false and the constituent arguments are invalid or unreliable. It is hard to justify an explanation in which the general law (major premise) has a questionable truth value. The problem with universal scientific laws is that, in principle, they cannot be verified. As a consequence, explanatory adequacy hinges on the extent to which their reliability or truth value can be assured as compared to, say, single observations to which they may be applied.

In the example given in Table 8.1, the truth value of the explanandum statement can be determined more by observing class, ethnicity, and gender relationships in the society in question, rather than by relying exclusively on its logical deduction from the premises of the explanans, the major one being the universal generalization: "all societies are stratified by class, ethnicity, and gender." The adequacy of the explanation partly depends on the truth value of the lawlike generalization. The latter is not only unconfirmed, but can be falsified by one single observation to the contrary. The point of emphasis is that the logical justification of an explanation does not constitute a sufficient condition of explanatory adequacy or soundness. In the final analysis, the latter must depend on the truth value of the general laws involved, and therefore on their empirical verifiability.

Table 8.1

The Covering Law Model of Explanation

Explanans	
$L^1L^2L^3 \ldots L^m$	General laws
Example: "All societies are stratified by class, ethnicity, and gender."	
$C^1C^2C^3 \ldots C^m$	Antecedent conditions
Example: "This collectivity is a society."	
Explanandum	
E	Description of explained or predicted phenomenon
Example: "This society is stratified by class, ethnicity, and gender."	

This raises a question about the empirical content of the explanans or the fact that it should be capable, at least in principle, of being tested through experiment or observation. Contextually, statistical laws are allowed in some variants of the Covering Law model. The implication is that the occurrence of the phenomenon described by the explanandum is accorded only a certain degree of probability. In cases where heavier reliance is placed on highly probable statistical laws, statements describing the explanandum are deduced "with a high degree of inductive probability" from the explanans. Under statistical or probabilistic forms of explanation the general laws can take either of two forms: (i) theoretical laws or principles from which empirical laws could be derived; and/or (ii) inductive generalizations based on observation.

The implication of the Covering Law model for the study of development is that the explanandum (underdevelopment) can be subsumed under (a) nomic regularities, such as the uniform historical "stylized facts," or stages of growth discussed in the previous chapter; and (b) a set of cognitive statements based on presuppositions about what is taking place in the developing world. As noted in Chapter 5, these essentially connote sets of economic, political, and sociocultural attributes that are antithetical to the modernization ideals inculcated in the West.

By contrast, the realist-existentialist mode of interpretation postulates that explanation and understanding need to penetrate behind external appearances or "surface structures" of phenomena as a result of chains of causal connection (Keat and Urry 1975: 27-45). The focus therefore shifts to the identification and investigation of basic and detailed causal mechanisms and underlying structures whose external representations are more often than not imperfect artifacts. Contextually, two elements of theory are highlighted. One is the "deep structure" which forms its essential underpinning. Thus, explanatory adequacy or success depends significantly on the ability of the social scientist to understand the deep, but sometimes hidden, structures lurking behind observed reality - systems of power, unequal economic relationships, and forms of dependency. As mentioned above, the other refers to the surface structure, or mechanisms that link the deep structure to particular observations in the real world - competitive markets, and the situational or textbook exposition of relationships among demand, supply, and price.

Structuralist interpretations of development are grounded in the realist-existentialist conception of scientific knowledge. In this analytical mode, the particular phenomenon to be explained is not subsumed under some general law, but rather emphasis is placed on the particular circumstances that are deemed sufficient to explain the phenomenon in question. For example, if it is hypothesized that social inequality causes underdevelopment, the validity of this statement is not attributed to some nomic regularity, but to the assumption that the structures (processes and relations) comprising the condition of social inequality tend to produce the state of underdevelopment. In other words, the structuralist theoretical perspective posits that the underlying structures (explanans) have causally produced underdevelopment (the explanandum). Moreover, having identified the structural causes, an attempt is made to show how and why particular structures come about, and why, given these structures, they tend to generate the conditions of underdevelopment.

The emphasis placed on structures means that it is necessary to come to grips with the non-economic parameters of economic models. A central assumption is that economic outcomes are significantly influenced by social, organizational, and political parameters. In identifying the limitations of neo-classical analysis, for example, Hla Myint (1987) attributes superior development performance to improvements in the organizational framework of the economic system. Where the framework is functioning well, increases in long-run capacity will be better able to utilize the potential sources of growth in output and productivity. As Myint points out, however, this way of interpreting economic development is implicitly ruled out in orthodox theoretical models, notably the model of "perfect competition." The latter assumes a highly developed organizational framework, or an ideal which cannot be improved upon.

The organizational framework underlying economic decisions puts in bold relief the fact that markets are essentially social processes. This was explained in Chapter 5 in terms of the embeddedness of economic transactions in social relations. For purposes of the present discussion, the latter constitute the non-economic parameters or "structural matrix" of the economist's model. As Latin American structuralists argue, they cannot be delinked from the historical contexts constraining opportunities and actions that can be potentially pursued. This interpretive mode bears a close affinity to the Marxian paradigm which places particular emphasis on social structures as a means of understanding the behavior of economic agents. Elements of the structural matrix include, inter alia, the land ownership system, imperfect commodity and factor markets, labor force composition, the government fiscal system, and unstable foreign markets for exports.

Such factors were originally highlighted in studies of the inflation problem in Latin America, and formed a focal point in the heated controversy between "monetarists" and "structuralist" perspectives. The former, identified with the Chicago School of thought, explains inflation in terms of an expansion in the volume of money in relation to the rate of growth in real output. Substantial and continuous increases in the general price level are considered to be a direct consequence of monetary expansion, and any monetary policy that permits such a state of affairs will accelerate the inflationary impetus. Since the power to determine the money supply rests in the hands of government, the latter must bear the responsibility for the inflation that results when the money supply grows too rapidly. Monetary expansion occurs because of the capricious folly of governments and their irrational behavior in relation to market forces (Friedman 1956, 1969).

The main proponent of the structuralist view of inflation was V. Noyola (1965) who argued that inflation was not a monetary phenomenon, but the result of interaction between two factors: "basic inflationary pressures" stemming from structural rigidities, and the "propagation mechanism" of competing income claims. Osvaldo Sunkel viewed the "basic inflationary pressures" as "fundamentally governed by the structural limitations, rigidity or inflexibility of the economic system." He continues, "[i]n fact, the inelasticity of some production sectors to adjust to changes in demand--or, in short, the lack of mobility of productive resources and the defective functioning of the price system--are chiefly responsible for structural inflationary disequilibrium" (Sunkel 1960: 120).

Both Noyola and Sunkel cited as their authority for the structuralist explanation a paper published by Michael Kalecki in Mexico in 1955 where he argued that the inelastic supply of food had been a major factor causing inflation (see Kalecki 1976). While visting the Economic Commission for Latin America (ECLA), Hollis Chenery also expounded the general structuralist perspective by advocating the use of input-output analysis and linear programming for investment planning in developing countries. As he stated (1961: 51), "a central problem in developing policy is the adequacy of free market forces in allocating investment resources. . . . These kinds of defect in the price mechanism . . . combine to produce a rigid market structure. . . . Serious structural disequilibrium in the use of labor, natural resources and foreign exchange represents one of the situations requiring state intervention in investment decisions."

The basic inflationary pressures represent points in the economic structure that typically provide the most resistance to the changes required for development. They are exemplified by economic factors - a sharp rise in export prices, as well as by non-economic ones - government action, or food shortages after a drought. The general structuralist interpretation is that inflationary pressures always start when one or more of these factors frustrate conventional expectations. For example, the additional public revenue generated from a rise in export prices may induce a government to launch a public works program. This, in turn, increases urban employment, changes conditions in the labor market, raises the demand for agricultural surpluses, and provokes shifts in the import schedule. Hence, a number of expectations may be frustrated, causing resistance to changes needed to achieve an efficient allocation of resources.

Once the inflationary process is set in motion, it tends to create unforeseen circumstances that react upon the initial inflationary impulse, leading to a cumulation of the inflationary impact. As an instance, the rise in money costs resulting from the inflation may have negative consequences for an economy's ability to compete in international markets, reducing both import and export capacity, thereby aggravating the inflationary process itself. Furtado (1970: 100) paints the relevant picture in the following terms:

> The most rigid points in the economic structure are like a barrier damming up the accumulated potential energy of a constantly rising level of water. In some circumstances, this energy can be diverted and

> the economic system will continue to operate as though it did not exist. It is far more likely, however, that the pressure will spread and affect other points of the economic structure, the course taken being dependent on the propagation mechanisms that it uses.

A host of psychological and sociological factors are involved in the propagation of inflation. Once the process is initiated, business firms continue to raise their prices in anticipation of higher wage and material costs. Labor responds by demanding increases in wages based on past increases in the cost of living and on the anticipation of further increases in the future. Thus, a continual tug of war develops among various economic interests, with each perceptible advance by one group countered by the moves of others to prevent a reduction in their real income. Government decision making with respect to credit, exchange, and wage policies, and the methods used to finance deficits in the public sector tend to define the environment within which the economic struggle takes place.

For example, if the decision is to introduce monetary restraint, the likely result will be a halt in the cost-price spiral but at the expense of creating unemployment and a fall in profits, resulting in discontent among politically powerful groups in labor and business sectors. The other alternative would be for the government to fix wages, other costs, and prices. In doing so, however, it would no longer be acting impartially, and would have to enforce its decisions through authoritarian measures. It is in this way that public sector deficits have historically become the main mechanism by which inflation has been institutionalized in Latin America.

Theory of the Socio-Economic Surplus

Latin American structuralists assign a pivotal role to the dynamic structural phenomenon termed the "social" or "economic" surplus, which highlights the relationship between accumulation and distribution in the development process. It refers to "that considerable portion of successive increments in productivity that is appropriated by the owners of the means of production, especially those concentrated in the high social strata" (Prebisch 1984: 185). The inherent dynamism of the surplus is inequality. Its growth follows a dynamic sequence: accretions in reproducible capital accumulation, increases in employment and productivity, further increases in capital accumulation, and so on.

The rate of growth and continuous expansion of the surplus depend on successive increments in productivity that are added to it. With capital accumulation, the labor force that was previously employed in low-productivity activities is gradually absorbed into occupations with higher productivity. However, remunerations do not increase proportionately because of the competition which has to be faced with those workers who have remained in occupations with a low productivity. As a result, only a relatively small proportion of the labor force can share spontaneously in the fruits of technological and productivity development. It is at this point that the theory of accumulation joins hands with the theory of social stratification. The latter not only explains the factors giving rise to inequalities in the distribution of the surplus, but also defines the options that are open for its utilization.

Increases in the surplus are accompanied by changes in the social structure due to industrialization, technological penetration, and changes in occupations and incomes. Thus, powerful forces typically emerge in the quest to share increases in productivity. Over time, they tend to weaken the rate of growth of the surplus and reproducible capital. An important contributory factor is considered to be the growth of a relatively privileged consumer class that promotes a premature and dysfunctional diversification of demand, with adverse social consequences. The historical evolution of the process is thought to have been exacerbated by the proclivity of industrial centers to siphon off a disproportionate share of income, especially through the activities of transnational corporations that are closely tied to the privileged consumer society in the periphery.

In some accounts, this phenomenon has been interpreted as an integral part of an overarching global process in which the growth and spread of transnational enterprises have been accompanied by the extrusion of global networks for the electronic transmission of information and values among members of a corporate elite, as well as for purposes of cultural penetration. In the latter context, the globalization of consumer culture continues to have a growing and irreversible effect in transforming consumer tastes in the periphery. Among other things, this is suggested by the rapid spread of marketing "know-how" from the headquarters of Madison Avenue advertising agencies to their branch offices around the world and the perpetual creation of demand for consumer goods. The same firms that are responsible for developing global marketing strategies tend to utilize new and innovative technologies as weapons of mass media control in the periphery. With the spread of these technologies to peripheral states in Asia, Africa, and Latin America, they have been effectively utilized by consumer-orientated transnational firms.

Global advertising through standardized subliminal images has sometimes been interpreted as part of a quiet revolution designed to create a "global village" whose inhabitants internalize not only Western-style consumerism, but also shared economic, political, and moral ideals. What seems to be sold, it is opined, is not so much an array of consumer goods, but more a way of life predicated on consumerism. From this perspective, global advertising not only transcends selling of material consumption goods, but attempts to homogenize cultures by transmitting a system of values. In this context, Schiller (1986) contends that the concept of "cultural imperialism" perhaps best describes the totality of the processes by which societies in the periphery have been successively incorporated into the world system. In the evolving pattern of global relationships, it is argued, the dominant stratum has utilized a variety of mechanisms to shape institutions that correspond to, or even promote, the values and structures of the center.

Whatever its intent, the argument continues, the transnational process tends to be buttressed by an internal system of social stratification that increasingly limits the use of the surplus generated in the periphery, thereby making it unavailable to satisfy the essential needs of the larger population. The overall tendency has been for different forms of private and public consumption to increase, but not at the expense of the consumption of high-income groups who share and enjoy the surplus. As a matter of fact, each form of consumption tends to be superimposed on others. From the perspective of sustained economic development, the various forms of consumption cannot increase indefinitely without encroaching on the rate of accumulation of reproducible capital. If this occurs, the result will be an impairment of the dynamic sequence of accumulation, employment, productivity, and further accumulation. All evidence points to the entrenchment of this cumulative and vicious structural circle in the developing world.

As Furtado (1987) emphasizes, how the relationship between accumulation, consumption, and distribution is eventually played out depends largely on the nature of the democratization process, or the interplay of factors defining the changing intensity of power relations among the various economic interests. When a situation of genuine democratization prevails, the redistributive power of labor is augmented and cumulates over time. However, this redistributive potential may be reduced to the extent that the top social strata in society have the power to manipulate or hamper the process. The state also has the power to share in the fruits of accumulation and productivity. Across developing countries, the nature of state appropriation of the surplus has varied, ranging from extreme forms of authoritarianism to more salutary and democratic arrangements. In the typical case, the growth of the state in the periphery has been associated with its role as employer of last resort for the manpower that could not be absorbed in the private sector because of an insufficient or overly capital-intensive accumulation of reproducible capital.

While the democratic process tends to play a crucial role in improving the real earning power of workers and in the evolution of the state, it has to be recognized that there are certain limits to the redistributive process. It may not be possible to correct maladjustments in the system through democracy, the play of market forces, or government monetary and fiscal policy. As previously noted, increases in the money supply may be needed to pay a growing wage and salary bill accompanying pressures for more redistribution of the surplus. But such an increase must be just sufficient to match the growth of final output that results from the increase in employment. If it is more, any increase in productivity will result in structural inflation; if it is less, the increase in productivity will be accompanied by falling prices.

Structuralists recognized that monetary expansion is a motive force in the production process, and therefore becomes a primary mechanism whereby the surplus is appropriated by owners of the means of production. It can experience continual growth, depending on the extent to which it is allocated to consumption or accumulation. The dynamics of the economic system are put in constant jeopardy, however, when the surplus itself and the activities of privileged groups reach such critical thresholds that the income redistribution process must come to a grinding halt. Moreover, the market is not the supreme regulator of the economy. What ultimately matters, structuralists contend, is the *deep structure* behind the market and the arbitrary play of power relations. While it is possible to preserve the market or even create a more efficient one, what may be needed in the long run is a change in the structure itself.

Center-Periphery Relations and the Structuring of International Inequality

Structuralist diagnoses of the development problem also found a foremost representation in analysis of the structure and functioning of the world economy in terms of asymmetrical relationships between industrial nations (center) and their less developed counterparts (periphery). The most prominent of these reinterpretations emanated from the Economic Commission for Latin America (ECLA) and have been championed by Raul Prebisch (1950, 1959), Hans Singer (1950), among others. The starting point is a realist-existentialist view of the world in which center-periphery relationships are used to define patterns of differentiation or deep structures. In the relatively developed center, development and change are construed as endogenous, that is, based on their own internal dynamism. By contrast, the same processes have been largely exogenous or externally propelled in the relatively underdeveloped and agrarian periphery. This, in turn, has resulted in relatively low levels of capital accumulation, little or no technical progress, low employment and productivity levels, and a lack of structural and institutional change.

As detailed elsewhere (see David 1986: 137-52), the Prebisch-ECLA-Singer perspective is based on a general opposition to orthodox liberal ideas about comparative advantage on the grounds that the economic relations between center and periphery nations tend to reproduce the conditions of underdevelopment and increase the gap between them on a cumulative basis. The argument, supported by Gunar Myrdal (1957) and others, is that the invisible hand of the market tends to aggravate inequalities rather than correct them. This arises because center nations tend to appropriate the fruits of technological progress, and this, in turn, results in a deterioration in the terms of trade between primary products and manufactured goods.

Some of the main historico-structural mechanisms have been identified as follows: (i) insufficient stimulus for economic growth in Latin America through primary commodity exports, due to a decline in the import coefficients of center nations; (ii) higher productivity in manufacturing compared to agricultural production, and the corresponding failure of the rising productivity in manufacturing to be translated into lower prices for manufactured goods; and (iii) the tendency for wage levels in industrial countries to be maintained due to trade union pressure, and for industrialists to defend their profit rates because of their oligopolistic power. Thus, the political and organizational strength of employers and workers in center nations were thought to enable them to block the functioning of the market, thereby producing a specific unequalizing effect on international trade.

International disparities and lagging economic performance in the periphery were therefore attributed to market failure, or the perception that private expectations and market incentives failed to guide resources into avenues where the long-term social returns would be optimal. The unfair operation of the international economy was blamed on market imperfections, for example, monopolies and oligopolies at the center and segmented capital and labor markets in the periphery, resulting in inordinately high prices for manufactures and an excessively high production of low-priced primary commodity exports. This unequal partnership was reinforced by the activities of transnational corporations which, while introducing technical progress, were able to earn excessive profits, reflecting a deviation from the conditions of perfectly competitive comparative advantage. The overall result was a smaller gain from trade for the periphery.

However, the disparity was not necessarily reflected in the commodity or barter terms of trade (the ratio of exchange between commodities), but more in the factoral terms of trade (relating to the interchange between resources, and therefore reflecting changes in productivity in the tradable goods [export and imports] sector). Prebisch's assumption was that such productivity increases most rapidly, if not exclusively, in the center. Contextually, the terms of trade argument can be divided into two parts--one historical, the other theoretical. The historical argument is that primary production should be avoided because the commodity terms of trade have had a long-term bias against agriculture. The theoretical argument is that whatever the past experience, if primary producers develop their exports faster than the corresponding demand in industrial countries, it is inevitable that the terms of trade would move against them. In the long run, however, it is the factoral terms of trade that determine the commodity terms of trade, and not the other way around. Since the factoral terms of trade have moved continually against the periphery since the beginning of the nineteenth century, the basic way to stop this is through sustained increases in the productivity of farmers producing for the domestic market, thereby raising the supply price of export crops.

The Prebisch-ECLA-Singer perspective was based on what is sometimes termed "elasticity pessimism," or the perception of disparate income and price elasticities of demand for primary commodities vis-à-vis manufactures. In mainstream economic theory, the dynamic gains from trade were predicated on two related premises. One concerned the likelihood that the gains from trade would grow over time if the earnings are saved and invested efficiently. The other suggested that the introduction of new goods and technology can have a positive effect on a country's rate of technological progress and per capita income level. In such a situation, differences in elasticities would predictably guide dynamic comparative advantage, and by implication, generate relatively large market-signalled investments in primary production for export relative to investments in manufactures. The Prebisch-ECLA-Singer argument was that such a consistent trend in the terms of trade made prices inappropriate signals for investment decisions. If such a course were to be followed, the development process would come to a grinding halt. Under the circumstances, public intervention was needed to limit imports and promote industrialization.

Arguments based on elasticity pessimism were also used by Nurkse (1959), who proposed a strategy of inward-looking balanced growth and industrialization. While accepting the theoretical implications of comparative advantage, he raised the question whether trade could still be considered an "engine of growth." He explained the link between trade and economic growth by citing factors operating on the demand side, and in terms of the positive effects that could be transmitted by a rapidly growing world demand to an open, developing economy. He posited that trade was such an engine of growth in the white settler colonies during the nineteenth century, but also predicted that this would no longer be the case for developing nations in the twentieth century.

Later, Irving Kravis (1970) questioned the view about the link between trade and economic growth, and especially Nurske's thesis, on the grounds that growth is determined predominantly by internal factors. In his view, foreign trade merely provides an extension of the domestic opportunities available for converting resources into goods and services. This comes close to the classical view that trade widens the market and therefore enables countries to produce goods and services at a decreased cost. Thus, the benefits stressed by Kravis refer to the efficient use of resources available to a country, and are therefore more concerned with the supply side of the economy. This is not to deny that the exposure to international competition that accompanies increased trade may help to prevent the growth of monopoly, thereby acting as an antidote to the development of relatively high-cost industries.

Returning to the case of center-periphery relationships, it should be noted that Prebisch's argument, in particular, was strongly influenced by the experience of Latin American countries during the Depression. The foreign exchange scarcity created by the fall in primary commodity exports and the decline in import capacity, combined with the limited access to foreign goods during the Second World War, gave a boost to import substitution and several Latin American countries achieved notable successes in the production of import substitutes. However, Prebisch placed more emphasis on the negative effects of "cyclical fluctuations." He explained the structure of the center-periphery system in terms of its cyclical character, which was supposed to reflect the active role of industrial centers and the passivity of the periphery, where the consequences of economic fluctuations emanating from the center are intensified.

Fluctuations in the terms of trade and primary commodity prices bear a close relationship to movements in the trade or international business cycle. Prebisch's claim was that national trade cycles, such as those in Argentina, primarily reflected those of industrial centers, and especially the United States, which was considered the "cyclical center" of the international economy. The argument can be generalized to explain the special predicament that typically faces countries in the periphery. When the cycle turns into a recessionary phase, it is these countries that tend to be most affected. Their lack of market power means that they have to absorb severe losses due to price reductions. By contrast, the monopolistic control of markets by industrial center firms enables large exporters of manufactured goods to maintain prices in line with their cost structure, enabling them to guarantee normal profits. This represents part of an endemic structural situation in which relative prices obtained during the upswing of the business cycle tend to favor producers of manufactures more than proportionately, without equally compensating losses during periods of contraction.

Under the circumstances, Prebisch and other proponents of industrialization questioned the wisdom of an international division of labor that implied specialization in primary commodity production and exports. Given the relatively limited domestic flexibility, balance of payments fluctuations due to falling export prices implied smaller incomes than a more diversified economy would earn. While recovery in the international economy during the immediate postwar period was accompanied by a favorable terms of trade for many Latin American countries, as well as by an expansion in their exports and trade prospects, Prebisch's structuralist orientation impelled him to invoke an argument based on long-term trends as a means of counteracting predictions relying on the short-term force of market signals.

As he stated in the World Bank's *Pioneers* volume (1984: 178), "[t]heoretically, the problem was put in the following dynamic terms. What is to be done with productive resources when further expansion of primary exports would bring a fall in prices? Should these resources be used to generate additional exports, or should they be allocated to industrial production or domestic consumption? The answer was to propose a set of policy measures designed to promote industrialization linked to foreign currency allocation, import substitution, and adequate protection for domestic industry."

The Policy of Import Substitution Industrialization

Proposals for import substitution industrialization (ISI) emerged as a response not only to the Prebisch-ECLA-Singer perspective, but also to the rise in nationalism and a serious desire to raise living standards for the masses in the periphery through employment creation. This was accorded primacy since the technological centers had penetrated mainly export enclaves, and not into other activities where a large proportion of the labor force existed. As mentioned earlier, a basic problem involved raising the productivity of the entire labor force. Industrialization had a pivotal role to play in providing employment for the burgeoning numbers of low-productivity workers as well as the manpower released by further technological progress in both export activities and the production of agricultural commodities for domestic use.

Implementation of the industrialization program implied a shift in the centers of decision making to the periphery as well as a strengthening of the capacity of the state for decision making and regulation. At the same time, Prebisch emphasized the need for a certain amount of competition and expressed a basic dislike for over-centralization and state control. He thought that precedence should be given to the enhancement of internal creativity in the capital accumulation process, with the state acting as the primary catalyst. Thus, some degree of planning and coordination was necessary. As he stated, "[p]lanning was compatible with the market and private initiative. It was needed to establish certain basic conditions for the adequate functioning of the market in the context of a dynamic economy. But it did not necessarily require detailed state investment, except in infrastructure and development promotion" (1984: 180).

Such ideas, though innocuous enough, were extensively criticized by orthodox economists who defended the idea of a free market as the best mechanism for guaranteeing authentic development. In their view, the Prebisch-ECLA-Singer perspective was too doctrinaire, and provided one of the most subtle guises for introducing bureaucratic socialism into the fabric of the developing world. The primary reason was that it defended protectionist economic policies and advocated state intervention as a means of correcting market distortions and for mobilizing internal resources.

The developing countries were therefore urged to drop the idea of industrialization. One is not sure whether such an idea still persists. Nevertheless, the dominant worldview was that such a strategy held out little hope for profits and no promise for success when interpreted from the perspective of the traditional theory of comparative advantage and the competitive alternative. Contextually, orthodox economists assailed protectionism in the periphery as being inexpedient and unprofitable. Protectionist measures, it was argued, did not stimulate the development of domestic industrial activity, but tended to raise artificial barriers to foreign competition and paved the way for the introduction of "restrictive monopolies." In addition, protectionist policy, by raising prices in protected industries, was likely to raise the national cost structure. This was a burden that the entire nation would be forced to bear.

Under the circumstances, peripheral countries were advised to produce and export the kinds of commodities that required relatively less capital per unit of output and import needed intermediate and capital goods. In other words, the production and export of agricultural products would bring higher profits than investment in industry; and, in general, investment in manufacturing industry would be disadvantageous according to the principles of static comparative advantage. In the extolment of this perception, less concern was shown for the structuralist interpretation, which, as previously mentioned, was based on observable and potential divergences between theory and reality in the economic relations between center and periphery.

Two versions of the radical heterodox critique should also be mentioned. One was the classical Marxian view that the scarcity of capital did not pose a problem for the process of industrialization. This perspective suggested that capital expansion would occur in the periphery because the rise in the organic composition of capital in the center would tend to accelerate the falling rate of profit there. Investment would occur in the periphery in order to avoid the tendency for the rate of profit to fall. Moreover, countries in the periphery would prove attractive to foreign investors because the former boasted a combination of a lower organic composition of capital and the availability of abundant and cheap labor.

An alternative critique emphasized the inadequate use of the socio-economic surplus in the periphery. As indicated earlier, this surplus is often used irrationally, that is, in the form of luxury consumption by the upper classes in the periphery. As a result, foreign investment tends to aggravate rather than resolve problems connected with the use of the surplus. On this basis, Baran (1957) saw the problem as not so much one of capital shortage or the narrowness of internal markets, but rather one of properly reallocating the surplus. Thus, in contrast to the Prebisch-ECLA-Singer perspective, Baran's view was that protectionist and other policy reforms could not alter the prevailing conditions of underdevelopment. Any attempt to reallocate the existing surplus and promote foreign capital inflows would be ineffective unless power structures were changed.

The process of industrialization in Latin America took place in two stages. The first or "easy" stage was based on the establishment of industries that were more or less synergetic with the production possibilities of the countries in question. By 1950, many of these countries were semi-industrialized and had established a nucleus of industries producing nondurable consumer goods, such as processed foods, textiles and clothing, leather and shoes, and wood and furniture. The process of import substitution was largely completed in these industries. Since there was relatively little need to use sophisticated technology, and the optimum scale of output was relatively low, these industries required very little protection.

However, industries based on nondurable consumer goods did not provide the momentum necessary for self-sustained economic growth. They failed to produce the genuine industrial outlook and knowlegeable cadres of managers and skilled personnel. The domestic linkage effects were also tenuous. Increasing urbanization created a demand for building materials and their manufacture largely replaced the traditional materials produced by local artisans. Industrial activity was limited to the processing of local raw materials or to the finishing of semi-manufactured consumer goods, with all the needed equipment purchased from foreign suppliers.

As alluded to above, the first stage of industrialization, at least in the more advanced Latin American countries, had exhausted the possibilities for further import substitution based on the internal market for nondurable consumer goods.

It became necessary, therefore, to enter into the more complex and difficult forms of industrialization requiring larger markets. The second stage was predicated on import replacement through domestic production of intermediate goods (steel, petrochemicals, etc.), producer durables (machines, machine tools), and consumer durables (automobiles, refrigerators, and the like). Economies of scale are of considerable importance to such industries and efficient plant size relatively large compared to the size of the domestic market. Moreover, the manufacturing processes required an industrial structure of considerable technical sophistication based on the managerial and labor skills mentioned earlier.

Recognizing the importance of economies of scale, ECLA proposed the establishment of a Latin American Common Market and industrial programming at the regional level. However, neither of these initiatives met with much success, so that industries had to be established within the framework of national markets. The overall result was escalating production costs due to the loss in economies of scale, the high capital requirements for manufacturing intermediate goods, and the technological sophistication required for manufacturing producer and consumer durables. Correlatively, establishment and maintenance of these second-stage import substitution industries necessitated a considerable degree of protection. This was provided more or less automatically to would-be industrialists and reflected a policy of "import substitution at any cost."

Given the limited size of domestic markets, some industries became virtual monopolies, and there was little effective competition among the small number of other firms, including subsidiaries of foreign corporations attracted by the policy of high protection. The industrial structure was isolated from the outside world, and in the absence of foreign and domestic competition, there was little incentive for technological innovation and improvement. The policies that led to this situation were described by Prebisch (1964: 7) as follows:

> The criterion by which the choice was determined was based not on considerations of economic expediency, but on immediate feasibility, whatever the cost of production. . . . [T]ariffs have been carried to such a pitch that they are undoubtedly--on average--the highest in the world. It is not uncommon to find tariff duties of over 500 percent.
>
> As is well known, the proliferation of industries of every kind in a closed market has deprived the Latin American countries of the advantages of specialization and economies of scale, and owing to the protection afforded by excessive tariff duties and restrictions, a healthy form of internal competition has failed to develop, and to the detriment of efficient production.

In essence, the policy of high protection produced a concerted stream of negative results. These include: (i) a discrimination against primary production, since protection and export taxes turned the internal terms of trade (i.e., the ratio of prices of primary commodities to prices of industrial products) against primary activities; (ii) the ease with which profits based on low turnover could be made by catering exclusively to domestic markets hindered the development of manufactured goods that could be sold abroad at world market prices; and (iii) the export potential was further damaged by currency overvaluation and domestic inflation, which resulted in considerable risk and uncertainty for would-be exporters. Thus, rather than improving the internal terms of trade, as was presumed under the Prebisch-ECLA-Singer thesis, the policies for import substitution industrialization led to a decline in world market shares for the major primary exports of Latin American countries.

The slowdown in the growth of primary commodity exports, combined with the failure to develop exports of manufactured goods, severely limited import capacity and the availability of the foreign exchange needed for sustained economic growth. With the decline in net import savings, the situation was exacerbated by the increased demand for imported machinery and other materials in import substitution industries. At the same time, a relatively high-cost and capital-intensive method of production raised the capital requirements of additional increments of output in a situation where large segments of the labor force remained unemployed or otherwise employed at low productivity levels.

Radical Structuralism: Interpretations of Dependency

Following upon the center-periphery dichotomy, there was an extension of the structuralist conceptual framework to the study of the dialectical interaction between internal and external forces impinging on the development process. In particular, it was thought that the Prebisch-ECLA-Singer thesis lacked a sufficient analysis and exposure of the mechanisms of social and economic exploitation that perceptibly perpetuate class divisions within peripheral economies, their uneven development, and unequal exchange relationships with the center. This formed the starting point of an influential dependency perspective, which interpreted the structure and functioning of the capitalist system and its expansion overseas in terms of dichotomous relations of dominance and dependence, development and underdevelopment.

The evolution of this interpretive mode was substantially influenced by Marxian skepticism about the viability of capitalist development in peripheral countries that were integrated into the world economy. Early Latin American formulations of the dependency thesis started out with a basic challenge to the "classical Marxist approach" which had "restricted itself mainly to the role of international monopoly capital," neglecting its effects on the periphery (Sunkel 1969: 32). Nevertheless, the home-grown reinterpretation was Marxist in orientation. Accordingly, its domain assumption was grounded in the argument that the "basic structural elements" associated with the historical evolution of international capitalism have given rise to underdevelopment, which is part and parcel of the globalization of the international system.

Therefore, development and underdevelopment can be simply construed as two faces of one single universal process. The evolution of this global system based on a structural matrix of development-underdevelopment has, over a period of time, systematically produced two visible types of polarization: (i) the asymmetrical division of the world between countries--the developed, industrialized, advanced, or "central Northern" vis-à-vis the undeveloped, poor, dependent, and "peripheral Southern" ones; and (ii) a polarization within countries--between advanced and modern groups, regions, and activities vis-à-vis backward, marginal, and dependent groups, regions, activities.

In his *Economic Growth of Brazil* (1963) and subsequent studies, Celso Furtado defined center-periphery relationships not only in terms of unequal sharing of the benefits of development, but also as forms of dependency involving domination and economic exploitation. His formulation of the theory is based on a comprehensive approach to capitalism as an economic system that has expanded horizontally as well as vertically, and as a constellation of heterogenous social formations. This inclusive theoretical framework provides a basis for studying the diversity of the accumulation process over space and time and its effects on latecomers to the industrialization process. It also forms the essential background for investigating links between internal and external forms of economic and social dominance, and other related matters such as the role of the state and activities of transnational corporations.

The argument is that, apart from colonial domination, the phenomenon of dependence was initially manifested in the cultural area through transplantation stemming from the surplus generated from foreign trade. The chief mechanism of dependence, therefore, is the "demonstration effect," whereby the lifestyles of a small country in the periphery are ostensibly "modernized" through the internationalization of Western consumption patterns, while transnational corporations control access to modern technology. As Furtado states (1987: 211):

> It is the highly dynamic nature of the modernized component of consumption that brings dependence into the technological realm and makes it part of the production structure. Indeed, it is when countries attempt to substitute domestic manufactures for imported goods through industrialization that the production apparatus divides into two parts: one tied to traditional economic activities for export or for the domestic market, and the other comprising industries that produce for the modernized sector of consumption.

This dependence has been constantly reinforced by the introduction of new products, whose production calls for allocation of more capital and sophisticated techniques. The overall result has been the growth and spread of a peripheral capitalism in which the advance of industrialization has been accompanied by increasing income concentration. The process has little internal dynamism and has been unable to generate innovations. It has therefore become dependent for transformation on decisions emanating from abroad. To quote Furtado again, "I call external dependence the structural situation in which such peripheral capitalism prevails in certain countries" (1973: 120).

External dependence refers to the patterns and concentration of external reliances in areas such as trade, technology, finance, and even in terms of political and social ideology. These, in turn, tend to have certain internal developmental consequences that reflect "internal dependence." The latter pertains to restricted choice or vulnerability, or to the difficulty that a peripheral country would face in having to adjust to a break in relations. It is typically manifested by internal fragmentation, a lack of integration among social and economic sectors, and a distorted pattern of development in which islands of economic growth coexist in veritable seas of poverty and underdevelopment.

The negative consequences of lopsided, uneven, or what has been termed "disarticulated" development have been a central theme in radical heterodox interpretations of dependency and underdevelopment. In this context, some well-known scholars, notably Paul Baran, Samir Amin, Immanuel Wallerstein, and Andre Gunder Frank, have advanced the thesis that hierarchial center-periphery relations are necessary for accumulation on a world scale and survival of capitalism itself. While the world system continues to develop through the globalization of capital, it is argued, the center-periphery hierarchy remains a structured feature of the larger system, that is, it is continuously reproduced through an array of interactive mechanisms that are endemic to the domination of the capitalist mode of production in the world. Hence, dependency and underdevelopment are viewed as inevitable effects of the capitalist mode of production itself.

This interpretation has resulted in a generalized thesis about the "development of the underdevelopment," first proposed by Frank (1967), or the claim that there is an inevitable deepening of the conditions of underdevelopment as long as the center dominates the periphery. Accordingly, development and underdevelopment are interpreted as opposite faces of the same coin, or as products of a single but dialectically contradictory economic structure and process of capitalism. While this process includes the integration of disparate elements, it is thought to be responsible for generating and perpetuating a center and a periphery within the same overall framework.

This perspective has also been used to explain the fact that a substantial number of so-called "newly industrializing countries" (NICs) were to experience relatively long periods of economic growth within the capitalist system. According to Frank (1981), such countries (for example, Brazil, Argentina, India, Iran, Israel, and South Africa) should be categorized as "semi-peripheral" or "sub-imperialist" centers that not only occupy an intermediate place between center and periphery, but also act as political intermediaries in the unequal bargain between the two poles. Under the circumstances, the emergence of these economies should be considered a result of the sharpening of the unequal nature of capitalist accumulation and development that is always associated with world capitalist crises.

Contextually, Frank advances a gloomy prognosis that none of these new semi-peripheral countries is likely to attain the status of an industrial center in the near future. As he states, "[f]or any country to do so it would have to reverse its internal disarticulation of the economy, which excludes a majority of the population from benefits, and successfully outcompete countries in Southern and Eastern Europe, including the Soviet Union, and perhaps China, where opportunities for emergence from semi-peripheral status to a central role in the world economy are very much greater" (1981: 61). Of course, this comment (while somewhat dated) raises the question whether industrial centers boast a uniquely benevolent fabric that enables the majority of the population to participate meaningfully in the benefits of capitalist growth.

This issue aside, Frank attributes the parlous situation facing semi-peripheral countries to all the major political and economic forces operating in the periphery, including things such as the destruction of village and traditional family structures. From this perspective, the inevitable condition of disarticulation and degradation is not only inherent in the long-wave crisis of capitalism, but also has taken a turn for the worse, thereby leaving the countries in question with no freedom of maneuverability. This inevitable result, it is argued, is objectified through the activities of "dependent states," which are more often than not the creation and usually the instruments of an imperialist bourgeoisie. Within this conceptual framework, the dependent nature of the economy and society as a whole is construed as a major factor determining the subordinate status of dependent states (see also Chase-Dunn 1989).

In general, the dependency perspective has been criticized on the grounds that it glosses over the need to make the important distinction between the unpleasant aspects of capitalist-oriented growth and the viability of capitalism itself. Marxian critics, such as, Laclau and Brenner, and dependency theorists, such as Cardoso and Faletto (1979), have pointed to the pervasive tendency to overemphasize "circulation" (as distinct from production) as well as the stagnationist proclivities of the dependency perspective. On the other hand, hard-nosed neo-classical economists tend to ignore the historical role of trade, investment, and social class relations in altering the structure of property rights in developing countries.

In the latter context, the structuralist or dependency theorist has been described as a person who "sees the world as inflexible. Change is inhibited by obstacles, bottlenecks and constraints. . . . In economic terms, the supply of most things is inelastic" (Little 1982: 20). From this perspective, the inflexibility and lack of responsiveness in the market mechanism are thought to provide the structuralist rationale for intervention designed to remove the constraints and facilitate the process of growth and change. It may be commented that, like neo-classical economists themselves, dependency theorists have no monolithic view of the complex role of the state in the development process.

Dependency theorists such as Cardoso and Faletto have posited that new trends in international capitalism have been associated with an increased level of interdependency and a corresponding modification of traditional patterns of dependency. They are credited with using dependency as "a methodology for the analysis of concrete situations of dependency" (Palma 1978). As such, they continue to view Latin American economies as integral constituent parts of the world capitalist system, with options for each country conditioned by developments taking place at the core or center. However, it is claimed that the changing nature of the world capitalist system has rendered dependency and industrialization or development less contradictory.

In particular, it is argued that dependency, especially in areas such as capital and technology, can be made compatible with capitalist development. This makes it possible for countries to follow a path of "associated dependent development." Of course, such a strategy would call for a redirection of analytical and interpretive efforts toward (i) understanding the specificity of the interaction between internal and external factors; and (ii) explanation of the particularity of social, political, and economic processes in dependent states. In a similar vein, the highly deterministic orientation underlying radical heterodox variants of the dependency perspective has been challenged on the grounds that too heavy a reliance is placed on undifferentiated global forces and the analysis lacks sufficient specificity.

In the latter context, it can be argued that interpretation of the relationships among capitalism, dependency, and underdevelopment promises to be much more fruitful and informative if it is executed on a case-by-case basis. In each such case, the outcome can be explained as resulting from a particular configuration of economic and non-economic conditions. As Brenner (1977: 61) states, "neither economic development nor underdevelopment are *directly* dependent upon, or caused by, one another. Each is the product of a specific evolution of class relations, *in part* determined historically "outside" capitalism, in relationship to noncapitalist modes." This can be interpreted as part of a more thoroughgoing critique of the historical Marxian thesis. According to Laclau (1971), the latter sees capitalism everywhere and makes the social structures of peripheral countries capitalistic from the very inception of their incorporation into the world economy.

On a related basis, serious doubts have been expressed about the strong Marxian thesis that capitalism has led to the continued impoverishment of the periphery. Based on empirical analysis of the postwar (pre-1980) development trends, Warren (1980) has shown that countries in the periphery experienced unprecedented economic growth, industrialization, technological progress and other forms of development. Echoing Marx's historical predictions, he interpreted these trends to mean that poor countries were being transformed into robust capitalist societies, and that this represented a necessary prerequisite for their eventual conversion to socialism. However, the experience, especially since the 1970s, has clearly demonstrated that while some peripheral countries may be industrializing and developing in a limited sense, this should not be taken to mean that all countries can or will follow the same path, unless they are *forced* to do so, in some sense.

Structuralist (North-South) Economic Models

The structuralist analysis of dependency and underdevelopment does not constitute a mere descriptive or discursive account of the internal and external forces underlying capitalist growth on a world scale. Over the years, the perspective has been reformulated in a number of "North-South" economic models that attempt to capture and rigorously analyze one or more of the structural asymmetries defining center-periphery relations. Our objective in this final section of the chapter is not to provide a detailed blow-by-blow account of the internal technical factors relating to model specification, but rather to determine the extent to which the theoretical underpinnings provide an adequate interpretation and understanding of the complex realities involved.

One variety of radical heterodox models is grounded in the assumption that asymmetrical relationships tend to lurk behind the veil of the market, and can be explained by differential influences of historical and institutional processes among trading partners. Emmanuel's model of *Unequal Exchange* (1972) can be used as an example. The model turns on the following assumptions about international resource flows. First, capital is internationally mobile and tends to move around in such a manner as to equalize profit rates. Second, while capital is mobile, the labor force is immobile. Even though there is a "seepage" of labor across national frontiers, this tends to be insignificant so that wages tend to be unequal at both national and international levels. By and large, labor remains a national factor of production.

In essence, Emmanuel's model rests on the premise that rewards to factors of production such as capital and labor are the main determinants of exchange values. This reverses the traditional Ricardian assumption about comparative costs and international division of labor. Ricardo had assumed capital immobility and the equalization of wages at subsistence in a full employment economy. A third assumption in Emmanuel's model is that wage differentiation is determined by social, historical, and institutional forces, such as exogenous differences in wage and worker bargaining power, center monopoly power in commodity markets, commercial policy, and so on. Fourth, the center-periphery wage differential produces a dynamic type of relationship in which the total size of the center market grows proportionately more than that of the periphery. Fifth, with wage rates in the periphery stagnating at a relatively low level, international trade and exchange typically result in a hidden transfer of resources from poor to rich countries.

Thus, the bedrock of center-periphery relations is provided by a law of price formation that allows for unequal rewarding of factors of production. The basic thesis is that members of the labor force in the periphery normally exchange the produce of their labor at an unfavorable rate compared to their counterparts in the relatively high-wage center. This "unequal exchange" is interpreted as the elementary mechanism underlying the transfer of exchange values from the poor to the rich, and therefore as defining the conditions of misery and underdevelopment in the periphery. Under the circumstances, it is reasonable to expect that trade between center and periphery would shift the terms of trade against the latter region, as Prebisch had predicted. The gains from trade and income levels in the periphery would be lower compared to some ideal (the economist's criterion of Pareto optimality) configuration in which both capital and labor are internationally mobile. In the latter case, there will be a tendency toward international equality in both profits and real wage rates, and a corresponding movement in the periphery's terms of trade and income to a more optimal level.

The model of unequal exchange suggests that it is possible to achieve this result by (i) raising wages in the periphery; and (ii) international labor migration. The effect of raising wages in the periphery will depend on the price elasticity of center demand for exports from the periphery. Simply raising wages in the periphery to improve the terms of trade can have adverse consequences for employment if such center demand for exports is price-elastic. In other words, to the extent that wage costs constitute an important element in the export production in the periphery, the consequent upward pressure on export prices can adversely affect competitiveness and employment. The other economically viable, but politically and socially difficult, option is free migration of labor from the periphery (Findlay 1982).

In the latter case, it is estimated that at least 35 million people have migrated from the South to the North over the past three decades or so--at least 6 million illegally. Roughly 20 million more work overseas on fixed-term contracts (UNDP 1992). Such immigration has taken two basic forms: (i) from poorer countries to richer ones; and (ii) from countries in Southeast Asia and North Africa to the oil-rich countries in the Middle East. Such labor movements, whether short- or long-term in nature, may affect a country's economy through a number of channels, including: (i) the effect on the labor supply in the home country--while relieving pressure on surplus unskilled labor, migration heightens the loss of valuable skills; and (ii) through remittances--in terms of the salutary effects on the income and balance of payments of the home country.

Traditionally, migrant workers (especially illegal aliens) have been employed in the unattractive low-paying jobs that citizens in the richer countries decline. Over time, however, the recipient countries have come to place more emphasis on the import of skills. Some industrial countries are now not just asking for labor, but for money. For example, Canada and the United States now give preference to potential investors and attract millions of dollars through this mechanism. Of great significance is the fact that the developing countries lose thousands of valued personnel each year through the push-and-pull factors associated with the "Brain Drain." Successive cadres of engineers, physicians, scientists, managers, and technicians who are frustrated by low pay and limited opportunities at home migrate to richer countries that offer better working conditions and financial rewards.

In some cases, the loss to the economy may not be too significant, since the jobs of workers who migrate can be immediately filled by the unemployed. This is the case for countries such as India and Pakistan which have an oversupply of skilled workers whose emigration does not necessarily affect national economic development. By contrast, countries in Africa, such as Ghana, and other nations, such as the Philippines, have suffered significant losses of their skilled personnel. While there are no firm estimates of the effects of such losses on the national development potential, they have to be juxtaposed against the positive effects of migrant remittances.

According to UNDP estimates, the developing countries received about $25 billion in official remittances from the industrial countries and the Gulf States in 1989. On average, this amounts to $700 per worker on a yearly basis, or about $1,000 if unofficial remittances are taken into account. As is well known, some workers remit monies clandestinely because they are illegally employed. In general, while remittances account for only about 5 percent of the GNP of developing countries, they are a significant source of improvement to their foreign exchange and balance of payments positions.

Uncertainty remains, however, about the impact on overall economic development. Most domestic expenditures stemming from such flows can augment demand and therefore provide a stimulus to the local economy. The total impact ultimately depends on whether the funds are channelled into productive investment or otherwise used to finance conspicuous consumption, luxury imports, or even speculative activities. The gains from any multiplier effects would have to be offset against the reduced growth opportunities attendant upon the loss of skilled labor. In any event, the international labor market continues to be controlled by the industrial countries. In this regard, it is estimated that the barriers to entry associated with forms of immigration control deny developing countries about $250 billion a year (UNDP 1992).

Returning to the central issue of North-South models, it would be remembered that the original Prebisch-ECLA-Singer thesis focused on the effects of differential elasticities of demand for importables and exportables. Accordingly, unequal exchange was interpreted in terms of the unfavorable terms of trade facing the periphery on account of its high income elasticity of demand for imports vis-à-vis the center's relatively low demand for its exports. Bacha (1978) uses an extended Prebisch-ECLA-Singer framework to reformulate Emmanuel's problem of unequal exchange based on a simple neo-Ricardian wages fund model in which the center completely specializes in steel and the periphery in coffee. There are exogenous wages in both regions and profit rates are equated by international capital mobility.

Emmanuel's argument was that the center derives inordinate benefits from technical change in both regions. Moreover, rising real wages in the center are a cause of development rather than being the effect of technical progress and industrialization. Bacha's model specifies two elasticity conditions for the center to appropriate the benefits of technical change. These depend on the relative rates of technical change in the center and periphery. When technical change is faster in the center than in the periphery, the market in the former will grow relatively faster if its income elasticity of demand for imports is less than unity. This result does not depend on adverse movements in the terms of trade. Conversely, where technical change is faster in the periphery than in the center, and if it is assumed that the greater bargaining power of center workers enables them to appropriate a disproportionate share of the benefits, the likely result will be an adverse effect in terms of both employment and market size.

A related category of mainstream North-South models utilizes an open dual economy framework defined by asymmetric production structures and labor market conditions (see, for example, Bardhan 1982; Findlay 1973, 1980). Following Lewis's dual labor surplus model, a common assumption is inelastic labor supply in the center and unlimited labor supply in the periphery, with the real wage pegged at some institutionally determined subsistence level. This assumption is relaxed in Chichilinsky's model (1980) where the periphery is characterized by "abundant" labor, that is, the supply of labor is responsive to the behavior of real wages. Under conditions of abundant labor supplies, generalized dualism in the periphery, and differential capital/labor ratios and rates of technological diffusion between center and periphery, the general conclusion is that trade between the two regions typically leads to a worsening of the terms of trade, income distribution, and unemployment in the periphery, thereby fuelling the cumulative process of uneven development.

Another type of North-South model, for example, Krugman (1981), analyzes uneven development in terms of differential levels of capital availability and external economies in the production of manufactures. The model demonstrates that under certain conditions - a larger initial stock of capital, larger external economies of scale in manufacturing, and reinvestment of profits - the center is likely to experience a pronounced cumulative advantage based on a lower unit cost in manufacturing and a higher rate of profit. With classical savings behavior, the higher rate of profit will translate into a higher growth rate and the advantage will become cumulative as time passes. In a similar vein, the lagging periphery will experience a decline in the competitiveness of its manufactures. The missive is that, given certain conditions, uneven development can occur between two regions with only small differences in initial capital endowments. The historically famous example is the destruction of the once flourishing Indian textile industry by competition from Lancashire.

At least three important lessons or generalizations seem to emerge from models of this kind. First, and in concert with the endogenous growth models discussed in Chapter 3, there may be cumulative developmental advantages associated with economies of scale in production, the gathering and spread of information, acquisition of technological capacity, and the diffusion of technological innovations. Second, Gunnar Myrdal's thesis about the operation of cumulative and circular causation still seems to provide a potent explanation of the structural relations between rich and poor countries, and therefore of the apparent decumulative effects of the development process itself. Third, and as a corollary, more credence can be lent to the biblical saying: "To them that hath shall be given, and from them that hath not shall be taken away, even that which they hath."

Chapter 9

Paradigm Shift to Human Development

The ruling paradigm of development was essentially based on a "cost-of-production" value perspective, which focused primarily on material economic growth as the fundamental objective of development. As early as the 1960s and 1970s, skepticism surfaced in both academic and policy circles as certain perverse effects of the growth-oriented development style began to emerge. The attendant misgivings led to a rethinking of dominant preconceptions and a concomitant paradigm shift or reorientation of concerns toward the imperative of achieving broad-based human or people-centered development.

The implementation of orthodox policies and strategies seemed unable to offer productive and remunerative employment to major segments of the labor force. In the eyes of many, poverty and inequality were also on the increase. Rising unemployment was linked to rapid population growth and extensive rural-urban migration, which was traced to the primacy of place accorded the implementation of the dual labor surplus model. In this context, concentration of modern sector development in the majority of developing countries resulted in a visible "steel-and-glass" enclave with high productivity, a capital-intensive technology, and respectable growth rates. However, the dualist strategy revealed a great inability to create sufficient productive employment, among other things.

Population explosion arrived much sooner than was predicted by demographic transition theory. The lag between perception and occurrence of the demographic explosion, combined with a development style based on modernization, produced a number of systematic effects on the development process, including: (i) a concentration of income and wealth in a relatively small but highly visible and dynamic sector of the economy; and (ii) emergence of hordes of people, mostly young, trying to enter the labor market. A veritable paradox therefore surfaced, with relatively high rates of economic growth coexisting with worsening unemployment, income distribution, and poverty. These intractable problems have persisted.

Economic Growth and Declining Human Welfare

In the majority of developing countries, the sources of economic growth are still concentrated in a few export-oriented production sectors. In many cases, the production of commodity staples is highly lucrative, but there is lack of integration with a coherent and differentiated domestic economy. The absence of depth and diversity in the production structure is traceable to the fact that the pattern of industrialization has not been based on efforts to produce mass consumption goods. Rather, priority has been given to satisfaction of the conspicuous consumption proclivities of high-income strata and urban middle classes. As a result, the masses of the population have not been successfully integrated into the capital formation process. A substantial part of the latter, such as the production of technologies, equipment, and intermediate goods, still takes place in the industrial centers, so that the potential economic spinoffs from the reproductive process are entirely lost.

In Latin America, for example, the modernization process has been accompanied by the creation of visible forms of physical and financial wealth. Some notable signs are modern cities dotted with skyscrapers and sophisticated nuclear, electronic, computer, and aircraft industries, as in Brazil. The other side of the coin is depicted by massive pollution, urban congestion, shanty towns, persistent poverty, and what many knowledgeable observers interpret as a monumental waste of resources. What is certain is that the majority of people have not benefitted significantly, if at all, from the modernization and wealth-creation process. Some scholars view this as "mal-development," or an extremely faulty orientation in which material economic growth has brought in its wake a ruthless and destructive capacity and the most glaring forms of inequality. In other cases, the process has been labelled "mis-development" or a condition connoting the mismanagement of resources in countries with disparate ideological orientations.

Across developing countries, the economic growth process might have benefitted certain entrepreneurial and urban cadres, but it has by and large impoverished the masses and bypassed the majority of the population living in rural areas. In many cases, traditional forms of production have been destroyed, capital rendered idle, employment reduced, and underemployment increased. Thus, the growth process proved incapable of relieving mass poverty by redistributing the fruits of production, or by reducing the gap between the few enjoying relatively luxurious consumption patterns and the larger majority of the population. As income and wealth distribution worsened, malnutrition and undernutrition increased, more children were out of school than in school, and health standards deteriorated.

It was envisaged that modern sector development would enable the fruits of modernization to rapidly trickle down to the poor. The overwhelming evidence, however, is that growth did not raise the income share of the poorest members of society. Indeed, economic growth tended to work to the disadvantage of lower income groups in poor countries with sharply dualistic economies. Calculations show that it takes at least one generation for such groups to recover the loss resulting from the imposition of a relatively small modern sector on a largely traditional form of socio-economic organization.

Thus, trends in inequality raised the question whether development in the past was accompanied by such a worsening of income distribution that the poor benefitted little from the fruits of economic growth. As discussed in Chapter 7. the pertinent debate originated with Simon Kuznets's hypothesis about the inverted S-curve of income distribution. In the case of poorer countries, this led to the following extrapolations. First, economic growth is likely to produce a more rapid increase in the demand for skilled vis-à-vis unskilled labor, leading to widening inequality when the supply of skilled labor expands relatively slowly. Second, these unequalizing factors tend to be exacerbated by a policy and institutional framework that is biased in favor of modern and urbanized sectors, leading to an excessive flow of resources to them and the corresponding provision of incentives for capital-intensive production. Third, when these a priori considerations are combined with the available evidence, the conclusion emerges that the singular pursuit of the aggregate economic growth objective in poor countries is more than likely to be associated with increased inequality.

A vigorous empirical research program emerged around this perspective. The Kuznets hypothesis received some measure of support from a number of studies, but there was no agreement about the extent of the increase in inequality that accompanied economic growth. For example, Adelman and Morris (1973) and Griffin and Khan (1978) viewed the relationship between economic growth and income equality as conflicting, that is, economic growth tends to be accompanied by a protracted process of absolute and relative impoverishment for large segments of the population. By contrast, studies by Chenery and Syrquin (1975) and Ahluwalia (1974) argued that while the cross-sectional evidence pointed to increasing inequality during the early stages of development, this did not completely offset its effect on economic growth. While relative inequalities might have worsened, it was claimed, this was not necessarily the case for absolute inequality.

The general explanation is that the absolute levels of income of the poorest groups in society tend to rise, but much more slowly than the average. Some individual countries, especially in East Asia, have been able to establish the preconditions for a more egalitarian distribution of income and sustained economic growth in such a policy environment. A reasonable judgment, therefore, is that they may well have been able to avoid or moderate the phase of increasing income inequality. The experience of such countries suggests that economic growth was accompanied by relatively high rates of labor absorption and a rapid movement toward full employment. This is in stark contrast to the sharp inequalities in income and asset ownership that emerged in the majority of developing countries.

It is evident that policy plays a critical role in shaping the profiles of factor proportions underlying the growth process, that is, whether a capital-intensive or labor-intensive form will predominate. As previously noted, in countries that implemented policies geared toward modern sector industrialization, the aggregate capital-output ratio rose even as the rural sector stagnated through neglect. Some of the perverse effects on employment, income distribution, and poverty were also attributed to factors associated with patterns of trade, foreign investment, and aid.

A general concern surfaced about the distributional impact of free trade policy, both within and across countries. The argument was that orthodox interpretations of the gains from trade did not give sufficient consideration to how the gains were distributed among trading partners, and the fact that world market imperfections systematically biased the gains from trade against weaker bargaining partners. Some degree of intervention was therefore advocated as a means of correcting market imperfections and to shift more of the gains from trade toward developing nations. It was also recognized that the distribution and size of such benefits were influenced by the pattern and degree of foreign participation in the industrialization process, that is, the contribution of foreign-owned factors of production, foreign ownership and control of marketing distributional networks for exports, and the degree of reliance on imported technology.

Concern was also expressed over the tendency of foreign firms to invariably use the capital-intensive technology available to them through prevailing intra-corporate transfer arrangements. As a result, it was argued, they turned a blind eye to the economic, political, and social problems that might arise when substantial numbers of people remain unemployed. Tax holidays, accelerated depreciation, and related fiscal incentives were also thought to be counterproductive in the sense that they helped to perpetuate enclavism, increased capital intensity, and inflation.

These misgivings marched in tandem with a perception that comparative advantage as a fundamental pillar of liberal trade theory had lost its relevance and predictive power. While the emphasis of trade theory from Ricardo to the Hechscher-Ohlin-Samuelson model was based on inter-industry trade, newer theories and perspectives increasingly focused on inter-industry, inter-firm, and intra-firm trade. In classical and neo-classical theory, it is assumed that labor and capital are immobile and only finished products are exchanged. By contrast, modern theoretical perspectives take account of the fact that we live in a world in which factors of production are highly mobile and commodities are exchanged at various stages in the production process, for example, technical knowledge, intermediate goods, and components of final products. Furthermore, while older theories neglected foreign investment and overseas production, newer ones interpret foreign trade and production as complementary to the strategies of transnational corporations and powerful nation states.

In the case of official aid, the perverse effects were thought to stem from policies governing the forms and methods rather than the quantities disbursed. For example, the Articles of Agreement of multilateral lending agencies such as the IMF and World Bank stipulated that loans should cover only the foreign exchange costs of projects financed. Since most of the import content of development projects takes the form of equipment, such requirements tend to favor projects requiring more capital-intensive (import-intensive) technologies. This tends to reduce the employment effects associated with a more intensive use of local resources in the developing world. In this connection, the 1969 Pearson Commission on International Development had urged donors to encourage local procurement wherever economically feasible, and to remove regulations that prevent or limit contributions to the local costs of projects.

In general, more official aid was available for a few large projects compared to numerous smaller ones. The latter boast at least two important advantages: they tend to be more labor-intensive; and since they are normally located in rural areas or small towns, they can be instrumental in reducing urban unemployment stemming from rural-urban migration. Related to the arguments about foreign costs and project size was the fact that more aid was available for investments in the modern or urban sector, adding more fuel to the "urban bias" in world development. The overall effect was to diminish the attractiveness of rural or traditional activities. In general, there is a direct relationship between the employment-intensity of aid and the proportion that is channelled into projects for agricultural and rural development.

The Dethronement of GNP Fetishism

The ascendancy of egalitarian worldviews was accompanied by a shift in development thought and policy from the conventional concern with highly aggregated indicators such as gross national product (GNP) and macroeconomic growth rates to more disaggregated magnitudes such as different types of employment and the basic needs of poverty groups. This inevitably evoked interest in the quantitative measurement of human well-being. The received practice relies on a measure based on the level of income attainment, defined by average GNP per person. GNP is the proportion of a country's gross domestic product (GDP) - a measure of the total value of final goods and services produced by its domestic economy over a given period of time - claimed by its residents. It is usually calculated in three ways (in terms of production or value-added, income, and expenditure), with each producing equivalent results. The three methods are illustrated in Table 9.1.

Table 9.1

Summary of Three Ways of Estimating GNP at Market Prices

Production		**Income**		**Expenditure**
Net output of: Agriculture		Wages and salaries of employees		Private consumption
+ Mining and manufacturing		+ Profit and income from		+ General government
+ Construction		self-employment		consumption
+ Utilities	=	+ Rent and interest	=	+ Investment
+ Trade and transport		+ Depreciation		+ Exports of goods and
+ Government services		+ Net indirect taxes		non-factor services
+ Other private services				- Imports of goods and
				non-factor services
= GDP at market prices		= GDP at market prices		= GDP at market prices
+ Net factor income from		+ Net factor income from		+ Net factor income from
abroad		abroad		abroad
= GNP at market prices		= GNP at market prices		= GNP at market prices

The production method focuses on the net output produced by an economy's various sectors, such as agriculture, industry, and services. This is a measure of value-added, that is, the value of gross output of goods and services produced, less the value of the goods and services used as inputs or factors of production in the generation of this output. The income method measures the earnings received by the various inputs, such as land (rent), labor (wages and salaries), and capital (profits). The expenditure method is concerned with measuring the final expenditures that are made in terms of private consumption and investment, government consumption and investment, exports, and imports. Given these measures and the size of a country's population, the GNP per person yardstick has come to be used as a primary determinant of a country's development status as well as the social well-being of its citizens. A common practice is to arrange countries in league tables based on their income statuses - low, middle, and high - with each used as a proxy for the level of development attained.

The emphasis placed on GNP attainment via production, income, and expenditure tends to highlight the fact that opulence and the availability of material goods and services are typically considered primary determinants of human well-being. In this interpretive mode, the material goods and services are thought to constitute wealth, so that its accumulation becomes of strategic importance. In a very general sense, the stock of wealth constitutes all the material goods and services that people in a given society use to satisfy their various wants and needs, including the means of producing them, such as land, labor, and capital. When properly used, the stock of wealth produces a flow of income, so that there is a direct relationship between wealth and income creation. Other things being equal, a larger stock of wealth is likely to produce a greater flow of income. When a part of this income is saved, it can then be used to augment the stock of wealth and therefore the flow of income in the future. The interaction between wealth and income creation then becomes an integral part of a dynamic, cumulative relationship, which is ultimately reflected in the size and pace of growth of a country's GNP.

Accordingly, increases in GNP (economic growth) are assumed to make a positive contribution to living standards and the overall quality of life by enabling people to provide for their basic necessities and the prerequisites for a full and enjoyable life. In this context, the assessment of GNP growth and its desirability is usually made from two related angles. The first is in terms of its contribution to the maintenance and strengthening of the economy as a whole, and, in particular, its potential for creating and enlarging a democratic and free society. Second, the direct impact on the individual is also emphasized. From this perspective, the more indirect social and political effects of GNP growth are deemed to be as important as the direct effect on individual welfare.

The underlying assumption is that there is always a harmonious relationship between the "social" and the "individual," or between the "macro" and the "micro." This puts into bold relief the age-old problem in philosophy and the social sciences concerning the relation of the individual to society, or parts to the whole. Ever since the days of classical political economy, the view has held sway that the structure and change of all social phenomena can in principle be explained in terms of the properties, goals, beliefs, and actions of individuals. This "methodological individualism" has been interpreted as an essential antidote to the excesses of holistic and grand theories of historical and social change, including orthodox Marxism. Instead of attributing motivations to collective socio-economic units such as "developed" and "underdeveloped" countries, or "East" and "West," it is argued, individual persons alone are motivated, and therefore have international properties.

Thus, all social and economic theories have what may be termed "micro-foundations," that is, their explanations and interpretations entail, or are ultimately reducible to, explanations of individual behavior. At the same time, all persons are "social individuals" or have what Elster (1985) calls "relational properties." If this is true, then the proper theoretical, methodological, or "metaphysical" question is not how to reduce the social to the individual, but rather to show interconnectedness and linkage between the macro and the micro.

In terms of this chapter's central focus, the fusion between these two aspects of reality can be expected to take place through a "trickle down" or "diffusion" process because of the conventional belief that there are few, if any, innocuous or corrupting influences associated with the drive toward income and wealth creation. The dominant philosophy is that a wealthy or opulent society offers the best avenue for expanding the range of individual human choice, presumably because it enables people to gain a better control of their environment, thereby enhancing the possibilities for freedom. However, there is now widespread agreement that human social well-being or authentic development encompasses much more than aggregate income or wealth creation, as reflected by increases in levels of per capita GDP or GNP attainment.

While the latter provides a broad or average picture of the means or income available to individuals in a country, little or no indication is provided of the quality of life they actually succeed in living. This conclusion follows from the limited information provided by the GDP or GNP measure. It reflects the average income accruing to a person over a specific time period, usually a year, but this says nothing about his or her achievements in terms of enhancing living standards. It remains true that income availability enables individuals to expand their purchase of basic commodities, such as food, clothing, housing, and transportation, that are an integral part of human needs. The point of emphasis, however, is that purchasing power, as reflected in the income measure, tells us nothing about other dimensions of human welfare. In the latter context, it is meaningful to ask whether people are better educated, living longer, or in general, whether they are enjoying life to the fullest.

From a statistical angle, the GNP yardstick is primarily concerned with material production. As such, it captures only those elements of human welfare to which a price tag or monetary value can be attached, or which can be otherwise traded in the market. As indicated in Chapter 3, there is an array of unmeasured activities or "non-marketed outputs" that are clearly important to the majority of people in the developing world. To reiterate, these encapsulate a variety of activities in the non-monetized sector, including: (i) unpaid labor services of women for household and farming activities; (ii) agricultural production for family subsistence and home consumption needs; and (iii) a wide array of personal and communal services for which no monetary payments are made or expected.

The market bias inherent in the GNP measure rests on the corresponding assumption of a homogeneous and organized market, and that fairly accurate comparisons can be made about the relative prices of goods and services within the economy. This assumption does not hold true in cases where prevailing markets are segmented. The presence of market segmentation means that prevailing prices do not reflect their true economic opportunity costs. This is exemplified by the phenomenal growth and entrenchment of what has come to be variously termed the "underground economy," "parallel," or "black" markets. In many cases, transactions taking place in these markets tend to overshadow those in their more formal counterparts. While these activities can be described in several ways, their presence and increasing significance suggest that a growing proportion of income earned in many economies is not reported, and is therefore not captured in the GNP figure.

Across countries, such activities are typically stimulated by government controls and regulations, prohibitions and bannings, and bureaucratic corruption. In the case of the goods market, for example, a substantial flow of goods and services usually takes place at prices that are higher than officially reported ones, and the true income earned is not reported. In a similar vein, workers employed in the black market for labor usually receive lower wages than in the formal market. In the typical case, these and other forms of income are not reported to the official authorities, since income, social security, payroll, and other taxes do not have to be paid on them.

Because the GNP measure is biased in favor of goods and services provided by the private market, it does not normally reflect real levels of "social income" provided by government services, such as education, health, and other public goods. These goods are usually provided through the expenditure, tax, and budgetary policies of government, and are typically treated in national accounts. However, their full benefits cannot be adequately measured because of the presence of externalities. While they may be reflected in the expenditure side of the national accounts, they do not normally show up on the income side since they are not counted as part of receipts.

The GNP per head measure is commonly used to make comparisons of the relative levels of development attained by countries. The standard statistical procedure is to convert the GNPs per head of different countries into a common international currency (usually the U.S. dollar) using official currency exchange rates. However, these exchange conversions may be highly misleading for the following reasons: (i) they do not always reflect income and price differentials among countries, that is, the real purchasing power of the respective currencies; (ii) as indicated above, the presence of illegal, "non-price," and "underground" activities in many countries means that a large part of the total income earned may not be reported. Correlatively, when a significant portion of a country's GNP does not enter into world trade or the domestic and international market, official exchange rates will not necessarily reflect the domestic purchasing power of currencies; (iii) there is a lack of consistency among countries in calculating changes in real output over time; and (iv) where there are excessive fluctuations in exchange rates, the relevant conversions may show substantial changes in relative "nominal" GNPs between pairs of countries, even though no "real" change has actually occurred.

As mentioned above, the official exchange rate may not necessarily reflect the domestic purchasing power of a currency. The latter can be several times its dollar exchange rate. As a consequence, the real GNP per head reported for a country may be several times the value shown in the exchange rates conversion. As a hypothetical example, the price of a pair of shoes in the United States may be, say, five times higher than in India, but this is not taken into account when one says that the GNP per person in the United States ($21,790 in 1990 dollars) is more than sixty-two times that of India ($350 in 1990 dollars). More generally, GNP comparisons do not adequately reflect certain realities about living conditions across countries. For example, people need relatively less to survive in tropical environments compared to more temperate climes where they need to spend more on items such as fuel, food, clothing, and housing. For these and related reasons, analysts connected with the International Comparison Project have concluded that the reported per capita GNP of most developing countries should be adjusted upwards by a factor of two, three, or more in order to capture more adequately the true relative purchasing power parities (Kravis, Heston, and Summers 1982).

In statistical terms, the GNP per head figure is an average, or arithmetic mean, that is obtained by dividing the annual value of a country's total income or output equally among its population. This average share is not a true reflection of the incomes people actually receive, and therefore does not show how income is actually distributed among different segments of the population. A country's GNP per person may expand while its distribution becomes more unequal. This can happen if, for example, wealthier segments of the population become better off while the poorer members continue to receive less in terms of absolute real incomes. Under the circumstances, expansion of GNP per person may be accompanied by an increase in poverty. Hence, the measure may conceal more than it reveals about the condition of the poor.

As an illustration, consider a hypothetical country with a population of one million people. In this country, 900,000 people, or 90 percent of the population, receive an average income of $100 each (a total for the group of $90 million), while the remaining 100,000, or 10 percent of the population, receive an average income of $20,000 each (a total of $2 billion for this group). Such a country would have an average GNP per person of $2,090, with the average income of the richer minority nearly ten times that of the average for the country as a whole, which is roughly twenty times that of the average for the poorer majority. From this it can be surmised that the average GNP per head figure tells us nothing about the living standards or overall quality of life that can be enjoyed by either the rich or the poor. The data in Table 9.2 can also be used to throw some further light on this burning issue.

In this case, a comparison is made between the GNP per person in a select group of countries and the percentage of income accruing to the poorest 40 percent of households. It is evident that, across countries, poverty and inequality are inextricably linked, though their incidence is much more pronounced at low levels of development. In the latter context, the GNP per person in a country such as Brazil is double that of Thailand, while the share of income going to the poorest 40 percent of households in Thailand is more than two times (15.2 percent) that of Brazil (7 percent). The GNP per person in Kenya is slightly higher than that of India, but the average income received by the poorest households in the latter country ($101) is higher than the former ($65). In India, the poorest households received 16.2 percent of the total compared to 8.9 percent for Kenya. The Philippines and Cote D'Ivoire have about the same level of GNP per person, but the average income received by the poorest households in the Philippines is $213 compared to $132 for Cote D'Ivoire. By the same token, the share of GNP accruing to the poorest 40 percent of households in the Philippines is 14.1 percent compared to 8.6 percent for Cote D'Ivoire.

A conclusion germane to the above interpretation is that the ramifications of poverty cannot be fully grasped unless a full account is taken of the behavior of incomes, wealth, and living conditions in society as a whole, as well as the access of individuals, groups, and regions to the available resources. Correlatively, policies designed to reduce or eradicate poverty are likely to prove ineffective unless corresponding steps are taken to reduce or eliminate inequality. On the other hand, it is sometimes argued that poverty and inequality should be treated separately, and that the problem of inequality is less urgent than that of poverty. The reason advanced is that since inequality is an inevitable human condition, the focus should not be on lowering the incomes of the rich but rather on raising the incomes of the poor to some minimum acceptable level. As a corollary, it is argued that we can live with inequalities among people as long as all members of society achieve some minimum acceptable levels of income and basic needs fulfillment.

The debate on the interpretation and measurement of poverty has remained a controversial one, and a full account cannot be provided here. The usual starting point inheres in the distinction between "absolute" and "relative" poverty. As a general proposition, people who are absolutely poor cannot enjoy a minimum standard of living that is consonant with human dignity. They live in destitution and do not enjoy even the biological level of subsistence. Life in general is liv-

Table 9.2

GNP per head and Poverty

Country	GNP per head (in 1985 US dollars) Total	Poorest 40%	Percentage accruing to poorest 40% of households
Netherlands	9,180	5,141	22.4
Japan	11,330	6,203	21.9
Sweden	11,890	6,094	20.5
Germany, F.R.	10,940	5,579	20.4
Switzerland	16,380	8,231	20.0
Norway	13,890	6,563	18.9
United Kingdom	8,930	3,880	18.5
Finland	10,870	5,000	18.4
Denmark	11,240	4,889	17.4
USA	16,400	7,052	17.2
Canada	13,670	5,844	17.1
France	9,550	3,915	17.0
Korea, Rep. of	2,180	921	16.9
Hong Kong	6,220	2,519	16.2
India	250	101	16.2
Sri Lanka	370	147	15.9
Thailand	830	315	15.2
Philippines	600	213	14.1
Costa Rica	1,290	387	12.0
Venezuela	3,110	801	10.3
Mexico	2,080	515	9.9
Kenya	290	65	8.9
Cote d'Ivoire	620	132	8.6
Brazil	1,640	287	7.0

Source: UNICEF: *The State of the World's Children 1989.*

ed in a constant struggle against misery, and is defined by the cumulative interplay of a host of undesirable elements: inadequate income to purchase basic necessities, a lack of assets, low productivity, malnutrition, disease, short life expectancy, and high mortality rates. These conditions typically coalesce in a seamless web that denies the victims their humanity. The cumulative or self-reinforcing nature of the seamless web means that once people are caught in absolute poverty, they are likely to remain trapped in this state of deprivation.

Thus, in the attempt to define some minimum acceptable level of income or basic needs, it is often necessary to identify some absolute core, which may or may not have relativistic connotations. For example, two individuals living in a developed and less developed country, respectively, may be equally poor, even though the income of the poor person living in the former country is several times that of his or her counterpart in the latter. The existence of relative poverty can be traced more to the influence of the "demonstration effect," or the perception that one is faring worse than others - those "having" or "having more." Accordingly, it is not just a matter of having access to a minimum level of income and supplies of basic necessities, but how one perceives the gap between oneself and others. As a mental phenomenon, it tends to generate shame, envy, and even rage.

Where people perceive that they are not fully enjoying life through no fault of their own, or that others are much better off for no good reason, their relative deprivation can prove to be as equally deleterious (at least to their mental state) as if they were in absolute poverty. Both within and across countries, the state of relative poverty tends to be fuelled by expectations. At the intra-country level, poor people compare themselves with elites and members of the upper classes, and may feel deprived because they live in substandard housing, cannot afford transportation or to drive expensive cars, or send their children to private schools. At the international level, the most important causal factor is probably the role of the communications media in transmitting cultural values and lifestyles from reference group countries.

While the broad dichotomy between absolute and relative deprivation maintains its tenacity, a further refinement is necessary to capture some significant changes in the structural conditions of the poor that have emerged since the 1980s, and especially with the implementation of structural adjustment programs. First, the lot of the hard core or "structural" poor has hardly changed. They continue to occupy the bottom 20 percent of the income distribution profile and typically struggle under the seamless web of poverty mentioned earlier. These cadres have been traditionally left out of the development process.

A second category includes the "borderline" poor or vulnerable. They consist of low-income vulnerable groups who have been affected most severely by changes in the prices and availability of major items of consumption, especially food, cutbacks in social programs, and adverse shifts in the internal terms of trade. This borderline group includes a substantial proportion of the general public. Some of its members move in and out of poverty, while others never cross the poverty threshold. Examples are low-income government employees, casual workers, pregnant and lactating mothers, and poor farmers. There is a very thin dividing line between the borderline poor and a third group - the "new" poor.

They consist predominantly of urban personnel who are direct victims of the austerity and belt-tightening associated with structural adjustment programs. One subgroup comprises workers who have experienced cuts in wages and salaries, retrenched civil servants, and private sector employees who have lost their livelihood because of a shift in economic priorities. The majority used to enjoy some reasonable standard of living before the age of adjustment. While by no means rich, most in their midst have definitely become "poorer," even though it is difficult to speculate whether their new state of pauperization will become more extreme with the passage of time. Another subgroup consists of those who always lived on the borderline anyway. They constitute disadvantaged urban groups, mostly self-employed, who are no longer able to sell their services, engage in petty trade, or otherwise work on a casual basis because of economic retrenchment.

Search for Yardstick of Sustainable Human Development

Since the 1970s, the increasing concern for the well-being of the poor has given rise to a search for alternative indicators of human social welfare. A focal point has been on the minimum standard of living that any developing society should set for the poorest groups of its people. This resulted in a basic needs approach to human development, which stressed the necessity for societal restructuring and the reallocation of resources to the marginalized sectors of society, especially the urban poor and rural areas where the majority of the poor live. The shift to basic needs carried the important implication that human development would become a primary end of social life and not just a mere byproduct of economic growth defined in terms of GNP attainment. It also meant a reorientation toward a set of development indicators that would reflect the results of human strivings and not just the means, such as income attainment.

The results or achievements inhere in certain aspects of basic needs fulfillment, such as levels of literacy (freedom from ignorance), average life expectancy, and the nutritional status of the population. The results measured by such indicators can be considered the outcomes derived from a variety of means. However, the usefulness of basic needs indicators depends on the extent to which they can overcome a basic dilemma that faces most measurement yardsticks. On the one hand, they must be capable of fully reflecting the ideal of human development, or the essential but ultimately immeasurable goal of a full and enjoyable life for all. On the other hand, if they are to serve as a useful guide to policy, they must have some practical and operational significance, and therefore be capable of measurement.

The basic needs indicators would seem to meet both requirements in many respects. Not only do they provide some indication of the end results of human development, but they also provide some reasonable proxies of what we are ultimately trying to measure. For example, the achievement of a certain literacy rate not only provides some direct indication of the proportion of a given population that is benefitting from basic education and schooling, but also the capacity of people in general to participate meaningfully in other aspects of social and economic life. A measure of a nation's average life expectancy rate provides a fairly good indication of the health and nutrition status of its population. If there is a significant rise in the average life expectancy rate and/or a fall in the infant mortality rate, this can be interpreted to mean that a substantial proportion of the population must be sharing in the advances that make such changes possible.

As direct measures of human well-being, the basic needs indicators have the advantage over the GNP per head measure in that they are not subject to the fallacy of averages. Even if the distribution of income is unequal, reliance on such measures means that the rich cannot affect a nation's average life expectancy, literacy rate, or nutritional status. As shown earlier, the GNP per head measure has little meaning if the distribution of income is highly unequal. Furthermore, the basic needs indicators are particularly useful in making inter-country comparisons of socio-economic well-being. One reason is that they do not suffer from the exchange rate and purchasing power distortions that are associated with the GNP per head measure.

On this basis, the search for a results-oriented indicator of human welfare culminated in the construction of a Physical Quality of Life Index (PQLI) by analysts at the Overseas Development Council in Washington, D.C. (See Morris 1979; Grant 1978). The PQLI is an average measure based on three indicators: longevity or average life expectancy at age one, the infant mortality rate, and the adult literacy rate. Both life expectancy and infant mortality are considered good indicators of the results of the total social process. They sum up the combined effects of social relations, nutritional status, public health, and family environment. To the extent that income and nutritional intake do result in changes in patterns of life and death, they are reflected in infant mortality rates. It can even be argued that these two indicators also reflect qualitative desiderata such as social order and personal stratification. As indicated earlier, literacy provides information about the potential for human development and the extent to which the poor and disadvantaged can share the possibilities and advantages of development activity.

In the construction of the PQLI, each of the three indicators is indexed as a scale from zero (the most unfavorable performance in 1950) to 100 (the best performance expected in the year 2000). For life expectancy at age one, the most favorable figure expected to be achieved by any country by the year 2000 (77 years) is valued at 100, and the most unfavorable performance in 1950 (38 years for Guinea-Bissau) is valued at zero. Similarly, for the infant mortality rate, the best performance expected in the year 2000 (7 per 1,000 live births) is rated at 100, and the poorest performance in 1950 (229 per 1,000 live births) is rated at zero. The literacy rate is a percentage figure and is therefore automatically scaled from zero to 100. The three scores for each of the indicators are then averaged to give the PQLI on a scale from zero to 100 for each country.

The data in Table 9.3 show some of the results of the computations, together with comparisons of GNP attainment. It is evident that, compared to the GNP measure, the PQLI is very sensitive to the distribution of benefits among segments of the population. While GNP per head and PQLI scores are closely correlated, there are a number of exceptions. For example, the performance of countries such as the People's Republic of China, Sri Lanka, and Tanzania show that low per capita income and the worst consequences of poverty and deprivation need not go hand in hand. Both socialist-oriented countries (People's Republic of China, Cuba, Sri Lanka, and Tanzania) and high-growth, capitalist-oriented ones (South Korea, Hong Kong, and Singapore) recorded relatively high PQLI scores. Despite variations in income attainment and in their economic, social, and political structures, the combined experiences of these countries demonstrate the difference it makes when basic social services are made available to all segments of the population as a matter of deliberate government policy.

As a composite indicator of human development, the PQLI suggests that it is possible to satisfy the basic minimum needs of a population through a variety of ways, such as better nutrition, health care, and education. These are the means for achieving the ends of human social well-being. The mix of means chosen must ultimately depend on the resources, culture, and priorities of an individual country. In any event, it is the task of policymakers to choose those mixtures of policies that promise the best results in terms of the ends to be achieved. While the human development goal must be kept at the forefront of consciousness, it is impossible to escape value judgments even at the level of the public policy decision-making process.

However, while the PQLI is relatively simple to construct, it suffers from a number of technical limitations. In the first place, the equal weighing accorded the three basic needs indicators introduces some measure of subjectivity and arbitrariness into the analysis. Second, there is no agreed theoretical basis for combining the three indicators into a single composite index that can potentially rival the GNP per head measure. The evidence suggests that the three indicators may be highly inter-correlated for some countries, which means that there may be no substantial difference in the scores for each indicator. When this happens, it may be better to use one of them as a single overall index of human development. On the other hand, given that each indicator carries an equal weight, where a marked difference occurs in the three scores, the interpretation of the PQLI must rely on value judgments.

For example, a country with a high average life expectancy and a low literacy rate may register the same PQLI score as one with the opposite characteristics. In such a situation, interpretation of the PQLI must rely on the judgmental conclusion that the two indicators represent more or less equal levels of human

Table 9.3

GNP per Head and the PQLI

Country	GNP per head average in 1970 US dollars	PQLI
Ethiopia	97	22
India	133	43
Zaire	136	32
Tanzania	154	53
Haiti	176	36
Sri Lanka	179	82
Kenya	213	53
People's Republic of China	350	69
Cuba	800	85
Taiwan	847	87
South Korea	797	82
Jamaica	1,037	85
Hong Kong	1,624	87
Singapore	2,111	86
Japan	4,146	96
U.S.A.	7,024	95

Sources: Grant (1978); Morris (1979)

development (Streeten 1982). Finally, there are misgivings about the statistical bases underlying the construction of the PQLI index. Questions may be raised about the reliability of the statistics, the depth of their coverage, and the different definitions that are typically used in their calculation. In the latter context, problems concerning the definition of literacy are particularly acute in African countries where official languages are not the primary media of communication in the daily rounds or work environment.

The procedure used in constructing the PQLI index bears a close similarity to the one employed by analysts at the United Nations Development Programme in their design of the Human Development Index (HDI). The HDI is based on three indicators--life expectancy at birth, literacy, and GDP per capita. The latter is used as a measure of the command over resources needed for a decent living, or the purchasing power to buy commodities needed to satisfy basic needs. The composite HDI index is constructed by specifying a minimum value (the maximum deprivation set equal to one) and a desirable or adequate value (no deprivation set equal to zero) for each of the indicators. The minimum values were chosen by taking the lowest 1987 value for each indicator. In the case of life expectancy at birth, the minimum value was 47 years (Sierra Leone, Afghanistan, and Ethiopia); for adult literacy, 12 percent (Somalia); and for GDP [adjusted for purchasing power], $220 (Zaire). The yardsticks for desirable or adequate achievement were Japan's 1987 life expectancy at birth of 78 years, an adult literacy rate of 100 percent, and the average official "poverty line" income in nine industrial countries of $4,861, adjusted by purchasing power parities.

As mentioned above, the minimum and desirable or adequate values are end-points on a scale indexed from one to zero for each of the indicators. A country is then placed at the appropriate point on each scale, the three scales are then averaged, and the average "human deprivation index" obtained. When subtracted from one, this yields the HDI index. The data in tables 9.4 and 9.5 show the HDI scores and rankings for developed and developing countries, respectively. As in the case of PQLI scores, the world's leaders on the human development front are the developed market economies. Those at the top of the list are known for their consistent commitments to social investments. In general, the proposition is substantiated that both basic needs provision and access to resources can make a substantial difference to the overall quality of life people are able to enjoy. In the case of developing countries, examples that stand out are small countries such as Barbados, Costa Rica, Sri Lanka, and Jamaica. Historically, people in these countries have had a relatively greater access to basic goods and services compared to those in larger ones such as Nigeria, Brazil, Saudi Arabia, and South Africa.

Finally, we return to the problem posed by non-marketed goods and services. Even if they could be included in the GNP measure, the computation would be meaningful only if appropriate market prices can be imputed to them. It is difficult to find such prices for a large number of goods and services that have economic value. A primary example relates to the critical services provided by the biophysical environment. Environmentalists have been constantly grappling with the problem of devising technically sound ways of altering the per capita income measure so that it can properly reflect the requirements of environmental integrity. This is an integral part of a more embracing search for a measure of what is now termed "sustainable development," that is, meeting the development needs of the present generation without unduly compromising the welfare of generations yet unborn.

The corresponding issues of inter-temporal choice and inter-generational equity inhere in the fact that human beings must constantly interact with the wider world of nature as a means of guaranteeing their survival and future development. The quality of human life has always depended on the continuous and diverse flow of material and biological resources, that is, those elements in the biophysical environment that produce valued commodities designed to support life-sustenance needs, other material wants, and leisure. Thus, the interface poses a central problem of continued human existence and authentic development.

Table 9.4
HDI Ranking for Industrial Countries

Country	HDI rank	HDI value
Canada	1	0.982
Japan	2	0.981
Norway	3	0.978
Switzerland	4	0.977
Sweden	5	0.976
U.S.A.	6	0.976
Australia	7	0.971
France	8	0.969
Netherlands	9	0.968
United Kingdom	10	0.962
Iceland	11	0.958
Germany	12	0.955
Denmark	13	0.953
Finland	14	0.953
Austria	15	0.950
Belgium	16	0.950
New Zealand	17	0.947
Israel	18	0.939
Luxembourg	19	0.929
Italy	21	0.922
Ireland	22	0.921
Spain	23	0.916
Greece	26	0.901
Czechoslovakia	27	0.897
Hungary	28	0.893
Poland	32	0.874
U.S.S.R.	33	0.873
Bulgaria	35	0.865
Yugoslavia	37	0.857
Malta	38	0.854
Portugal	39	0.850
Albania	49	0.791
Romania	60	0.733

Source: UNDP (1992)

Table 9.5

HDI Ranking for Developing Countries

Country	HDI rank	HDI value	Country	HDI rank	HDI value	Country	HDI rank	HDI value
Barbados	20	0.927	Sri Lanka	76	0.651	Cameroon	118	0.313
Hong Kong	24	0.913	Ecuador	77	0.641	Ghana	119	0.310
Cyprus	25	0.912	Paraguay	78	0.637	Pakistan	120	0.305
Uruguay	29	0.880	China	79	0.612	India	121	0.297
Trinidad and Tobago	30	0.876	Philippines	80	0.600	Namibia	122	0.295
Bahamas	31	0.875	Peru	81	0.600	Cote d'Ivoire	123	0.289
Korea, Republic of	34	0.871	Oman	82	0.598	Haiti	124	0.276
Chile	36	0.863	Dominican Republic	83	0.595	Comoros	125	0.269
Singapore	40	0.848	Samoa	84	0.591	Tanzania, U. Rep. of	126	0.268
Brunei Darussalam	41	0.848	Iraq	85	0.589	Zaire	127	0.262
Costa Rica	42	0.842	Jordan	86	0.586	Nigeria	128	0.241
Argentina	43	0.833	Tunisia	87	0.582	Lao People's Dem. Rep.	129	0.240
Venezuela	44	0.824	Mongolia	88	0.574	Yemen	130	0.232
Kuwait	45	0.815	Lebanon	89	0.561	Liberia	131	0.227
Mexico	46	0.804	Iran, Islamic Rep. of	90	0.547	Togo	132	0.218
Qatar	47	0.802	Gabon	91	0.545	Uganda	133	0.192
Mauritius	48	0.793	Guyana	92	0.539	Rwanda	134	0.186
Bahrain	50	0.790	Vanuatu	93	0.536	Bangladesh	135	0.185
Malaysia	51	0.789	Botswana	94	0.534	Cambodia	136	0.178
Dominica	52	0.783	Algeria	95	0.533	Senegal	137	0.178
Antigua and Barbuda	53	0.781	El Salvador	96	0.498	Ethiopia	138	0.173

Table 9.5 (continued)

HDI Ranking for Developing Countries

Country	HDI rank	HDI value	Country	HDI rank	HDI value	Country	HDI rank	HDI value
Grenada	54	0.758	Nicaragua	97	0.496	Angola	139	0.169
Colombia	55	0.758	Indonesia	98	0.491	Nepal	140	0.168
Suriname	56	0.749	Maldives	99	0.490	Malawi	141	0.166
United Arab Emirates	57	0.740	Guatemala	100	0.485	Burundi	142	0.165
Seychelles	58	0.740	Honduras	101	0.473	Equatorial Guinea	143	0.163
Cuba	59	0.739	Viet Nam	102	0.464	Central African Rep.	1444	0.159
Panama	61	0.732	Swaziland	103	0.458	Sudan	145	0.157
Jamaica	62	0.731	Cape Verde	104	0.437	Mozambique	146	0.153
	63	0.722	Solomon Islands	105	0.437	Bhutan	147	0.146
Fiji	64	0.713	Morocco	106	0.429	Mauritania	148	0.141
Saint Lucia	65	0.712	Lesotho	107	0.423	Benin	149	0.111
Saint Vincent	66	0.693	Zimbabwe	108	0.397	Chad	150	0.088
Saudi Arabia	67	0.687	Bolivia	109	0.394	Somalia	151	0.088
Saint Kitts and Nevis	68	0.686	Egypt	110	0.385	Guinea-Bissau	152	0.088
Thailand	69	0.685	Myanmar	111	0.385	Djibouti	153	0.084
South Africa	70	0.674	Sao Tome and Principe	112	0.374	Gambia	154	0.083
Turkey	71	0.671	Congo	113	0.372	Mali	155	0.081
Syrian Arab Republic	72	0.665	Kenya	114	0.366	Niger	156	0.078
Belize	73	0.665	Madagascar	115	0.325	Burkina Faso	157	0.074
Libyan Arab Jamahiriya	74	0.659	Papua New Guinea	116	0.321	Afghanistan	158	0.065
Korea, Dem. Republic of	75	0.654	Zambia	117	0.315	Sierra Leone	159	0.062
						Guinea	160	0.052

Not only are we what the environment has made of us, but we are also what we make of it. On the one hand, people are dependent on nature for the wide variety of goods and services they need in order to survive and prosper. On the other hand, nature is dependent on humans for enhancing its productive potential and the quality of resources that can be made available for the support of human life. The march of civilization has required the development of forms of knowledge to modify or better control the biophysical environment as a means of guaranteeing human survival and progress. Without human ingenuity and intervention, nature's productive inputs and life-sustenance qualities cannot make an optimal contribution to human welfare, that is, in the form of land, food, energy, water, air, and other things that are valuable to human life.

The irony is that if these resources are overexploited or mismanaged, the very possibilities for a sustainable life will be compromised. The problem has been captured in the *Economist* (September 16, 1989: 77) in the following terms:

> Once upon a time, an entrepreneur was cast away on a desert island. By good chance, the island lay on a busy sea route, in a convenient time zone. The entrepreneur cut down all the trees and exported them to Japan, sold off all the coral for jewelry, dug up the island's gold and used the proceeds to set up schools, homes and factories for a new Hong Kong, where everybody lived prosperously ever after on the product of their brains, high technology and imported materials. Is this sustainable development?

The question is particularly relevant to developing countries because the exploitation of natural resources accounts for a substantial proportion of their national output. At the same time, damage to the natural environment continues to impose considerable costs on their development potential. In this context, the conventional approach to national income accounting has been found wanting in at least three respects. First, essential assets such as clean air and forests are not counted as part of national wealth. Yet, it can be assumed that people are likely to feel worse about the quality of their lives if they live in a polluted and barren country. Second, manmade capital is depreciated but not natural resources. A country which exhausts its manmade capital without replacing it will evidently become poorer but, on the basis of conventional economic measures, one which depletes, say, its non-renewable minerals or fish stocks will appear to be more prosperous. Third, while the costs of cleaning up environmental damage are usually recorded as an addition to GNP, the environmental loss caused by the original degradation is not subtracted.

To some extent, the United Nations has revised its system of national accounts (SNA) to address these concerns A fair comment is that this approach has not fully integrated economic and environmental accounts. The new SNA still faces the basic difficulty of determining a common measure of value for physical goods and environmental services. Many statisticians continue to harbor deep skepticism about "green national accounts," or attempts to assign monetary values to environmental benefits and costs. The primary reason is that such exercises do not compare like with like.

In its report on "Monitoring Environmental Progress" (1995), the World Bank has attempted to integrate economic and environmental indicators by breaking down national wealth into three broad categories: (i) "produced capital," or the economic value of physical capital assets such as machinery, factories, roads, and other aspects of a nation's infrastructure; (ii) "natural capital," or the value of forests, mineral deposits, land, water, and other environmental assets; and (iii) "human resources," or investments in human or social capital such as education, nutrition, and health care. While the "produced capital" component comes closest to the conventional measure of national wealth, comparisons reveal that it accounts for only about 20 percent of real wealth in most countries. The latter is reflected primarily in hidden values on the human and social side, such as the skills of educated cadres.

The overall message is that national wealth is enhanced through investment in people and not just in machinery, buildings, and other physical assets. On this basis, it is argued that natural resources can be depleted as long as the proceeds derived from their exploitation are invested in building human capital. In this process, nations would be giving future generations the same, if not more, opportunities than we found ourselves. In what is perceived as a "birthright approach" to development, it would be beneficial to cut down trees or deplete the amount of oil in the ground in order to invest in human resources, for example, in the education of women and children.

In order to create new wealth, countries must engage in what the World Bank terms "genuine saving" by producing more than they consume. Beside the utilization of goods and services, such consumption includes the gradual depreciation of a country's produced assets and the depletion of its natural resources. Based on this formula, it is envisaged that countries which use their natural resources wisely will ultimately become wealthier because they would have invested in people. By contrast, those that squander the proceeds would be "dissaving" and are likely to become poorer. Thus, it is argued, while both East Asian and Latin American countries have been depleting their natural capital, the investment in human resources undertaken by the former has brought handsome dividends in terms of economic progress while Latin America is still caught in an economic backwater. The same is true of Africa.

Chapter 10

Egalitarian and Meliorist Reforms: Restructuring Growth

As we have indicated, policies based on the modernization ethic generated a phase of widening inequality. The relative rise in incomes per person was accompanied by a limited increase in employment. While inequality per se may be undesirable, its reduction may not necessarily lead to a corresponding eradication of poverty or improvements in the overall quality of life. In this context, two broad policy scenarios were to gain ascendancy: (i) the "redistribution with growth" (RWG) strategy of the World Bank; and (ii) more direct "people-centered" orientations, including the "basic needs" perspective of the International Labour Organization (ILO) and others that variously stressed community development, people participation, and unified and decentralized development.

Redistribution with Growth (RWG)

Table 10.1 summarizes essentials of the RWG perspective. The corresponding strategy emerged from a questioning of the growth-oriented approach. Observation of the development experience had indicated that: (i) income did not trickle down to the poor; (ii) economic growth was not accompanied by poverty redressal; and (iii) growth of production in developing countries was still based on a lopsided economic structure and not matched by sufficient access to international markets or internal market development. Therefore, careful consideration was given to the international mechanisms and domestic economic

Table 10.1

Redistribution with Growth

Primary Objectives	• GNP per capita growth • Asset redistribution • Increasing productivity of the poor
Development Values	• Mutual self-interest • Egalitarianism
Performance Criteria	• Minimum income for all • Economic efficiency • Employment creation • Poverty redressal
Policy Instruments	• Social sector investment • Incomes policy • Land reform
Principal Mechanisms	• Public policy reform • Appropriate technology • Unimodal pattern of agricultural development • Export of labor-intensive manufactures
Agents of Change	• Market agents • Rural dwellers • Formal and informal institutions • Activist state

reforms that could help to promote a genuine productivity dynamism among the bottom 40 percent of the population. Contextually, an influential study by Hollis Chenery (then vice-president for development policy at the World Bank) and his associates advocated a fundamental reorientation of development policies and strategies toward expanding the productive use of resources in urban and rural areas containing the principal poverty groups, that is, the urban informal sector and small-scale agriculture (see Chenery et al. 1974).

Some of the assumptions about the possibilities of redistribution need recounting. As is well known, the distribution of income among households depends of the availability of assets (land, capital, and labor), since the latter determine the distribution of earnings - land rent, capital income, wages and salaries. In other words, people's incomes consist of the value of the services of assets owned by them and that are sold in the market. In this sense, the problem of poverty can be interpreted as a situation in which both the quantity and volume of market sales are too low, and/or the market price is not adequate. Thus, how the poor fare during the course of economic development depends on the impact of the overall development style on the distribution of assets as well as the prevailing institutions determining asset accumulation and access to markets.

Contextually, the experience across developing countries had thrown up the following stylized facts. First, the distribution of land is a major determinant of poverty and the incidence of inequality. The pattern of land distribution has not been highly skewed in countries that have been able to maintain economic growth with a relatively equitable pattern of income distribution, such as Taiwan, South Korea, and Costa Rica. The development style followed by such countries has relied on policies that equalized rural income distribution and kept rural-urban income differentials much narrower compared to other developing countries with a relatively uneven distribution of land. This was matched by both an unequal distribution of income and a high incidence of poverty. Landlessness has been a major cause of increasing poverty in developing countries.

Second, the distribution of capital has been even more unequal than that of land, and has cumulated over time. The main causal factors are traceable to higher rates of saving by the rich, a financial system that has provided them with better access to credit and, as previously emphasized, the overall reliance on dualist-oriented and urban-based development strategies. Third, the distribution of human capital over the labor force has more or less paralleled the distribution of other assets. Other things being equal, the uneven pattern of asset distribution has shown a positive association with the unequal distribution of labor incomes. In turn, the smaller share of income accruing to the poor has been associated with an unequal access to education and therefore an uneven spread in the ownership of human capital.

The quantity of assets owned by the poor can be increased in various ways. One method is by redistributing assets to them, for example, through land reform. Another is by creating opportunities for the accumulation of more assets, for example, through wider access to primary education, subsidized credit, and the like. The RWG strategy of the World Bank relied on policy instruments that emphasized the latter, that is, differentially allocating a larger share of the proceeds of economic growth to incremental asset accumulation by, and investment in, the poor. The rural strategy focussed on increasing the productivity of the small farmer and self-employed through better access to land, water, credit markets, education, and so on. It was also recognized that the urban poor required a more diversified strategy since, even with optimal policies, the modern sector could not provide adequate employment for the bulk of the growing urban labor force.

The preferred policy mix resulted from a simulation model of distribution and growth in which three alternative policy scenarios were considered: consumption transfers to the poor, wage restraint, and investment transfers to the poor. The policy that transferred investment assets to the poor proved superior to the other two, both in terms of growth and equity. Compared to consumption transfers and wage restraint, the asset transfer alternative improved the asset distribution profile and caused no perceptible reduction in aggregate investment and economic growth. Thus, considerable emphasis was placed on the necessity for an incremental redistribution of income and assets to the poor during the growth process. The policy proposals emanating from these simulations were implemented through a massive increase in World Bank lending for poverty-oriented projects in small-scale agriculture, and for social, educational, and health services. The expectation was that such initiatives would help to get resources to small farmers and, in general, upgrade the productive capacity of the poor.

The model of change is one that promises to improve the labor power or human capital of the poor through institutions that enhance their access to income-earning opportunities. The focus is on employment generation through greater reliance on agricultural development, light manufactures, and labor-intensive services such as transportation. The diffusion of technology is also deemed a primary catalyst of development. But, the technology chosen must be appropriate in terms of its employment-creating effects and potential for channelling income into people's hands. Under the circumstances, public policy is expected to play a pivotal role in restructuring the mix of domestic production, exports, and the distribution of attendant benefits. While the institutional structure remains a market-oriented one, the government enters as a key player in guiding investment policy and explicitly advocating mechanisms for asset redistribution.

This reflects a basic philosophical difference between the standard growth-oriented approach and the RWG strategy. In the latter case, the emphasis is shifted toward means, or the critical role of public provisioning. This is based on a recognition that the market sometimes functions better with the help of some degree of stimulus from public economic policy. Indeed, this is borne out by the East Asian success story. That experience also raises an important question about the salutary effects of the right initial conditions, that is, about the relative merits of a strategy emphasizing "redistribuion *with* growth" vis-à-vis one based on "redistribution *before* growth." By sheer force of historical accident, massive investments in rapid industrialization and extensive land reform preceded policies designed to improve agricultural output and productivity.

It is well-documented that Japan, South Korea, and Taiwan were goaded by the U.S. authorities to institute fundamental land reforms during the late 1940s and early 1950s. This resulted in a virtual elimination of prevalent forms of farm tenancy. The reforms created a cadre of small, independent, and proprietary farmers who became strong allies of the national governments, thereby ending seemingly endless cycles of rural violence and instability. The evidence suggests that the reforms resulted in a substantive narrowing of the income distribution and had a pervasive long-term effect of increasing the political clout of the massive class of small and prosperous peasants, who could now demand changes in their own interests. After the reforms, government policies in all three countries provided positive protection to agriculture, and a relatively large proportion of public infrastructural development was channelled to the rural sector.

In essence, perspectives on the issue of land distribution have varied, depending on whether the land-scarce Asian or land-abundant Latin American and African countries were the subject of discourse. There is a long and convoluted history of failed attempts at reform in Latin America where land distribution patterns remain highly skewed. During the early 1970s, open land frontiers still prevailed in Africa, and it was therefore still possible for poor farmers to maintain or even increase output without any major land redistribution. However, the situation became progressively worse, since major land grabs were organized by powerful groups of people who obtained bureaucratic monopolies and used the rents extracted to make substantial purchases of land in rural areas. As a result, the land frontier has been successively pushed back, and its potential development by small farmers foreclosed.

In principle, policies aimed at both redistributing the existing stock of assets and investing in the creation of new productive assets can have both growth-augmenting and growth-reducing effects. For example, in the spirit of the Cambridge-Lewis capitalist-centered savings perspective, it can be argued that since the poor tend to save a smaller proportion of their income than the rich, land reform might reduce saving and therefore dampen the growth rate. On the other hand, it might have a salutary effect on growth if it encourages a more efficient use of land. Investment in education and other forms of human capital can be good for growth over the longer term since it promises to improve the quality of the labor force. However, it may be bad for growth in the short run since it requires higher taxes to finance the increase in public spending.

From the broader perspective of political economy, the two types of policy tend to differ in terms of their effects on income distribution, and therefore, political feasibility. Land redistribution typically leads to an immediate and permanent loss in incomes and consumption for the non-poor and vested interests. This explains why it encounters such strong opposition by more powerful groups in society. Extra taxation to finance increased human capital in the poor is sometimes resisted for the same reason. The differences between the two options are essentially political. The latter approach is usually judged to be more politically feasible because the extra investment in human development can be passed on more gradually, so that the increased burden of taxation on the non-poor is paid entirely out of future increments in income. Moreover, some non-poor groups, such as industrialists, are likely to support such a policy because of the potential gains to be realized from the availability of a more skilled labor force.

The two scenarios mentioned above are not meant to suggest that asset redistribution and investment in the poor are mutually exclusive alternatives. Indeed, a relatively egalitarian redistribution of land assets may help to enhance the effectiveness of other policies designed to alleviate poverty. The bone of contention among economists has centered around the inter-temporal trade-off between growth and equity. The two options can become complementary rather than substitutive. Better tenurial arrangements and improvements in human capital can produce positive effects on output growth and productivity. More income in the hands of producers would not only increase effective demand, but also give a further fillip to savings and investment.

Be that as it may, the design of the World Bank's RWG strategy had to face the basic problem of choosing between two options: giving adequate incentives to the poor, or providing them with adequate access to the means of production, such as land. The Bank's leading executive directors seemed unwilling to sanction policies designed to forcibly effect land redistribution. Since incentives were viewed as the key to agricultural and rural development, more emphasis was placed on measures to liberalize markets, for example, by dismantling marketing boards and privatizing parastatal organizations. Nevertheless, access to the means of production, especially land and capital, remained the central issue. Any credible theory or policy must take account of the fact that both market prices and resource availability determine the possibilities for authentic development.

The political and ideological orientations of influential policymakers evidently ruled the roost. As a result, the philosophy behind World Bank lending fell short of the fundamental and thorough-going redistribution of assets that the original theoretical framework of RWG had envisaged. In pragmatic terms, while large redistributions of land assets have been associated with rapid reductions in poverty, they have invariably occurred only in times of great political upheaval. Under the circumstances, the distribution of capital or investment in favor of the poor has been the more favored approach. In particular, investment in human capital through primary and vocational education has been the standard approach followed by most countries and international lending agencies. Whether this option raises incomes, however, ultimately depends on the real returns to education and training, that is, whether adequate opportunities exist, or can be created, for people to effectively utilize their acquired skills.

Basic Needs and the Right to Development

Implicit in the RWG strategy is an egalitarian ethic that has as a goal the promotion of mutual interests rather than mere individual self-interests. While the strategy is grounded in some notion that basic opportunities and a reasonably decent standard of living should be afforded all peoples, the case for redistribution is essentially argued on utilitarian grounds, that is, in terms of means and ends. The discourse has been extended one stage further by what we term "people-centered" interpretations of development, which are based on the imperative of economic and social justice. From this perspective, development becomes a fundamental human right whose ultimate foundation is constituted by the essential needs of each individual.

As previously mentioned, consensual agreement about the evils of inequality does not mean that its reduction would necessarily lead to poverty alleviation or improvements in the overall quality of life. Under the circumstances, the direct provision of basic human needs becomes a sine qua non of social survival and authentic development. The overriding normative implication is that development efforts should focus directly on people and not just on the production of goods and services, countries, and nation states. Table 10.2 provides an illustration of the basic needs and related people-centered development styles. They collectively reflect the necessity to foster societies built around people's genuine needs.

At the conceptual level, it may be useful to reemphasize the distinction between "means" and "achievements" alluded to in the previous chapter. The means refer to the income that people use to purchase basic necessitites. However, this tells us nothing about the quality of life they succeed in living, or what sociologists term their "life chances" (Dahrendorf 1979). The latter refer to the opportunities offered individuals to share in the basic economic and cultural goods of society. The life chances are reflected in the fact that, across countries and civilizations, people have always valued their ability to perform certain acts and achieve a variety of ends, such as being able to live a full and enjoyable life, being well nourished, or being free to express themselves.

Thus, the overall quality of life that a given people succeed in living at a particular point depends on what Sen calls their "beings" and "functionings." Achievement of these depends on: the commodities they own and how they are used; the public or government provision of goods and services; and the possibility of using private goods not freely provided by the state. For example, the achievement of *being* healthy, well nourished, or literate depends on the public or private provision of health services, opportunities for purchasing or growing food, the availability of educational facilities, and so on. From this perspective, authentic development can be interpreted in terms of the "functionings" *achieved*, and viewing these in the light of the *means* to such functionings (Sen 1981a, 1988).

Table 10.2
People-Centered Development Styles

	Basic Needs	Development from Below and Self-Reliance
Primary Objectives	• Improvement in the overall quality of life • Participatory economic and social relations	• Sustainable human development • Building a viable economy • Participatory economic and social relations
Development Values	• Priority to human concerns • Economic, social, and political rights	• Priority to human concerns • Balance between individual rights and communal self-determination
Performance Criteria	• Needs achievement	• Meeting needs • Popular self-determination
Policy Instruments	• Social sector investment • Development of target groups • Markets guided by public policy • Integration of economic and social policies	• Decentralization and localization of decisions • Grassroots organization • Markets guided by communal decisions • Integration of economic and social policies
Principal Mechanisms	• Diffusion of human values • Public institutions	• Diffusion of human values • Participatory democracy • New educational socialization
Agents of Change	• Target groups • Poor people • Local organizations	• Organized and special publics • Local organizations

This implies a raising of the overall standard of living through the expansion of people's capabilities, entitlements, and ownership rights. Entitlement systems represent beliefs and rules about things individuals and groups ought to receive and under what circumstances. At the practical level, they tend to be created by political practice and are typically embodied in socio-cultural, legal, and economic processes. Examples are land tenure rules, notions of family obligations, and rules governing market transactions, employment, and labor standards. These are usually specific to particular cultural milieux and historical circumstances. As such, they cannot be predicted from economic models, and do not necessarily work according to the absolute standards of equity.

In economies subscribing to some measure of private ownership of the means of production, how much basic necessities such as food people can command depends on their "ownership rights" and "exchange entitlements," or what they get in exchange for what they own either through production and/or trade. Under such conditions, people may find themselves facing food deprivation--hunger, starvation - or other threats to their basic needs fulfillment for at least two reasons: that is, land alienation to creditors, or in the exchange entitlement of their ownership, that is, a loss of control over what they own. The latter may result, for example, when they become unemployed and are not able to sell their labor power, or because of an increase in the relative prices of basic necessitites vis-à-vis other commodities in their consumption baskets.

One policy implication is that, across countries and cultural environments, careful assessments have to be made about the ownership patterns facing different classes and occupational groups, as well as the exchange markets they face. In the majority of cases, income provides a very inadequate measure of the entitlement structure. The reason is that the latter depends not only on people's ability to sell their labor power and prices of commodities in the market, but more importantly, on factors such as the structure of power relations in society, the spatial distribution of resources, and the nature of public goods provision, that is, what people can garner from the state.

In the initial conceptualization of basic needs and related policy proposals, the ILO emphasized not only the earning opportunities to purchase life-sustenance necessities, but also access to the provision of public services. The list included "certain minimum requirements of a family for private consumption: adequate food, shelter, and clothing as would be certain household equipment and furniture . . .[and] essential services provided by and for the community at large, such as safe drinking water, sanitation, public transport, health and education facilities" (ILO 1976: 31). Thinking was that these would figure on a comprehensive list of the urgently felt needs of poor people. In addition to being valued in their own right, they were also thought to be a necessary prerequisite for meeting "higher order" needs such as self-determination, self-reliance, freedom, security, and participation.

In this context, Goulet (1978) identified three basic components, or core values, that any definition of development must embrace: life-sustenance, self-esteem, and freedom. Life-sustenance is axiomatic, in the sense that it deals with the basic necessities of life. Self-esteem refers to feelings of independence, self-respect, identity, integrity, and a sense of people's own worthiness. Freedom connotes people's ability to make choices governing their lives. Thus, there is a synergy between Sen's vision of development in terms of the expansion of people's entitlements, capabilities, and functionings. Entitlements give rise to life sustenance, while capabilities and functionings provide the prerequisites for achievement of freedom.

From this perspective, the ILO's basic needs approach emphasized not only a minimum level of economic security, but also the creation of conditions that would allow continuing equal access of opportunities as a means of fostering self-actualization and authentic development. Like the World Bank's RWG strategy, however, the possibility of meeting basic needs was essentially linked to the necessity of generating genuine productivity increases among the poor. Under the circumstances, considerable significance was attached to the production of goods and services and their distribution in favor of the poor and underprivileged. More specifically, the approach was predicated on the achievement of per capita physical production targets for food, education, housing, and other primary goods in different regions by the end of the century through alternative policies stressing rapid economic growth alone and some redistribution combined with growth. Both policies were found to require historically unprecedented growth rates ranging between 6 and 11 percent per annum to achieve the basic needs targets within the set time frame.

The appropriateness of stressing economic considerations, at least in the short run, was defended on the grounds that no matter what deficiencies exist in the institutional system, provision of goods and services that enter into the basic needs basket can never be ensured without a corresponding increase in production. More generally, the approach was based on a recognition that there is a high degree of mutual causation or interdependence among elements of basic needs. For example, while investment in health may be considered as socially useful, people's state of health determines the extent to which they can be economically active. The symbiotic relationship between the "economic" and the "social" was forcefully championed by United Nations development agencies (see, for example, UNRISD 1980).

However, it should be reiterated that from the more embracing perspective of human development, basic needs represent things to which people have a natural right, whether or not they are directly involved in the production process. Therefore, their provision does not constitute a charitable option. The fruits of production cannot improve human well-being or social welfare unless there are some effective institutional mechanisms for distributive and social justice. The latter operates as a set of "claims" based on principles and percepts such as fairness, needs, duty, equality, equity, and rights. Contextually, what is now termed the *right to development* is seen as setting a new moral and legal basis for the articulation of authentic development.

As enshrined in the United Nations Declaration of the Right to Development of 1986, the philosophy does not turn a blind eye to economic necessity, but insists that the production and distribution of wealth cannot be divorced from democratic ethical norms. Therefore, the mutually reinforcing role of both the economic and moral dimensions of human social well-being is emphasized. Accordingly, a variety of ethical arguments can be used to support the existence of a right to development. These support the claim that development is the condition of all human life and an international duty based on solidarity and moral interdependence.

It is in this sense that the right to development asserts the right of every person to fully participate in and enjoy the fruits of economic, social, cultural, and political progress. Ideally, since this right places the welfare of the individual and the human condition at the center of the development stage, it is designed to achieve the potential realization of all fundamental freedoms and human rights. Such rights are inalienable, that is, they cannot be relinquished or taken away by individuals or nation-states. People have these rights by virtue of their common humanity. Every person is human by nature, as opposed to economic or social convention. In epistemological terms, the proposition that people are naturally human is an analytical one. While it is tautological, it can never be verified or falsified by empirical evidence or contingent facts.

A given person's social environment is determined by accident of birth. A person is only accidentally a native of the United States of America, England, or South Africa; or, for that matter, an African American, Indian, farmer, schoolteacher, or surgeon. By contrast, she or he is not accidentally human. In this context, both the United Nations Charter and the Universal Declaration of Human Rights have enunciated a set of rights that organized societies have a moral obligation to bring about, guarantee, and protect. The rationale is provided by the fact that we live in an interdependent world, and that this establishes a need for shared standards of human dignity and the embracement of the fundamental rights of people everywhere. For example, the Preamble of the United Nations Charter emphasizes the need "to reaffirm faith in fundamental human rights, in the dignity and worth of the human person, in the equal rights of men and women of all nations large and small." In a similar vein, the Universal Declaration of Human Rights contains thirty Articles highlighting basic rights and freedoms, or "inviolable" conditions reflecting "a common standard of achievement for all peoples and nations."

While these imperatives are self-evident and innocuous enough, different groups interpret them from their own perspectival interests. For example, philosophers and political scientists usually express concerns about the logical defensibility of such rights. Economists, political leaders, and businessmen tend to be more concerned about the implications for national economic growth and the profitability of private enterprise. Moreover, even if politicians pay lip service to human rights, some other members of society may accord a higher priority to other goals such as economic success and upward social mobility. More generally, while the goals of authentic development cannot be detached from the principles guaranteeing basic human rights, each society may subscribe to specific rules for distributing such rights.

Thus, even if it is accepted that there are certain universal rights that attach to people by virtue of their status as human beings, such rights should not be construed as abstract phenomena but as having practical and contextual relevance or meaning. The implication is that if universal standards are to be protected, some consideration must be given to how different peoples are perceived and how each group goes about the task of determining its own rights. It comes as no surprise, therefore, that the universality and inalienability of human rights tend to be frequently juxtaposed against the requirement that cultural and social differences manifested in specific societal settings should be respected. A particularly vexing question is whether the universalism derived from Western values and concepts of natural law and their peculiar assumptions can dictate how people should live in all societies.

The tension between the universal and the particular puts into bold relief a major difference between the basic needs and right to development approaches. The former focuses primarily on basic rights pertaining to food, clothing, shelter, and education, while the latter is much more inclusive and encapsulates cultural and political attributes of the overall development process. While the fulfillment of basic needs primarily concerns the rights of individuals within society, the right to development sets obligations for entire societies based on a cosmopolitan morality. It then becomes the moral responsibility of the haves, both nationally and internationally, to accord redistributive justice to the have-nots who suffer in an unjust world.

Governance and People Participation

From the above perspective, it can be said that there is one overarching or top-level basic need: to replace unjust and oppressive economic and political systems with fair and equitable ones. Only then can better housing conditions, health, and education be satisfied, resources effectively mobilized, and relevant policies and programs formulated to improve the overall quality of life. The principles of justice or fairness cannot be divorced from the wider framework defining the economic, social, and political policies of governments. In many countries, the problems of poverty, unemployment, and basic needs fulfillment remain intractable because most government policies tend to perpetuate inequality through a social and economic order that is maintained under a coercive political apparatus.

Under the circumstances, basic needs and other meliorist policies will always come to grief as long as a powerful and privileged few continue to appropriate a nation's resources to their own advantage and to the detriment of the population at large. Some influential participants in the development debate, including many political leaders of poor countries, have contended that any meaningful solutions to the problems would have to be comprehensive, since piecemeal "practical" responses to some problems as they arose would only make matters worse through their impact on other systematically related areas. However, questions have been raised about the capacity of human institutions to manage such comprehensive solutions, the reason being that social, political, environmental, and resource limits have the potential of crippling development. In some circles it was even opined that solutions guaranteeing human survival would require a high degree of regimentation and suppression of dissent.

Needless to say, under such conditions the values of human welfare, equity, and fairness would have to be dispensed with. What is more plausible and just is the creation of a relatively free and democratic environment in which each individual has a fair and equal opportunity to develop his or her potential to the fullest. At one level, the critical issue revolves around the possibility of inculcating the tenets of what is nowadays called "good governance." These are summarized in Table 10.3. At another, the crucial question concerns the links between good governance and a democratic environment, and how the latter is to come about. Throughout the tortuous development debate, the general perception prevailed that many policy failures in developing countries can be traced to the absence of democracy. While a few stable democracies have performed reasonably well, there is still a large number of unstable and incipient ones performing poorly in both an economic and political sense. The presumption of a positive linkage between democracy and authentic development has been based on a number of propositions extrapolated from the historical experience of the industrialized West.

One is that most industrial countries are democracies. The reason why they are apparently hospitable to democracy, it is alleged, is that they are economically wealthy. During the 1945-73 period, steady economic advancement of industrial capitalism was to lay the foundations for development of the welfare state, which has been a significant factor in easing class and interest conflicts. Since that time, however, industrial capitalism itself has been faced with an adjustment crisis due to prolonged recessions, concerted attacks on the welfare state, and heightened social schisms.

Second, a positive association is commonly assumed between democracy and political stability. A reasonable conclusion that can be drawn, at least from the more recent historical experience, is that democracies tend to be less prone to virulent upheavals and internecine conflicts when compared to authoritarian regimes. A basic reason is that when they are functioning well, democracies tend to create strong incentives for social cooperation and good governance based on values such as accountability, representativeness, the rule of law, institutional pluralism, and freedom--of speech, association, and to move about.

Moreover, conflicts among the diverse sectors of interest are more likely to be dampened because a prosperous economic milieu invariably circumscribes the boundaries within which differences are aired and resolved. Disruption of these boundaries damages the system that creates wealth, thereby limiting opportuni-

Table 10.3

Characteristics of Good Governance

Principles	Definition
Accountability	• Ensuring the legitimacy of government through open processes of public choice such as free and fair elections; making the state elite and public servants accountable for their decisions and actions through transparent processes.
Rule of Law	• Creation and maintenance of an objective, efficient, and reliable judicial system to guarantee the safety and security of the citizenry, and fair enforcement of contracts.
Equitable/Sustainable Development	• Ensuring that forms of economic and social development are promoted for the benefit of present and future generations; making all institutions responsive to the needs of the public.
Meeting Needs of Intelligence and Sociality	• Availability of information to ensure accountability is practiced, laws are correctly applied, markets function adequately, and to encourage creativity and innovativeness of the people; freedom of association, speech, and to move about.

ties for economic advancement. The stakes of the political and economic game tend to be lower when potential losers perceive that there are alternative channels of social, economic, and even political mobility. The "bounded" struggle for power that is typical of democratic systems is not a zero-sum game, and access to the state or bureaucratic apparatus is not necessarily viewed as a route toward upward mobility. Thus, there is a lower probability of destructive conflict.

We hasten to add that while a positive association between democracy and equitable development cannot be denied, the linkage is not necessarily a straightforward one. Many so-called democracies are not efficient or just, nor have they demonstrated any deep interest in fostering participatory forms of development. There is no firm or irrefutable evidence that the widely acclaimed model of multi-party democracy necessarily guarantees all the key ingredients of good governance, or is a necessary and sufficient condition for authentic, or people-centered, development. Examples of corrupt democracies abound, especially in the less developed sector of the world. At the other extreme, while a few economies are still run by authoritarian regimes, benevolent or progressive dictatorships are a rarity!

Over the past two decades, the issues surrounding the democracy-development nexus have intersected with a more far-reaching debate about the need to construct coherent alternative futures in the developing world. The meliorist option has emphasized the need to foster an appropriate balance between internal and international reforms based on the following policy prerequisites, among others: reorientation of policy toward reducing pervasive forms of inequality, and increasing the scope and depth of popular participation in decision making; promotion of self-reliant forms of development; and charting an economic development path that is in harmony with the biophysical environment.

It was envisaged that internal policy reforms would require deliberate attempts at transforming production and distribution structures, ending the protracted influence of powerful minorities, and introduction of a decentralized and democratic administrative structure. The latter was considered a necessary precondition for translating policies into equitable decisions and actions, and in order to ensure participation of disadvantaged groups in needed development efforts. In this context, it may be useful to note that early ideas about basic human needs emanated mostly from North America and Europe where the underlying processes of developmental change were viewed as operating mainly from the "top down" rather than from the "bottom up." This perspective was synergistic with the bureaucratic model of organization which formed the lynchpin of centralized planning.

As a consequence, the provision of basic needs was linked to paternalistic programs based on government "doing things for people" rather than "people doing things for themselves." This prompted a call for reformulation of the basic needs approach to reflect self-reliance, and the design of structures and institutions that would elicit and guarantee involvement of the people at all levels. The basic presupposition was that the masses of the people would become subjects or active architects of their own development and destiny rather than mere passive objects. As a corollary, popular engagement of the people at the local or grass roots level was considered a necessary prerequisite for development to become viable, acceptable, and sustainable. These conditions, in turn, would determine the extent to which society is able to function over the longer term for the well-being of all its members.

Viability of the development process depends on the extent to which a society's resources can be mobilized in building a productive capacity catering to requisite consumption and investment needs. Its sustainability depends on the balance that is fostered and maintained between present needs and those of future generations. Its acceptability depends on the weight given to human welfare and equity. On the one hand, a viable development style may not be acceptable, for example, where the economic growth process entails continuing inequities, impoverishment, and oppression. On the other hand, some modes of development may be acceptable but unviable because they overlook the necessity of building a coherent productive capacity. In a similar vein, the requirements of viability and acceptability may clash with the overarching need to foster sustainable economic growth over the longer term.

V

COUNTER-REVOLUTION AND BEYOND

Chapter 11

The New Orthodoxy: Classical and Neo-Classical Resurgence

While the development debate has remained a lively and controversial one, development economics has undergone notable changes over the past two decades due to a new paradigmatic shift within the field itself and its apparent "recapture" by the parent economics discipline. This has been fuelled by the forces of ideological hegemony and dominant political interests. These include, inter alia, rising conservatism in thought and policy in the West, precipitous rejection of central planning in the erstwhile socialist block, and the concomitant Western ideological domination in global economic and political relations.

Dissolution of the Development Consensus

As discussed in Chapter 5, the emergence of development economics as a distinct field of study was grounded in a dirigiste orientation, which emphasizes market imperfections and a necessary role of government in the development process. The presence of market failure was seen as providing signals for public investment allocation and coordination within a framework of coherent and consistent macroeconomic planning. Primary focus was placed on the potential role of government in exploiting the apparently large divergences between private and social rates of return caused by externalities. This optimism rested on a widespread belief that the unfettered play of market forces would yield inferior and suboptimal solutions to the development problem. From the very early days of its conception, therefore, the infant development economics was grounded in a "public interest" perspective based on a set of propositions about the role of the state.

First, and through the lens of neo-classical economic theory, the government was considered the most appropriate agency for removing market failures stemming from externalities, information asymmetries, and so on. As alluded to in Chapter 3, the prevalence of market imperfections means that all relevant information cannot be incorporated into prices, and the corpus of private information flows is unable to solve problems of coordination. Under the circumstances, some measure of central direction may be needed to handle urgent decisions, especially in crisis or emergency situations. This is not to deny that information problems may prove to be as acute and intractable for central government and planning authorities as for the private sector.

It is also now recognized that externalities relating to the processing of information, learning-by-doing, and the acquisition of technology can play a critical role in the development process. In the main industrial centers, such externalities tend to be internalized in large organizations such as transnational corporations which have access to the resources needed to invest in research and development. By contrast, information and capital markets tend to be small or even nonexistent in many latecomers to development. In such cases, the state can play a catalytic role in promoting the learning process.

Second, the state is an essential provider of public or collective goods since, if left to market decisions, such goods will be undersupplied or natural monopolies may develop. More generally, the structural changes inherent in the development process require investment in infrastructure, and rationality and foresight in government policy to obtain the proper relation among economic activities. In this context, state policy is needed in order to coordinate and intensify the rate of internal capital accumulation through adequate incentives and related policy measures. This means enhancing a country's capacity to save as well as attracting the international financial resources required to complement this. Finally, the concentration of wealth and economic power in the private arena may call for the redistributive hand of the benevolent state to effect outcomes that are more equitable and socially just.

The idea of an expanded role for the state became enshrined in the planning-centered approach adopted by the majority of developing nations, the subscription to industrialization, especially of the import substitution variety, and in general, the advocacy of state capitalism and forms of "national developmentalism." The latter refers to the model in which the ruling elite appropriates various policy measures to gain and maintain control of the local economy and development process, including increasing participation of the state in economic activity and selective nationalization of foreign corporations. The rapidly expanding role of the state was aided and abetted by the easy availability of external loans to governments and their agencies, and a corresponding officialization of public debt. Foreign lenders translated their natural propensity toward risk aversion into a redirection of their loans to the government sector.

Many knowledgeable observers of the development scene came to feel that during the 1960s and 1970s the governments of most developing countries became too bogged down in policies and strategies that were unworkable, resulting in colossal government failures and disasters of intervention. In many cases, what perceptibly went wrong was not the overall objectives advocated, but rather the specifics of the day-to-day process of implementation. In general, this process was marked by bureaucratic centralization, a lack of incentives to new producers, and a failure to sufficiently redistribute economic and political power. These outcomes, among other things, not only reflected a "poverty of development economics" (Lal 1983), but also signalled its death as a self-contained field of inquiry.

Hirschman (1981) has attributed the demise of development economics to the consequence of a strange and "unholy alliance" between neo-classical economics and Marxism. Indeed, not only do these two conflicting perspectives make strange bedfellows, but they have been locked in a perennial struggle for paradigm dominance, or what may be interpreted as a competition to provide an intellectual model that would adequately explain the causal mechanisms underlying the process of developmental change. Both the evolutionary (classical, neo-classical) and revolutionary (Marxian) perspectives of global development have been linked by a uniform desire to generate universally valid theoretical, historical, and empirical generalizations that are capable of capturing the forces of material economic progress.

From the classical/neo-classical perspective, economic development is an individual matter. The implication is that in all societies, irrespective of their standing in the development-underdevelopment nexus, the uniform goal should be to ensure that markets are free as possible, competition is perfect as possible, and an enabling environment exists so that independent individuals can realize their potentials to the fullest. Correlatively, material economic progress is interpreted as a rational process of evolutionary change based on the efficient allocation of resources and incremental or marginal adjustments through the manipulation of means to achieve related ends.

The Marxian alternative stands at the opposite interpretive pole. It posits the essential need to probe into the "deep structure" that lies behind market relations in the form of class asymmetries and unequal power relations. Under the circumstances, when individuals make decisions that are purportedly in their own interests, they are effectively blocked by a number of structural constraints historically put in place to preserve the status quo. It is in this sense that the social structure acts as a "fetter," or exogenous constraint, on individual initiative and the pursuit of human betterment. Change takes place through revolutionary struggle, or when individuals become aware of the structural constraints and mobilize through collective efforts to challenge dominant interests upholding the prevailing power structure. Thus, development should be interpreted as a discontinuous, disruptive, and disorderly process.

In passing, mention should be made of the middle ground taken by "neo-classical" or "rational choice" Marxism. Protagonists, such as Jon Elster (1979, 1985), point to important methodological similarities between sophisticated versions of the neo-classical and traditional Marxian paradigms. For example, while some modes of behavior, such as sharecropping and linkages among markets, are viewed by neo-classicals as inefficient and by traditional Marxists as exploitative, rational choice Marxists interpret them as rational responses of individuals to problems of risk, uncertainty, and economic survival. In a similar vein, the plausibility of the maximization assumption, it is argued, is not entirely divorced from the structure of markets or the mode of production (Bardhan 1988).

From the perspective of neo-classical economics, however, development economics has been blamed for having forsaken the true principles of efficient resource allocation, and in particular, for its hankering after inefficient forms of planning and import substitution industrialization. Through the lens of traditional Marxism, it was not sufficiently radical and failed to address the revolutionary changes needed to achieve authentic forms of development. Furthermore, the ostensible uniqueness of development economics has been increasingly challenged by the "universal/global convergence" thesis, which posits that the laws of economics are inexorable and immutable. In other words, the claim is that there is only one universal economics whose basic tenets apply to rich and poor countries alike. The universal applicability of certain theories, such as labor market segmentation, structural inflation, and dependency, is usually cited in this regard.

Under the circumstances, the death knell of development economics has been constantly ringing because of the resultant self-doubt and its apparent inability to mount a sufficiently vibrant counterattack. At the same time, the growing disenchantment with foreign aid has tended to undermine the credibility of the "mutual benefits" thesis and corresponding ideas about international cooperation and the harmony of interests among nations. As emphasized in Chapter 5, such ideas formed the foundation pillars for the evolution of a modern and self-contained development economics. Even more fatal, in Hirschman's view, were the political crises that faced the developing countries since the 1960s, as evidenced by civil wars, various forms of internecine conflict, and the rise of authoritarianism in some countries. To these influences should be added: (i) the ostensible death of the "Third World" idea; (ii) the concomitant differentiation among developing countries themselves; and (iii) the homogenizing influence produced by the global village and the global spread of capitalism.

As previously indicated, development economics was put on trial for having forsaken the principles of market and price adjustment that form the linchpin of both classical and neo-classical economics. As shown later in this chapter, the case for the prosecution has been championed by both economists with a conservative libertarian bent and more moderate analysts who maintain a dogged faith in the tenets of the standard neo-classical paradigm. The point of intersection rests on the argument that the analysis of development should be based on three related principles: (i) the operation of the market-price mechanism; (ii) the primacy of economic responses to individual incentives; and (iii) minimal government intervention in the market process. In this context, reference is sometimes made to the clash between the political objectives of state elites and the imperative of economic rationality. Policymakers and economic planners in the developing world increasingly realized that market prices were more powerful incentives than ministerial speeches and political rhetoric.

Government Failure and the "Dirigiste Dogma"

In the quest for paradigm dominance in economics and subdisciplines such as development economics, neo-classicism seems to have won out. The market-oriented thrust of the development "counter-revolution" is now reflected in the conditionalities underlying international policy reform, that is, the increasing pressure exerted on developing countries to reduce the scope of government intervention, craft more open policies, and the enlarged use of conditional development assistance as a means of enforcing compliance. This should be interpreted from the perspective of a more pervasive worldview that has perceived excessive government involvement as becoming more glaring in more developed and developing countries alike.

Contextually, many leading economists in North America and Europe contend that the main danger for the future of humanity has arisen from the zeal to bind the economy to various forms of regulation and control. In the major industrial centers, the dominant policy paradigm has been influenced by the generalized belief that undue advantages have been taken by the welfare state and its dispensation of social services. Accordingly, there has been a widespread perception that the smooth functioning of the economic system was unduly hampered by the disincentive effects produced by specific welfare-state measures, such as guaranteed minimum income, social security payments, and aid to families with dependent children (AFDC), or "welfare" for short. The climate of opinion was reflected in Milton Friedman's iconoclastic view that the growth of the welfare state in the United States not only undermined and destroyed the family, but also poisoned the spring of private charitable activity. His *Free To Choose* (1980) reached the conclusion that a winding down of the welfare state would help to eliminate the disincentive effects on employment and would eventually result in a larger national income.

Friedman's position somewhat mirrored the more embracing counter-revolution in economics which gripped North America and Europe. It rested on the belief that the burgeoning public expenditure associated with the rise of the welfare state was the primary cause of escalating budget deficits. In the larger arena of public opinion, confidence in the economic system had been shaken by two decades of stagflation, oil-price shocks, productivity declines, and perceptions of the loss of economic power by the United States and Europe. The period witnessed the emergence of supply-side economics and monetarism as a redressal to what was perceived to be the destructive effects of Keynesian-type demand management and regulatory policies which had been in vogue since the 1960s.

The new orthodoxy was predicated on the need to introduce a novel set of incentives into the economy through dismantling of the welfare state, privatization of economic activity, getting price signals right again, and the general pursuit of laissez-faire economic policies and strategies. The guiding premise is that "big" government results in inefficiencies, reduces personal freedoms, and threatens democracy. It is typically associated with a large and pervasive bureaucracy in which the right of decision making is transferred from individuals, acting on their own behalf and interests, to politicians and government bureaucrats who purportedly make decisions in the public or national interest. From the perspective of modern public choice theory, this results in a kind of behavior in which certain individuals and groups are able to capture property rights from the government, thereby undermining its legitimacy, and hence reducing its capacity to maintain law and contracts and to provide other services necessary for the smooth functioning of the economic system (Buchanan 1975, 1986).

In an early statement of this problem, Mancur Olson (1965) had opined that intervention originated from the lobbying activities of special interest groups and once initiated, they displayed a tendency to feed on themselves and cumulate. The thesis is that private interest groups come into existence as often as they do because of their ability to institute "select incentives." These refer to a class of private goods and benefits that can be restricted solely to those who have joined the group, and therefore denied to non-members. Olson (1982, 1989) also emphasizes the role of "distributional coalitions," which are primarily oriented toward struggles over the distribution of income and wealth. Such coalitions are more prone to spend their resources in redistributing society's resources in favor of their members, whereas if the same resources were to be spent in expanding the growth rate of the economy as a whole, all members of society would benefit.

Thus, once the process begins, beneficiaries usually organize in distributional and other types of coalitions and exert political, financial, and other pressures in order to maximize sectional benefits. As the process unravels, the government bureaucracy develops a momentum and power of its own by tailoring specific spending programs to the needs of beneficiary constituencies and clientele groups. In order to perpetuate the entrenched bureaucratic structure, public officials responsible for each spending program must constantly increase apparent needs for the services supplied. The overall result is that economic policy decisions are rarely made by disinterested economists or selfless public servants, but more often than not emanate from political pressures that are not necessarily consistent with the ideal goals of efficient resource allocation or sustained economic growth.

The overriding perception, therefore, is one of "government failure" rather than the "market failure" emphasized in mainstream neo-classical economics. One of the domain assumptions of what is now termed the "new classical political economy" is that the state is not necessarily "an exogenous force, trying to do good . . . . [but] is at least partially endogenous and the policies it institutes will reflect vested interests in society" (Collander 1984: 2). From this perspective, the neo-classical solution is a poor one for correcting market failure and the economics of Keynes is much more disastrous in its attempts to bring about full employment equilibrium. A central argument is that collective action and democratic participation designed to promote human welfare are incompatible with the greatest amount of individual liberty, which is assumed to be the driving force behind the self-interested motivation of rational economic agents.

Correlatively, notions such as the "general will" or "public interest" are deemed highly restrictive of liberty and impossible to justify without the "sword of Leviathan" or burgeoning state power. Accordingly, the application of decision theory to the solution of problems of collective welfare tends to mask the hidden operation of force and coercion in the centralized institutions of the modern state. In this regard, certain "demons" are thought to constantly plague the abode in which the conventional approach to politics still lives. The house is haunted, it is alleged, by a continued reliance on a utilitarian calculus ("the greatest good for the greatest number"), a related proclivity toward social engineering, and a "technocratic-elitist" type of mentality that makes economists believe that they have a special or unique perspective about the most appropriate social order that other people cannot conceive or understand.

Thus, to the extent that political action can be construed as a process of conflict resolution among individuals and groups, a "contractarian" view of politics becomes a necessity. From this has emerged the concept of a "minimal state" as "the necessary political role involved in enforcing individuals' rights and contracts and in producing those goods and services that are inherently public or collective in nature, including the legal system itself" (Buchanan 1986: 254). This view reflects the classical libertarian concern for protecting the rights and liberty of the individual. Therefore, expansion of the state beyond necessary limits is thought to produce unwarranted government regulation and illegitimate forms of coercion. This perspective suggests that government decision rules should be neutral, so that legislation may not take from some groups and give to others. The requisite rules should be there to enable individuals to organize themselves, and not to give special advantages to some over others (Hayek 1973, 1979).

It is evident that the perspective of the minimalist state rules out the Platonic "guardian state" that redistributes income and wealth in order to improve social welfare, but also practices that have become enshrined in all modern forms of government. There is an abiding faith in individualism, which translates into certain central theoretical tenets. First, economic and social inquiry should begin with propositions about individual behavior and welfare. Second, the concern for the individual basis of choice generates the proposition that individual preferences are the ultimate data. Moreover, such individual values are revealed in both the economic and political market. Third, social preferences do not exist because we cannot make use of social welfare judgments or collective preferences that are not derived from individual preferences. It follows that changes in the institutional framework can be accepted unambiguously only if they can command unanimous consent. Fourth, a system of voluntary exchanges based on market decisions is the most acceptable and desirable.

In the latter context, the claim is that the complexity of the institutional framework makes it possible only to analyze changes and not to make comparisons from scratch. Individuals are able to reap gains from trade only through voluntary exchanges. If A gives up something in exchange for other things that B has, both parties will end up at least as well off as before the exchange took place. In this regard, the concern of theory is not only with behavior in the private market, but also with the rules of "constitutional choice." Given such assumptions, it is argued that the study of government action should become an integral part of a unified theory of behavior in which the same motivational assumptions are made about the behavior of private individuals and public sector agents. The overall implication is that people honor contracts or pursue other ends not because of societal norms or sanctions but rather because the personal cost-benefit calculi suggest that those are the most appropriate or best courses of action.

"New classical" accounts about the disasters of dirigisme and state activism have carried over into the interpretation of government intervention in developing countries. The general consensus is that government failure has significantly outweighed market failure in the majority of such countries. The following types of evidence have been marshalled in support of this claim. First, there is the historical prevalence of exceptionally high-cost public enterprises engaged in economic activities which the private sector can manage more efficiently. Second, reference is made to the pervasive government controls on private sector activity, combined with socially wasteful government programs. Third, such practices, together with public enterprise deficits, have provided fuel for burgeoning government budget deficits. Fourth, such failures of "commission" have been complemented by failures of "omission" such as: the failure to maintain infrastructural facilities; maintenance of fixed nominal exchange rates in the face of rapid domestic inflation; credit rationing and fixing of nominal interest rates well below the rate of inflation, giving rise to negative real interest rates; and heavy reliance on exchange controls and import licensing (World Bank 1983: Srinivasan 1985; Krueger 1990).

The environment has been marked by an increasing propensity of political pressure groups to exert influence on decisions about development policy. As a result, many programs and policies ostensibly designed to help the poor have in fact benefitted the more affluent members of society disproportionately. In this context, some economists view the state in the developing world as passively responding to various forms of "rent-seeking" (DUP) activities (Bhagwati 1982), such as smuggling, underinvoicing, and lobbying to increase trade protection of various interest groups. Rent-seeking is explained by the fact that these policy constituencies are willing to expend resources to capture property rights from the government rather than devoting such resources to raising national output. The modern neo-classical literature on development is replete with accounts of the favoritism and corruption surrounding the bureaucratic allocation of import and investment licenses, and the awarding of government contracts. It highlights the misallocation and wastage of resources that have accompanied the "politics of clientage" in the developing world.

At the international level, therefore, the counter-revolution was translated into a revisionist approach to North-South relations based on an extolment of the advantages of Adam Smith's "invisible hand" over the disadvantages of the "visible hand" of statism. Contextually, the "poverty of development economics" has been attributed to the "policy induced, and thus far from inevitable distortions created by irrational dirigisme" (Lal 1983: 1). In his view, conventional development economics was not only too dogmatic and dirigiste in its orientation, but also supported by a number of "fallacies," including: (i) the belief that the price-market mechanism should be supplanted rather than supplemented; (ii) that the efficiency gains from improved allocation of given resources are quantitatively insignificant; (iii) that the case for free trade lacks validity for developing countries; (iv) that government control of prices, wages, imports, and the distribution of productive assets is a necessary prerequisite for poverty alleviation; and (v) that rational maximizing behavior by economic agents is not a universal phenomenon.

In inveighing against the distortions induced by government policies, Lal places particular emphasis on the failures of economic controls preferred by public bureaucracies in the developing countries. The perverse effects of such controls are attributed to the following factors; (i) their ineffectiveness in achieving the policy objectives to which they were assigned; (ii) counter-productive results, that is, many controls had effects that were opposite to those originally intended; (iii) undesirable spillover effects; and (iv) their excessive cost. In this context, it should also be mentioned that neo-classical economists had marshalled considerable evidence which pointed to the poor design of economic controls (see, for example, Little, Scitovsky, and Scott 1970; Bhagwati 1978: Krueger 1978). This formed the basis for Lal's case against all economic controls and forms of government intervention in industry and trade.

Besides advocating a smaller role for the state, Lal also joins hands with Hayek in arguing that nothing should be done about income distribution. "We cannot . . . identify equity and efficiency as the sole ends of social welfare . . . Other ends such as liberty are also valued. . . . [and] if redistribution entails costs in terms of other social ends which are equally valued it would be foolish to disregard them and concentrate solely on the strictly economic ends" (Lal 1983: 89). This argument can be interpreted to mean that no matter how substantial the welfare gains that are likely to accrue from redistributive policies, no liberty is ever worth trading or sacrificing. Besides the ideological tunnel vision that lies at the heart of such a claim, it can be argued that the possibilities of attaining authentic development depend as much on the sensitivity of the state to distributive justice as on the efficiency and allocative goals stressed in neo-classical economics or the "liberty" that is the focus of "new" classical political economy.

Peter Bauer, another central figure in the counter-revolution, contends that major variations in economic structure and levels of developmental achievement among countries should be explained in terms of corresponding differences in resource endowments and individualistic orientations. This perspective rests on a fundamental belief that the inherent potentials of individuals can be drawn out through the play of market forces. Contextually, he states (1981: 8), "the precise causes of differences in income and wealth are complex and various. . . . [I]n substance such differences result from people's widely differing attitudes and motivations, and also to some extent from chance circumstances. Some people are gifted, hardworking, ambitious, and enterprising, or had farsighted parents, and they are more likely to become well off."

In turn, such attributes are considered responsible for the East Asian success stories, or a demonstration of the validity and correctness of the individualistic free market approach to economic development. In more general terms, the success of these countries is interpreted as a confirmation of the domain assumptions of neo-classical economic theory: that efficient growth can be promoted by relying on free markets, getting prices to reflect real scarcities, liberalizing trade policy, and permitting international price signals to be more freely transmitted to the domestic economy. The overall idea, therefore, is that market-oriented systems with private incentives tend to show a superior performance in terms of growth achievement.

In general, critics of the "dirigiste dogma" such as Hayek, Lal, and Bauer contend that, compared to countries in the more developed sector of the world, most governments in the less developed sector lack the kind of knowledge and data needed for rational intervention, are often less democratic, and often display motives that are at variance with Keynesian-type or structuralist objectives of growth with redistribution and full employment. The response is that markets in both sectors of the world are less free than is commonly supposed, lack the capacity for making rational decisions, and especially in the developing world, not always sufficiently organized to effectively transmit the requisite price signals. There is some element of truth in both the anti-Keynesian and Keynesian/structuralist perspectives. Where the balance is finally drawn becomes a matter of ideology and subjective judgment rather than scientific economic analysis. In any event, the path followed by any particular country is usually constrained by its historical and socio-cultural circumstances.

Finally, the debate was further illumined by what can be construed as an interesting point of intersection among new classical, neo-classical, and Marxian dimensions of political economy. All three perspectives are apparently rooted in the preconception that the state is merely an arena of competition among interest groups and sectoral coalitions. In the Marxian case, forms of unequal or uneven development are directly traceable to the peculiar nature of the class structure found in the periphery. As Amin (1976) argues, this class structure lacks the classic nature of the industrial-capitalist class encountered in advanced industrial centers. His general thesis is that in developing countries members of this class are products of imperialism and colonialism, which created a mercantile and landed bourgeoisie out of the traditional upper and middle classes who were local guardians of international capitalist interests. One result was that the small proletariat in the periphery remained relatively well-off compared to the large numbers of marginalized peasants and urban unemployed. Members of the small proletariat were forced to cooperate with merchants and landlords in order to maintain their position of relative affluence.

In addition, the blockage of local forms of industrial development led to the formation of a modern middle class of "petit bourgeoisie" comprising army officials, government bureaucrats, civil servants, teachers, and similar cadres. In certain regions and countries, they included small traders, "progressive farmers," "middle peasants," and similar groups that come to acquire increasing importance in the absence of meaningful industrialization. They were to become the primary advocates of state capitalism and other forms of "national developmentalism." As previously mentioned, the very requirements of industrialization, the rules of profitability that determine the flow of foreign capital, and the insufficiency of private local finance were factors that fuelled the development of the public sector and an enlarged role for the state in economic activity. The subsequent entrenchment and strengthening of the state bureaucracy further promoted the growth of state capitalism.

A general point of convergence between orthodox and radical heterodox perspectives of development thought and policy is that the implementation of models of centralized planning, state capitalism, national developmentalism, and import substitution industrialization made very little change in the structural conditions governing the internal processes of capital accumulation, and only marginal changes, if any, in income and wealth distribution, employment creation, and poverty redressal. Even in those cases where the size of the socio-economic surplus available on the domestic front was increased substantially, it was eaten up by poorly conceived spending booms and/or otherwise recirculated among the ruling elite and consanguinal cadres in the form of rents or even open corruption. As a result, the larger majority of the population has been consistently denied participation in the distribution of benefits emanating from the development process.

In conclusion, almost all states in the developing world are interventionist in varying degrees. Some are classic cases of the predator or rentier state in which everything is part of a ruler's personal fiefdom and high offices are up for sale to the highest bidders. There are a few cases, however, where governments have demonstrated some measure of institutional coherence in the pursuit of collective development goals. Needless to say, the situation varies from one historical or political context to another. The majority of developing countries have no alternative but to rely on a strong and purposeful government to map out a strategic development course. The intractable theoretical and practical question remains why different types of interventionist states with command over similar resources and instruments of control tend to display extremely divergent development orientations and end up on dissimilar development paths.

The consensual view is that the large majority have remained "regulatory" or "obstructionist" and are far back on the road to becoming authentic "development states" that portray the vision and ability needed to promote essential development goals. Achievement of the latter depends not so much on the size of the government apparatus but more on its quality and effectiveness. This has been demonstrated by the development experience of Nordic and East Asian countries, which have been successful in meshing interventionist schemes with the market mechanism, as well as in nurturing durable coalitions of modernizing interests in the framing of national development agendas. Historically, such coalitions have derived their integrity, credibility, and political legitimacy from the nation's collective aspirations. The centralization of decision making has been effectively combined with a flexibility in dealing with technical and market conditions. Goals and policies have been constantly interpreted and reinterpreted on the basis of organizational networks between party organizations, public officials, and private entrepreneurs.

This is not meant to suggest that what has worked in the successful corporatist models of the Nordic countries and the Sinitic world, especially Japan, can or should be replicated in the late-developing world. In the first place, the social and cultural homogeneity in both regions have made the forging of a political consensus much easier. Second, the tensions that constantly arise between the articulated interests of organized classes, pressure groups, and the state elite responsible for policy formulation and execution cannot be resolved in a context-free or institutionally neutral manner. The state remains a "strategic actor in the game of mixed conflict and cooperation among other groups" (Bardhan 1988: 65). Under the circumstances, the nature of developmental outcomes ultimately depends on its ability to resolve conflicts and make compromises in an open political milieu. The openness of the political process determines the nature and effectiveness of the development delivery system and the extent to which consensual relationships can be established and nurtured with labor, business, people's organizations, and the rural sector.

End-Game Hegemony and the New "Global Consensus"

Many ideas perish or come to grief not so much because they are refuted by argument but more on account of extraneous influences related to time, place, circumstances, politics, and ideology. As argued in this book, the study of development, like any other theoretical or practical endeavor, cannot escape the sociology of knowledge, or the problems inherent in the symbiotic relationship between the growth of knowledge and the paradigmatic grip of dominant interests. In the final analysis, appraisal of the success or failure of theories and policies cannot be meaningfully divorced from the more embracing historical, socio-psychological, and political contexts in which they emerge, develop, change, and even die.

From this perspective, misgivings about the corpus of mainstream development economics were not only caused by what were perceived to be widespread failures in attempts to implement policies and strategies that were its offshoots. The field was also dealt a severe blow by a series of doubts that have been raised about the validity and efficacy of the "mutual benefits" thesis and the aid-centered development orientation in which it was ostensibly grounded. Contextually, at least three important foundation pillars undergirding the evolution of development thought and policy need reiteration. First, the theoretical focus of the nascent development economics was encapsulated in a belief or abiding faith in the ability of the benevolent state to correct market failures and effectively guide the investment process on to a path of self-sustained economic growth. Even in terms of its own internal development, the field never gained full independence and has always operated in the shadow of mainstream classical, neo-classical, Keynesian, and Marxian political economy. To some extent, this explains why its recapture has been easy.

Second, and at a more practical level, the field was developed mostly by economists in the West as a means of rationalizing the extended flow of financial resources from North to South. This, in turn, was linked to the strong belief that it was not only in the North's general interest to promote the development of the South, but that a positive-sum game would result from the corresponding benefits accruing to both parties from a truly symmetrical and interdependent world order. As previously emphasized, the rationale was stated in terms of the need to promote human solidarity based on "mutual interests" or benefits. Underlying this expectation was also an implicit moral obligation for the rich to help the poor, even though there might well be an enlightened self-interest in such a stance.

Third, the optimistic vision could only become practical reality within the ambit of the institutional pillars of the extant global political economy, or what Meier calls the "international public sector" (1984: 11). The reference here is to the matrix of institutions consisting of the Bretton Woods system (World Bank and IMF), the General Agreement on Tariffs and Trade (GATT), and the Organization for Economic Cooperation and Development (OECD). As alluded to in Chapter 4, the Bretton Woods institutions were designed to promote the multiple objectives of full employment, stable exchange rates, and freer and expanding world trade. These and others came to represent the ideological pillars of Western liberalism, and their policies have collectively reflected the philosophical underpinnings of a liberal international economic order.

A basic assumption underlying its creation was that the growth in the world financial and trading system would in time overcome the problems of international inequality and poverty through the massive transfer of private capital and official aid to the developing countries. Over time, the international order matured through a globalization process, the creation of an array of transnational economic linkages, and an increasing openness of national economies based on the integration of commodity and factor markets. Capital accumulation has increasingly transcended national boundaries, so that it has now become difficult to identify the countries of origin. At the same time, considerable skepticism arose about the ability of the changing global system to transform the asymmetrical relationship between rich and poor nations into a mutually beneficial partnership. Under the circumstances, challenges to the mutual benefits thesis have emanated from all sides of the ideological spectrum, and have been supported by rival interpretations of events taking place in the world order itself.

One set of arguments rests on the claim that morality cannot be reconciled with the mutual interests of rich and poor nations, since the activities of the two typically point in different directions. Evidence of this is provided by the fact that powerful governments in the North have been wont to support repressive and authoritarian regimes in the South in the name of mutual interests, that is, in terms of foreign policy and strategic considerations. Such support continued even when it became clear that such regimes were not bent on promoting the welfare of the majority of the people. In situations where the North helps to install and keep in power governments that are hostile to the poor and to the idea of guaranteeing their basic human rights, it is meaningful to ask whether the more developed world should not in fact bear some of the blame for the persistence of such inequities. Thus, while the need to help developing countries can be justified on moral grounds, the same moral principles cannot be used as a justification for keeping repressive and corrupt governments in power.

Correlatively, there may well be some inconsistency between aiding governments in developing countries, as distinct from the people, and especially the poor, living there. Most ethical arguments are meant to apply to individual persons rather than to governments or nation states. The common practice has been to anthropomorphize nations, that is, treating them as if they were individuals, and extending to them the same arguments on the basis of per capita income attainment. This approach has been dubbed as the "fiction of all nations throbbing as symbolic individuals in existence - 'fantasie' for short" (Sen 1981b: 477). It is this common practice of confusing governments with people that has precipitated the criticism of what Bauer calls "Third Worldism." As he states, "official aid does not go to poor people. . . . it goes instead to their rulers. . . . Indeed to support rulers on the basis of the poverty of their subjects is more likely to encourage policies of impoverishment than deter them" (1981: 111).

Across perspectival viewpoints, therefore, there has been no firm reason to believe that the philosophy of mutual interests or benefits based on a redistribution of purchasing power from North to South would automatically lead to a trickle down of benefits to the masses of the people. The realities of distributive justice, or lack of it, in the majority of developing countries continue to demonstrate that those who are well off tend to appropriate a disproportionate share of the benefits accruing from public expenditures. Since the urban and upper class "capture" may also be true of a number of countries in the more developed sector of the world, it may well reflect a universal or immutable law about human nature!

Be that as it may, the past few years have witnessed a considerable disenhancement with bilateral aid. In particular, U.S. foreign aid has declined substantially, with the lion's share now flowing to a few select countries. At the same time, the internationalization of capital proceeds apace, and most international resources flowing from rich to poor nations are now being channeled through the multilateral lending agencies, or "international public sector." In the overall scheme of things, the activities of transnational corporations (TNCs) now represent an essential symbol of what we may term the "globalization of being," and are thought to embody the logic inherent in the international expansion of capitalism. TNCs have now become the most efficient purveyors of goods and services, technology, knowledge, and finance on a world scale.

Transnational trends in production, trade, and payments have effectively transformed the practice of comparative advantage on a global scale. The creation of the liberal international order was predicated on specialization based on relative factor proportions and comparative advantage in trade among different companies and countries. For decades, however, such trade has been transcended by intra-corporate transfers within TNCs. Since they typically combine the highest, or capital-intensive, technology with least-cost labor, the capacity of developing countries to compete on an autonomous basis in the international area may have been profoundly compromised. The 600 biggest companies in the world - called the "billion-dollar club" because their annual sales exceed one billion dollars - still create more than one-fifth of the world's total value-added in agriculture and manufacturing.

By the early 1970s, the direct production of transnationals in different countries had already exceeded total world trade. By the early 1980s, the combined sales of the world's top 200 corporations were already equivalent to a third of world gross domestic product (GDP) and one and a half times the total production of developing countries. A United Nations study has reported that more than two-thirds of the global trade in minerals, commodities, and food products (especially exports from developing countries) is controlled by TNCs (Clairmonte and Cavanaugh 1984). The dire consequence for the developing world is that only about one-tenth of the final value of such products accrues, on average, to its producers. Furthermore, the transnationalization of capital has come to span the globe like a colossus. The vicissitudes surrounding such flows have had a dramatic impact on domestic development in almost every country, especially in the developing world.

As reported by the United Nations (1994), total net capital inflows (the sum of net foreign investment, net credit, grants, and other net financing) to the capital-importing countries in the developing world reached $154 billion in 1993. Net payments of dividend and interest amounted to $63 billion, or approximately 41 percent of the total. The total net transfer to the developing world amounted to

$91 billion, the highest figure ever recorded. Most of this took the form of private short-term capital and private direct foreign investment, with official credits lagging far behind. A dozen or so countries in Asia and Latin America, characterized by the international financial community as "emerging markets," received the lion's share of the capital inflow. The majority of developing countries have not been touched by the growth in financial transfers, and official development assistance (ODA) continues to be essential, especially for the poorest ones.

In cases where money is borrowed from private commercial sources, the resource flows are not necessarily determined by borrowers' demand, but more by factors operating on the supply side, including developments in world capital markets. A significant factor is related to shifts in the sources of net international savings among individuals and groups with different asset preferences. The relatively high financial return that can be potentially realized by investing in capital-poor nations rather than in their capital-rich counterparts has not changed the picture. This is due, in part, to the persistence of a perception that investing in some regions of the developing world, especially Africa, is fraught with greater political and commercial risk.

In the perfect international capital markets described in textbooks, private capital would flow naturally from the capital-rich core industrial nations to the capital-poor ones in the periphery, since returns would be greater in the latter. However, imperfections in world capital markets have historically limited the flow of private capital (at least to some world regions). This has spurred the officialization of development financing. In the unravelling of this process, the poorer countries of the world have had no alternative but to depend on official investment and concessional capital from the "international public sector." While these loans come at lower interest rates and less stringent borrowing terms compared to private capital, the conditions governing their orchestration continue to raise a fundamental issue about the ability of borrowing countries to formulate and execute sovereign development policies and strategies on an autonomous basis.

The philosophy of macroeconomic stabilization and structural adjustment has hardened from a "Washington consensus" to a "global consensus" or "universal convergence" of ideas about the most appropriate development styles that all countries should embrace. The corresponding list of mandated policy reforms is now ubiquitous, and includes: (i) achievement of internal and external balance through reductions in macroeconomic financial imbalance and payments deficits; (ii) financial liberalization and rationalization of monetary and credit policies; (iii) "getting prices right" by aligning domestic prices with those obtained in world markets; (iv) as a corollary, relative price correction, mainly through devaluation; (v) liberalization of trade and foreign investments; and (vi) institutional reform, domestic market deregulation, and privatization of state enterprises.

A fair comment is that the ideological presuppositions, values, and conceptual beliefs undergirding this list of policies are synergistic with those that now guide policy reforms in the more developed countries in the North. As we have also emphasized, the preferred policy mixes are a collective offshoot of mainstream economic theory, or an eclectic admixture of classical, neo-classical, Keynesian, monetarist, and "new" classical political economy (see David 1985). As such, the consensual economic policy paradigm seems to have turned a blind eye to the corpus of development economics, or has dismissed it as an irritable diversion from the harsh realities of economic rationality. If this is true, it is perhaps a reflection of the lack of practical success of conventional forms of development thought and policy and a concomitant decline in the original optimistic expectations of the "development revolution," at least as conveyed through the analytical visions and interpretations of its pioneers.

Nevertheless, the developmental consequences attendant upon the policies supporting the consensus remain a hotly debated issue. While the verdict is not finally out, there has been a growing concern that stabilization and adjustment programs tend to place a needlessly heavy burden on the poorest people. Due to the "conditionalities" mandated under such programs, government budgets have been squeezed, and welfare programs, food subsidies, and other public spending have been cut. In some countries, the poor are now worse off in terms of most objective indicators--unemployment, nutrition, infant mortality, and the overall quality of life. Furthermore, the austerity measures have been known to create political tension in a number of countries where riots have followed on the heels of attempts to raise the price of food and other basic necessities.

A counter-argument is that the conditionalities do not constitute anything economically or normally wrong, but are simply a consequence of borrowers' voluntary acts of economic mismanagement. Through the lens of the international public sector, an element of *coercion* is needed to counteract the private pecuniary and rent-seeking agendas of ruling elites. By contrast, many officials and groups in borrowing countries feel that coercion is either counterproductive or an unacceptable infringement on national *sovereignty*. Taking the middle ground, economic reforms and conditionalities cannot be sustained unless they are reflective of collaborative efforts, that is, acceptable to all players in the game. In the final analysis, conditionality remains a judgmental matter that depends not only on the circumstances and actions being sought, but ultimately on whose *values* should prevail.

Chapter 12

Alternative Futures

The competing paradigms and perspectives examined in this book clearly demonstrate that while ideas emanate from life, people tend to have different interpretations of life's experiences due to the differential influences of beliefs, preconceptions, and interests. In both academic and policy discourse, allowance has to be constantly made for the fact that alternative interpretations of the same phenomenon, such as development, may turn out to be incompatible. Thus, if destructive conflict is to be minimized, feasible compromises have to be forged and bridges continuously built across apparently conflicting perspectives. A modicum of tolerance for other people's positions, however reluctantly conceded, is the first principle of enlightened conversation.

Knowledge grows through an unending process of interpretation and reinterpretation of dominant interpretations. This involves a moving synthesis between perception and reality, theory and practice, and a constant juxtaposition of rival worldviews, theories, models, and policy scenarios. This involves critical reflection and recognition of persistence of the past, or the motive force provided by historical consciousness. In order to clearly discern the relative strengths of contemporary claims to truth and possibilities for future change, they have to be reinterpreted in the context of the truth claims and prior exaggerations that either support them or against which they might have revolted. What drives interpretation is a recognition that ideas are perennially changing and the fact that their collision represents an inevitable feature of human existence itself.

Whither the Conversation?

The dominant discourse now consists of a refinement of the postulates of neo-classical economics to deal with questions arising during the course of the development transition. It remains grounded in the ontological belief and epistemological presupposition that the laws of economics - such as those pertaining to capital accumulation, comparative advantage, and the market-price mechanism - have universal validity. The apparent neo-classical recapture of the development discourse raises some fundamental questions not only about interpretation of the development phenomenon but also about the future course of the development conversation. An array of issues surrounding the sociology of knowledge, economic theory, political economy, and hermeneutics take on added significance.

While it is too late in the day to provide any details in this book, a few general comments are proffered as a means of highlighting the nature of the impasse and suggesting some ideas that might guide the future course of interpretation and research. In this context, it should be noted that both Marxian and neo-classical perspectives of thought have traditionally rested on the premise that it is possible to generate broadly applicable theories and models. While Marxians attribute generality to the laws of historical motion, neo-classicism is embedded in supposedly universal postulates about human nature and behavior. The lesson from history is that development change based on such reductionist approaches is bound to fail. The primary reason is that their ideological preconceptions, methods, and assumptions become irrelevant when dealing with important historical specificities and localized contexts of socio-cultural and ecological dynamics.

Needless to say, cultural diversity is endemic to human history, which does not move in straight lines. There is no single key to the future or the past. Unlike the natural sciences, the laws of history do not open doors reflecting uniform causal chains which repeat themselves and can be formulated into general laws. In particular, the neo-classical paradigm essentially consists of a set of formalized economic models or "plausible typologies" that are supposed to lend intellectual rigor to, and provide a test of, the logical relations and consistency of specific sets of ideas. However, the fact that a model can be completely specified says nothing about the rightness or importance of the ideas on which it relies. Development problems are unlike those of chess, rule-governed games, or mathematics, which can be settled by the hypothetico-deductive method. They are of the same genre as questions about the ends of life and therefore cannot be arbitrated by recourse to even the most sophisticated mathematical or empirical reasoning.

Nevertheless, both modes of analysis and interpretation can help to throw light on the dynamics of developmental change. The direction of macroeconomic causality plays a pivotal role in determining the success or otherwise of most models. This, in turn, depends on the extent to which they are able to incorporate empirical generalizations about the development process. The manipulation of time-series and cross-sectional data can sometimes reveal significant general patterns that may be impossible to discern otherwise, thereby enhancing explanatory power or adequacy. However, forms of quantification do not provide the only answers to questions relating to causal structure. Besides the economist's time-honored criteria, such as internal consistency, coherence, and simplicity, judgments about the appropriateness of models cannot avoid confronting issues pertaining to historical relevance, the political conjuncture, and the institutional ordering of society.

Such factors have a critical role to play in selecting which models or theories best fit the situation at hand. It is probably easier to mathematize or quantify a false theory than to confront reality. In both mainstream economics and the development discourse, the plethora of theoretical and econometric models has undermined the necessity of either directly engaging in honest and open-ended conversation or dialogue with the human agents being studied, and/or conducting historical, institutional, and socio-cultural research in specific behavioral contexts. Inherent in the ruling epistemology of development economics is an implicit belief that all personal and human biases must be removed from the analysis.

However, the thralldom of scientific objectivity and technique has resulted in a one-sided and monologic discourse. As a consequence, development economists have distanced themselves from the human social objects of interpretation, their language, and how they view their own situations. A need exists, therefore, to tie theoretical and empirical concepts to the daily socio-economic round, and ordinary descriptions of human actions, events, and situations. This is germane to the fact that the success or failure of any particular economic arrangement ultimately depends on what it does to the lives of human beings.

From the very inception, development economics has been a developed country subject. Its major postulates have been shaped in the corridors of Washington, on the banks of the Cam (Cambridge), the Cherwell (Oxford), the Thames (London), the Charles (Harvard, Massachusetts Institute of Technology) and on the shores of Lake Laguna (Stanford University). At the extreme, one offshoot of this embeddedness in the temperate zone is that the dominant discourse is more often than not predicated on the need for analytical tractability. What is forgotten is that the human economic agents who are the objects of interpretation and understanding do not represent inconcrete and disconnected entities "out there," in the sense of being isolated from their environment in space and time, or from the theoretical and empirical constructs of would-be interpreters.

Both the growth of development knowledge and the future of development economics hinge on the imperative of conducting a more thoroughgoing interpretive analysis of, and conversation about, the perennial antinomies that continue to militate against authentic, or people-centered, human progress. These include, inter alia, the increasing gap between the rich and poor both within and across countries, between global prosperity and human misery, the powerful and the powerless, and ultimately between nature and nurture. The normative lesson revolves around the need for sustained improvements in the overall quality of life through policy priorities designed to restructure the "quality" of economic growth, create adequate employment, eliminate the most glaring forms of poverty and inequality, and promote environmental integrity.

These human goals of development cannot be effectuated unless a moving or dynamic synergy is forged between the historically and analytically separated "subjects" or "objects" of the development conversation. A useful starting point inheres in the necessity of effectively incorporating the needs, functionings, and capabilities of the distanciated objects who live on the banks of the Amazon, Demerara, Ganges, Nile, and Zimbabwe, or otherwise on the streets of Accra, Calcutta, Kingston, Lagos, and Rio de Janeiro. This is not a statement about human nature, since basic aspirations and motivations are probably the same throughout the globe. Rather, it is a plea for greater sensitivity to perceptions of those who suffer on a daily basis. According to World Bank estimates, they include more than 1.3 billion people in the developing world who live on one dollar a day and less.

More generally, the missive is that a concerted effort should be made in both development thought and policy to recapture what Aristotle a long time ago identified as phronesis. In Book IV of his *Nichomachean Ethics*, a sharp distinction is drawn between *episteme* ("scientific knowledge") and *techne* ("technical knowledge") on the one hand, and *phronesis* ("practical or ethical knowledge"), on the other. The latter differs from conventional forms of "objective knowledge" in the sense that it involves cognitive processes through which theoretical and technical reasoning are integrated into everyday experience and human action. It is not detached from the interpreter, but involves or engages his or her human consciousness, practical life, or *praxis*. From this perspective, the development conversation has faltered because of what Gadamer (1979) terms the "deformation of praxis" and the "falsehood of modern consciousness" in the contemporary world order.

At issue is a dialectical tension in which the very possibilities for the exercise of phronesis have become increasingly problematic, if not totally undermined or compromised. This is exemplified by the failure to directly confront what may be interpreted as a "deep moral crisis" engulfing a world order that is not prepared to do enough about inequality of opportunity and persistent poverty in a situation where global resources are available to turn the situation around. Breaking the impasse must ultimately rest on an optimistic belief or hope that it is still possible and desirable to foster the kinds of enlightened interpretive communities that are capable and willing to engage in a transparent dialogue about the norms that ought to govern our practical lives.

In a market-oriented environment, the traditional standard of promoting equal opportunity based on individualism, competition, and achievement motivation, while desirable, is oftentimes dehumanizing since the resultant striving may degenerate into a "rat race" based on a guiding premise of "win or perish." An environment defined by fewer "races" and more "dances" is likely to be much more pleasant and desirable because it combines the competitive values of the market with a more humanistic and dialogical consciousness based on social cooperation and solidarity. Thus, in what Okun (1975) terms the "big trade-off" between "equality" and "efficiency," or "rights" versus "dollars," efficiency and money will always win out over equality and rights. The plea for a more enlightened and emancipatory conversation about development is predicated on the imperative of according equal footing to efficiency, the freedom to choose (liberty), equality, justice, and fairness.

The Economic Challenge

The success or failure of countries in achieving authentic economic development is intimately bound up with their ability to combine growth-promoting strategies with others designed to remove debilitating structural and institutional bottlenecks from the economy and society. This involves a multidimensional or organic process of change inculcating output expansion, capacity utilization, and supporting changes in components that define the overall quality of life. As emphasized by Senghaas (1978, 1982), such a broad-based pattern of development inheres in the necessity to build viable, cohesive, and structurally differentiated economies. Despite inter-country differences in size, history, culture, and resources endowments, it is still meaningful to outline some broad elements of a coherent development strategy:

(1) restructuring economic growth by strengthening and diversifying productive capacity, improving income levels, and the pattern of its distribution;

(2) broad-based agricultural development designed to augment domestic food supplies and the production of raw materials for industrial use;

(3) development of an internal industrial capacity for producing goods to meet basic consumption needs and the demands for inputs into the production of intermediate and capital goods, as the case may be;

(4) supporting policies designed to promote the maximum feasible use of locally available resources, the design and construction of effective infrastructure and mass communication systems, the adaptation of existing technology and the invention of new technology that is appropriate to local needs;

(5) extensive reform of public expenditure patterns to provide an adequate mix of public goods to meet people's essential needs, such as decentralized and functional systems of public health, education, training, and other basic social services;

(6) the building up of an autonomous institutional capacity based on relevant requirements at the economic, political, and socio-cultural levels.

The elements of such a strategy are consonant with the economic structures built in the more developed sector of the world. A common feature of this experience is that all successful cases of economic development have involved a high degree of differentiation in the production structure and an organic interlinking of various sectors and subsectors. As emphasized in Chapter 6, a relatively high degree of congruence exists between the accumulation process, productive activities, employment levels, income distribution, and the structure of consumption. In the dénouement of this process, most people have been productively employed and are able to use their earned incomes to provide for their basic needs.

This suggests that a symbiotic relationship has to be forged and maintained between two basic structural elements of the overall development process. One relates to the imperative of guaranteeing rapid capital accumulation (physical, human, and social) to promote sustainable economic growth. The other connotes the prerequisite of steady and concerted improvements in the overall quality of life as a condition of economic justice and human freedom. The authenticity of the development process will ultimately depend on the kind of growth path that is pursued, or whether a balanced process of capital formation can be made synergistic with appropriate levels of resource mobilization and utilization, as well as distributive justice. It is a truism that there is no automatic tendency for the income and wealth distribution to improve with economic development. Under the circumstances, the overall objective becomes one of "restructuring economic growth," or improving the "quality" of GNP. This entails a progressive linkage to policies aimed at changing the structure of asset ownership through improved access by the poor and disadvantaged groups.

A central element in the autocentric development strategy centers around the need for internal restructuring of the production system and the achievement of a relatively high degree of sectoral articulation. The latter refers to the coherent intermeshing or balanced expansion of all appropriate production sectors. At one level, this connotes a possibility of achieving a differentiated pattern of agricultural and related resource-based development through the production, where applicable, of food and cash crops, livestock, fisheries, and forest products. The objective is to augment domestic food supplies and, where circumstances permit, to ensure a continuous supply of raw materials for local industrial processing. This necessitates the creation of an agrarian structure that is open and receptive to the forces of modernization based on: a modification of plantation agriculture; a predominance of small and medium-sized farms utilizing innovative techniques; eradication of village and rural penury; and the receptivity of landowners and tenants to institutional reforms and technical innovations.

At another level, and linked to broad-based agricultural transformation, is the necessity to establish an internal industrial capacity for producing goods catering to the mass consumption needs of the population as well as the demand for intermediate and capital goods. This entails the creation or upgrading of industries producing light and heavy industrial goods, such as manufactures, textiles, building materials, metal products, machine tools, petro-chemicals, and so on. As previously indicated, the nature of the sectoral transformation process, commodity mix, and scope of production ultimately depends on country-specific contexts. In general terms, however, its success or failure will hinge on the types of linkages that can be forged among various production sectors, including: agriculture (plantation, large-scale, and traditional), the rural non-farm sector, and the urban sector (formal and informal).

As the process of agricultural development gathers momentum, a variety of forward, backward, and final demand linkages can be forged with other sectors. Forward linkages can be effectively created as the supply of farm products overtakes local needs and demand requirements. Excess supply at the farm or local level will tend to induce a variety of non-farm activities such as processing, marketing, and transportation. In addition, backward linkages can be created through the increased demand for various kinds of farm inputs. The latter will in turn induce the establishment of non-farm economic activities geared toward the increased production of seeds, fertilizers, and agricultural implements. A self-sustaining process of sectoral development cannot take place in the absence of such linkages. The linkages must also be appropriate ones, otherwise the dynamic multiplier effects on the local economy will be lost and the potential gains from sectoral development will not be equitably distributed.

In the typical case of a growing economy with an advancing agricultural sector, the linkage processes tend to be associated primarily with employment creation in large cities and other urban places at the expense of the rural non-farm sector. Such a pattern can be reversed by policies designed to reorient spatial flows of goods and resources toward rural production and industrialization. The experience across developing countries has amply demonstrated that regional and rural-based industries tend to have greater effects on employment and income compared to industries in other sectors of the economy. Within such industries, the following activities have been found to generate the greatest beneficial effects on employment: manufacture of furniture, clothing, footwear, wood products, pottery, chinaware, leather, and leather goods. The most important indirect effects on employment seem to be produced by activities that are closely linked to labor-intensive agriculture, such as food and beverages. These, together with leather production, typically make the highest contribution in terms of raising income levels. Smaller industries also tend to have a greater employment potential compared to larger establishments (Michel and Ochel 1978).

A burning question concerns the relationship between the imperative of internal restructuring and the equally important development strategy of export-led growth. Smaller countries may have no alternative but to adopt an export-led growth strategy, while larger ones tend to have more leeway in orienting their industrialization toward domestic markets. Even where countries are dependent on foreign trade or have a dualistically structured economy, they cannot avoid the critical endogenous choices inherent in building internally coherent economic systems based on a gradual transition toward the finishing of goods originally exported in an unprocessed form. If this happens, the mix of exported products will become increasingly diversified, and to an extent compatible with a maturing domestic economy. The worst development scenario is where subscription to a full-blown export orientation leaves a country's production structure distorted, and its available resources untapped or misdirected.

Finally, the creation of coherent, differentiated, and integrated economic systems calls for a policy framework based on consistency planning and programming (Pyatt and Thorbecke 1976). This will ensure that the multifaceted goals of authentic development (economic growth, full employment, income distribution, basic needs fulfillment, and poverty alleviation) are suitably modelled and interpreted. Such a framework also provides the basis for evaluating the effects of economic change at several disaggregated levels: nationally, within regions and individual economic sectors, and in the institutions of society. Within a given economy, planners and policymakers would be able to specify a set of interrelated subsystems and major linkages among strategic variables both within and between them. It would then become possible to incorporate those policy instruments that can be manipulated to move the entire economy or parts of it in alternative or desirable directions.

A basic premise is that systemic transformation in the direction of authentic human development requires coherence and consistency among the policies, strategies, and programs that constitute the economic development matrix. National efforts should be integrated with several programmatic layers beneath this level, with the latter oriented toward specific local conditions. It is precisely at the local level that the managerial, administrative, and other attitudinal bottlenecks tend to be the greatest. It is also at the local and individual levels that various economic, political, social and other structural changes are likely to have the most profound and lasting impact.

The point of emphasis is that the policy formulation and planning system should be of a kind that allows for the coordination of its individual parts in accordance with the objectives a country sets itself in terms of national, regional, and local development. We hasten to add that this does not require the establishment of a giant bureaucratic machinery for policy formulation and planning. Rather, the exact opposite is the case. The activities of governments and policymakers at the national level will have to be coordinated with people's organizations and related decentralized institutional arrangements.

It is now part of the conventional wisdom that genuine participation of the people is a necessary prerequisite for achieving authentic development. This means that they have to be effectively involved in the policy formulation, planning, and implementation process. If national development is to move in tandem with people's aspirations and needs, then open consultations must constantly take place with representative organizations such as employers' associations, trade unions, local authorities, and village councils. It goes without saying that policies tend to work more effectively when the requisite institutional support can be garnered. This involves the strengthening of older institutions and the setting up of new ones. Examples include clear legislation about property rights, financial institutions for self-help programs, small farmers and industrialists, and indigenous non-governmental entities.

Bibliography

Adelman, Irma. 1961. *Theories of Economic Growth and Development.* Stanford, CA: Stanford University Press.

Adelman, Irma, and Cynthia Taft Morris. 1973. *Economic Growth and Social Equity in Developing Countries.* Stanford, CA: Stanford University Press.

Ahluwalia, Montek. 1974. "Income Inequality: Some Dimensions of the Problem." In *Redistribution with Growth*, edited by Hollis Chenery et al., 3-37. London: Oxford University Press.

Alexander, Sidney. 1952. "Effects of a Devaluation on a Trade Balance." *IMF Staff Papers*, 2: 263-70.

Amin, Samir. 1974. *Accumulation on a World Scale: A Critique of the Theory of Underdevelopment.* New York: Monthly Review Press.

______. 1976. *Uneven Development: An Essay on Social Formations of Peripheral Capitalism.* New York: Monthly Review Press.

Amsden, Alice. 1989. *Asia's Next Giant: South Korea and Late Industrialization.* New York: Oxford University Press.

Arndt, H.W. 1987. *Economic Development: The History of an Idea.* Chicago: University of Chicago Press.

Arrow, Kenneth. 1962. "The Economic Implications of Learning by Doing." *Review of Economic Studies*, 29: 155-73.

Atkinson, Anthony. 1991. "Comparing Poverty Rates Internationally: Lessons From Recent Studies in Developed Countries." *World Bank Economic Review*, 5: 3-21.

Bacha, Edmar. 1978. "The Interpretation of Unequal Exchange from Prebisch-Singer to Emmanuel." *Journal of Development Economics*, 5: 319-30.

Bairoch, Paul. 1975. *The Economic Development of the Third World since 1900.* London: Methuen.

Balassa, Bela. 1978. "Exports and Economic Growth: Further Evidence." *Journal of Development Economics*, 5: 181-89.

_____. 1979. "A Stages Approach to Comparative Advantage." In *Economic Growth and Resources*, edited by Irma Adelman. London: Macmillan.

_____. 1982. "Structural Adjustment Policies in Developing Economies." *World Development*, 10: 23-38.

Balassa, Bela, and Associates. 1971. *The Structure of Protection in Developing Countries*. Baltimore, MD: Johns Hopkins University Press.

Baldwin, Robert. 1956. "Patterns of Development in Newly Settled Regions." *Manchester School of Economic and Social Studies*, 24: 161-79.

Baran, Paul. 1957. *The Political Economy of Economic Growth*. New York: Monthly Review Press.

Bardhan, Pranab. 1982. "Economic Growth in a Lewis-Type World." In *The Theory and Experience of Economic Development*, edited by M. Gersovitz, et al. London: Allen and Unwin.

_____. 1988. "Alternative Approaches to Development Economics." In *Handbook of Development Economics*, Vol. 1, edited by Hollis Chenery and T.N. Srinivasan, 40-71. Amsterdam: North Holland.

Bauer, Peter T. 1976. *Dissent on Development*. London: Weidenfeld and Nicolson.

_____. 1981. *Equality, the Third World and Economic Delusion*. London: Weidenfeld and Nicolson.

_____. 1984. *Reality and Rhetoric: Studies in the Economics of Development*. London: Weidenfeld and Nicolson.

Baumol, William. 1959. *Economic Dynamics*. New York: Macmillan.

Beckford, George. 1972. *Persistent Poverty: Underdevelopment in Plantation Economies in the Third World*. New York: Oxford University Press.

Bhagwati, Jagdish. 1966. *The Economics of Underdeveloped Countries*. New York: McGraw Hill.

_____. 1978. *Foreign. Trade Regimes and Economic Development: Anatomy and Consequences of Exchange Control Regimes*. Cambridge, MA: Ballinger.

_____. 1982. "Directly Unproductive Profit-Seeking (DUP) Activities." *Journal of Political Economy*, 90: 988-1002.

_____. 1987. "Outward Orientation: Trade Issues." In *Growth-Oriented Adjustment Programs*, edited by V. Corbo, M. Goldstein, and M. Khan, 257-90. Washington, DC: International Monetary Fund and World Bank.

Boeke, J.H. 1953. *Economics and Economic Policy in Dual Societies*. New York: Institute of Pacific Relations.

Boserup, Ester. 1965. *The Conditions of Agricultural Growth: Economics of Agrarian Change under Population Pressure*. London: Allen and Unwin.

_____. 1981. *Population and Technological Change: A Study of Long-Term Trends*. Chicago: University of Chicago Press.

Boulding, Kenneth. 1952. "Religious Foundations of Economic Progress." *Public Affairs*, 14: 1-9.

Bradford, C., Jr. 1987. "Trade and Structural Change: NICs, and Next Tier NICs as Transitional Economies." *World Development*, 15: 299-316.

Brenner, Robert. 1977. "Origins of Capitalist Development: A Critique of Neo-Smithian Marxism." *New Left Review*, 104: 25-92.

Buchanan, James M. 1975. *The Limits of Liberty*. Chicago: University of Chicago Press.

_____. 1986. *Liberty, Market and State: Political Economy in the 1980s*. New York: New York University Press.

Cardoso, F., and E. Faletto. 1979. *Dependency and Development in Latin America*. Berkeley, CA: University of California Press.

Chase-Dunn, Christopher. 1989. *Global Formation: Structures of the World Economy*. Oxford: Blackwell.

Chenery, Hollis B. 1953. "Application of Investment Criteria." *Quarterly Journal of Economics*, 67: 76-96.

_____. 1961. "Comparative Advantage and Development Policy." *American Economic Review*, 51: 18-51.

_____. 1975. "The Structuralist Approach to Development Policy." *American Economic Review*, 65: 310-16.

_____. 1983. "The Evolution of Development Planning." Discussion Paper No. 158. Cambridge, MA: Harvard Institute for International Development.

Chenery, Hollis B., and Michael Bruno. 1962. "Development Alternatives in an Open Economy: The Case of Israel." *Economic Journal*, 72: 79-103.

Chenery, Hollis B., and Paul Clark. 1964. *Interindustry Economics*. New York: Wiley.

Chenery, Hollis B., and A. Strout. 1966. "Foreign Assistance and Economic Development." *American Economic Review*, 56: 679-733.

Chenery, Hollis B., and M. Syrquin. 1975. *Patterns of Development 1950-1970*. London: Oxford University Press

Chenery, Hollis B., and Lance Taylor. 1968. "Development Patterns Among Countries and Over Time." *Review of Economics and Statistics*, 50: 390-416.

Chenery, Hollis B., et al. 1974. *Redistribution with Growth*. London: Oxford University Press.

Chichilinsky, G. 1980. "Basic Goods, the Effects of Commodity Transfers and the International Order." *Journal of Development Economics*, 7: 505-19.

Chichilinsky, G., and G. Heal. 1986. *The Evolving International Economy*. Cambridge: Cambridge University Press.

Clairmonte, F., and J. Cavanagh. 1984. "Transnational Corporations and Services." *Trade and Development*, 5: 215-73.

Clark, Colin. 1940. *The Condition of Economic Progress*. London: Macmillan.

Colander, D., ed. 1984. *Neoclassical Political Economy*. Cambridge, MA: Ballinger.

Cole, Ken. 1995. *Understanding Economics*. London: Pluto Press.

Cole, Ken, J. Cameron, and C. Edwards. 1991. *Why Economists Disagree*. London: Longman.

Currie, L. 1986. "Sources of Growth." *World Development*, 14: 541-47.

Dahrendorf, R. 1979. *Life Chances*. London: Weidenfeld and Nicolson.

Dalton, G. 1971. *Economic Anthropology and Development: Essays in Tribal and Peasant Economies*. New York: Basic Books.

David, Paul A. 1992. "Knowledge, Property, and Systems Dynamics of Technological Change."In *Proceedings of the World Bank Annual Conference on Development Economics 1992*, 215-48. Washington, DC: The World Bank.

David, Wilfred L. 1979. "Agricultural Development and Structural Transformation." AGREP Division Working Paper No. 6. Washington, DC: The World Bank.

_____. 1985. *The IMF Policy Paradigm*. New York: Praeger.

_____. 1986. *Conflicting Paradigms in the Economics of Developing Nations*. New York: Praeger.

David, Wilfred L., and Pasquale Scandizzo. 1982. "Patterns of Growth and Structural Change in Middle Income Countries." AGREP Division Working Paper No. 30. Washington, DC: The World Bank.

de Janvry, A. 1981. *The Agrarian Question and Reformism in Latin America*. Baltimore, MD: Johns Hopkins University Press.

Denison, Edward F. 1962. *The Sources of Economic Growth in the United States and the Alternatives Before Us*. New York: Committee for Economic Development.

_____. 1979. *Accounting for Slower Economic Growth*. Washington, DC: Brookings Institution.

Denison, Edward F., and William Chung. 1976. *How Japan's Economy Grew So Fast*. Washington, DC: The Brookings Institution.

Diesing, Paul. 1982. *Science and Ideology in the Policy Sciences*. New York: Aldine.

Domar, Evsey. 1946. "Capital Expansion, Rate of Growth, and Employment." *Econometrica*, 14: 137-47.

Eckhaus, R. 1955. "The Factor Proportions Problem in Underdeveloped Countries." *American Economic Review*, 45: 539-65.

Elster, Jon. 1979. *Ulysses and the Sirens*. Cambridge: Cambridge University Press.

_____. 1985. *Making Sense of Marx*. Cambridge: Cambridge University Press.

Emmanuel, A. 1972. *Unequal Exchange*. New York: Monthly Review Press.

Evans, H.D. 1984. "A Critical Assessment of Some Neo-Marxian Models." *Journal of Development Studies*, 20: 202-26.

Faber, M., and D. Seers. 1972. *The Crisis in Planning*. 2 Vols. London: Chatto and Windus.

Feder, G. 1983. "On Exports and Economic Growth." *Journal of Development Economics*, 12: 59-74.

Fei, J., and G. Ranis. 1964. *The Development of the Labor Surplus Economy*. Homewood, IL: Richard D. Irwin.

Findlay, R. 1973. *International Trade and Development Theory*. New York: Columbia University Press.

_____. 1980. "The Terms of Trade and Equilibrium Growth in the World Economy." *American Economic Review*, 70: 291-99.

_____. 1982. "International Distributive Justice." *Journal of International Economics*, 13: 1-14.

_____. 1984. "Trade and Development Theory and Asian Experience." *Asian Development Review*, 2: 23-42.

Fishlow, A. 1984. "Some Comments on Adelman, Balassa, and Streeten." *World Development*, 12: 979-80.

_____. 1990. "The Latin American State." *Journal of Economic Perspectives*, 4: 61-74.

Foster-Carter, A. 1978. "The Mode of Production Controversy." *New Left Review*, 107: 44-77.

Frank, A.G. 1967. *Capitalism and Underdevelopment in Latin America*. New York: Monthly Review Press.

_____. 1975. *On Capitalist Development*. Bombay: Oxford University Press.

_____. 1978. *Dependent Accumulation and Underdevelopment*. New York: Monthly Review Press.

_____. 1981. *Crisis in the Third World*. London: Heinemann.

Friedman, Milton. 1953. *Essays in Positive Economics*. Chicago: University of Chicago Press.

_____. 1969. *The Optimum Quantity of Money and Other Essays*. Chicago: Adline.

_____. 1980. *Free to Choose*. New York: Harcourt, Brace, Jovanovich.

Friedman, Milton, ed. 1956. *Studies in the Quantity Theory of Money*. Chicago: University of Chicago Press.

Furtado, Celso. 1963. *The Economic Growth of Brazil*. Berkeley, CA: University of California Press.

_____. 1970. *Economic Development of Latin America: A Survey from Colonial Times to the Cuban Revolution*. Cambridge: Cambridge University Press.

_____. 1973. "The Concept of External Dependence in the Study of Underdevelopment." In *Political Economy of Development and Underdevelopment*, edited by Charles Wilber, 118-23. New York: Random House.

_____. 1987. "Underdevelopment: To Conform or Reform." In *Pioneers in Development*, Second Series, edited by Gerald Meier, 203-27. New York: Oxford University Press.

Gadamer, Hans-Georg. 1979. "The Problem of Historical Consciousness." In *Interpretive Social Science: A Reader*, edited by Paul Rabinow and William Sullivan, 103-60. Berkeley, CA: University of California Press.

_____. 1980. *Dialogue and Dialectic*. New Haven, CT: Yale University Press.

Geertz, Clifford. 1973. *Interpretation of Cultures*. New York: Basic Books.

Gerschenkron, Alexander. 1962. *Economic Backwardness in Historical Perspective*. Cambridge, MA: Harvard University Press.

Godelier, Maurice. 1972. *Rationality and Irrationality in Economics*. Trans. B. Pearche. New York: Monthly Review Press.

Goldsmith, Raymond. 1969. *Financial Structure and Development*. New Haven, CT: Yale University Press.

Goode, William J. 1986. "Individual Choice and Social Order." In *The Social Fabric: Dimensions and Issues*, edited by James F. Short, Jr., 39-62. Beverly Hills, CA: Sage.

Goulet, Denis. 1978. *The Cruel Choice: A New Critique in the Theory of Development*. New York: Atheneum.

Grant, James P. 1978. *Disparity Reduction Rates in Social Indicators: A Proposal for Measuring and Targeting Progress in Meeting Basic Needs*. Washington, DC: Overseas Development Council.

Griffin, Keith. 1974. *The Political Economy of Agrarian Change*. London: Macmillan.

Griffin, Keith, and A. Khan. 1978. *Poverty and Landlessness in Rural Asia*. Geneva: International Labour Office.

Griffin, Keith, and John Gurley. 1985. "Radical Analyses of Imperialism, the Third World, and the Transition to Socialism." *Journal of Economic Literature, 23:* 1089-1143.

Grossman, G., and E. Helpman. 1990. "Trade, Innovation, and Growth." *American Economic Review*, 80: 796-815.

Haberler, G. 1959. *International Trade and Economic Development*. Cairo: National Bank of Egypt.

Hamilton, Alexander. 1929 [1791]. *Report on the Subject of Manufactures*. Ed. A. H. Cole. New York: A. M. Kelley.

Harcourt, G. 1972. *Some Cambridge Controversies in the Theory of Capital*. Cambridge: Cambridge University Press.

Harris, Donald. 1975. "The Theory of Economic Growth: A Critique and Reformulation." *American Economic Review*, 65: 329-37.

Harris, J.R., and M.D. Todaro. 1970. "Migration, Unemployment and Development: A Two Sector Analysis." *American Economic Review*, 60: 126-42.

Harrod, Roy. 1933. *International Economics*. Cambridge: Cambridge University Press.

_____. 1939. "An Essay on Dynamic Theory." *Economic Journal*, 49: 14-33.

_____. 1948. *Towards a Dynamic Economics*. London: Macmillan.

_____. 1951. *The Life of John Maynard Keynes*. London: Macmillan.

Hayami, Y., and V. Ruttan. 1985 [1971]. *Agricultural Development: An International Perspective*. Baltimore, MD: Johns Hopkins University Press.
Hayek, Friedrich A. 1935. "Socialist Calculation: The State of the Debate." In *Collectivist Economic Planning*, edited by Friedrich A. Hayek. London: G. Routledge and Sons.
_____. 1944. *The Road to Serfdom*. Chicago: University of Chicago Press.
_____. 1948. "The Use of Knowledge in Society." In his *Individualism and Economic Order*. Chicago: University of Chicago Press.
_____. 1960. *The Constitution of Liberty*. London: Routledge.
_____. 1973. *Rules and Order*. Chicago: University of Chicago Press.
_____. 1979. *Political Order of a Free People*. Chicago: University of Chicago Press.
Helleiner, G. 1986. "Outward Orientation, Import Instability and African Economic Growth: An Empirical Investigation." In *Theory and Reality in Development*, edited by S. Lall and F. Stewart. London: Macmillan.
Heller, P., and R. Porter. 1978. "Exports and Growth: An Empirical Re-Investigation." *Journal of Development Economics*, 5: 191-94.
Hicks, John R. 1965. *Capital and Growth*. New York: Oxford University Press.
_____. 1974. *The Crisis in Keynesian Economics*. New York: Basic Books.
_____. 1979. *Causality in Economics*. New York: Basic Books.
Higgins, Benjamin. 1968. *Economic Development: Principles, Problems, Policies*. New York: Norton.
Hiley, D., J. Bohman, and R. Shusterman, eds. 1991. *The Interpretive Turn*. Ithaca, NY: Cornell University Press.
Hill, Polly. 1986. *Development Economics on Trial: The Anthropological Case for a Prosecution*. Cambridge: Cambridge University Press.
Hirsch, Fred. 1976. *The Social Limits to Growth*. Cambridge, MA: Harvard University Press.
Hirschman, Albert. 1958. *A Strategy of Economic Development*. New Haven, CT: Yale University Press.
_____. 1968. "The Political Economy of Import Substitution Industrialization in Latin America." *Quarterly Journal of Economics*, 87: 1-32.
_____. 1971. *A Bias for Hope*. New Haven, CT: Yale University Press.
_____. 1973. "The Changing Tolerance for Income Inequality in the Course of Economic Development." *Quarterly Journal of Economics*, 87: 544-66.
_____. 1977. "A Generalized Linkage Approach to Development with Special Reference to Staples." *Economic Development and Cultural Change*, 25: 67-98.
_____. 1981. "The Rise and Decline of Development Economics." In *Essays in Trespassing*. New York: Cambridge University Press.
_____. 1984. "A Dissenter's Confession: Strategies of Economic Development Revisited." In *Pioneers in Development*, edited by G. Meier and D. Seers, 85-111. New York: Oxford University Press for the World Bank.

Huntington, Samuel P. 1968. *Political Order and Changing Societies*. New Haven, CT: Yale University Press.

Independent Commission on International Development Issues (Brandt Commission). 1980. *North-South: A Program for Survival*. London: Pan Books.

Innis, H. 1915. *Essays on Canadian Economic History*. Toronto: University of Toronto Press.

International Labour Office. 1976. *Employment, Growth, and Basic Needs: A One-World Problem*. New York: Praeger.

Jameson, R. 1986. "Latin American Structuralism: A Methodological Perspective." *World Development*, 14:223-32.

Johnson, H. 1972. "Ideology and Economic Policy in the New States." In *Chicago Essays in Economic Development*, edited by D. Wall, 23-40. Chicago: University of Chicago Press.

Johnson, H., and E. Johnson, eds. 1978. *The Shadow of Keynes*. Oxford: Blackwell.

Johnston, Bruce. 1970. "Agricultural and Structural Transformation in Developing Countries." *Journal of Economic Literature*, 8: 369-404.

Johnston, Bruce, and Peter Kilby. 1975. *Agriculture and Structural Transformation: Economic Strategies in Late Developing Countries*. New York: Oxford University Press.

Jones, R., and P. Kenen, eds. 1984. *Handbook of International Economics*, Vol. 1. Amsterdam: North Holland.

Jorgenson, D. 1961. "The Development of a Dual Economy." *Economic Journal*, 71: 309-34.

_____. 1967. "Surplus Agricultural Labor and the Development of a Dual Economy." *Oxford Economic Papers*, 19: 288-312.

Jung, W., and P. Marshall. 1985. "Exports, Growth and Causality in Developing Countries." *Journal of Development Economics*, 18: 1-12.

Kaldor, N. 1955. "Alternative Theories of Distribution." *Review of Economic Studies*, 23: 83-110.

_____. 1957. "A Model of Economic Growth." *Economic Journal*, 67: 591-624.

_____. 1985. *Economics with Equilibrium*. New York: M.E. Sharpe.

Kalecki, M. 1976. *Essays on Developing Economies*. Brighton: Harvester Press.

Kanbur, S. 1987. "Measurement and Alleviation of Poverty with Application to the Effects of Macroeconomic Adjustment." *IMF Staff Papers*, 34: 60-85.

Kaplan, Abraham. 1964. *The Conduct of Inquiry: Methodology for Behavioral Science*. New York: Thomas Crowell.

Keat, R., and J. Urry. 1975. *Social Theory as Science*. London: Routledge and Kegan Paul.

Kelley, A. 1988. "Economic Consequences of Population Change in the Third World." *Journal of Economic Literature*, 26: 1685-1728.

Keohane, R. 1984. *After Hegemony*. Princeton, NJ: Princeton University Press.

Keynes, J.M. 1919. *The Economic Consequences of the Peace. The Collected Writings of John Maynard Keynes*. Vol. 2. Ed. D. Moggridge. London: Macmillan, 1971.

_____. 1933. *Essays in Persuasion*. London: Macmillan.

_____. 1936. *The General Theory of Employment, Interest and Money*. London: Macmillan.

Krasner, S. 1983. *International Regimes*. Ithaca, NY: Cornell University Press.

Kravis, Irving. 1970. "Trade as a Handmaiden of Growth: Similarities between Nineteenth and Twentieth Centuries." *Economic Journal*, 80: 850-72.

Kravis, Irving, Alan Heston, and Robert Summers. 1982. *World Product and Income: International Comparisons of Real GDP. International Comparison Project*. Baltimore, MD: Johns Hopkins University Press.

Krueger, Anne O. 1974. "The Political Economy of Rent-Seeking Society." *American Economic Review*, 64: 291-303.

_____. 1978. *Foreign Trade Regimes and Development: Liberalization Attempts and Consequences*. Cambridge, MA: Ballinger.

_____. 1990. "Government Failures in Development." *Journal of Economic Perspectives*, 4: 9-23.

Krugman, Paul. 1981. "Trade, Accumulation, and Uneven Development." *Journal of Development Economics*, 8: 149-61.

Kuhn, Thomas. 1970 [1962]. *The Structure of Scientific Revolutions*. Chicago: University of Chicago Press.

Kuznets, Simon. 1955. "Economic Growth and Income Inequality." *American Economic Review*, 45: 1-28.

_____. 1956-1967. "Quantitative Aspects of the Economic Growth of Nations." *Economic Development and Structural Change* (series of 10 articles).

_____. 1959. "A Comparative Study of Economic Growth and Structure of Nations." In *The Comparative Study of Economic Growth*. New York: National Bureau of Economic Research.

_____. 1973. "Modern Economic Growth: Findings and Reflections." *American Economic Review*, 63: 247-58.

Laclau, E. 1971. "Feudalism and Capitalism in Latin America." *New Left Review*, 67: 19-38.

Lal, D. 1983. *The Poverty of 'Development Economics.'* London: Institute of International Affairs.

Landes, D. 1990. "Why Are We So Rich and They So Poor?" *American Economic Review*, 80: 1-13.

Levins, R., and R. Lewontin. 1985. *The Dialectical Biologist*. Cambridge, MA: Harvard University Press.

Lewis, W. Arthur 1950. *Industrialization of the British West Indies*. Port of Spain: Caribbean Commission.

_____. 1954. "Economic Development with Unlimited Supplies of Labour." *Manchester School*, 22: 139-91.

_____. 1955. *The Theory of Economic Growth*. London: Allen and Unwin.

_____. 1958. "Unlimited Labour: Further Notes." *Manchester School*, 26: 1-32.

_____. 1978. *Growth and Fluctuations*. London: Allen and Unwin.

_____. 1979. "The Dual Economy Revisited." *Manchester School*, 47: 211-29.

_____. 1984. "The State of Development Theory." *American Economic Review*, 74: 1-10.

_____. 1988. "The Roots of Development Theory." In *Handbook of Development Economics*, Vol. 1, edited by H. Chenery and T.N. Srinivasan, 28-37. Amsterdam: North Holland.

Lipton, M. 1977. *Why Poor People Stay Poor: Urban Bias in World Development*. Cambridge, MA: Harvard University Press.

List, F. 1904 [1841]. *National Systems of Political Economy*. London: Longmans, Green.

Little, I.M.D. 1982. *Economic Development: Theory, Policy, and International Relations*. New York: Basic Books.

Little, I.M.D., T. Scitovsky, and M. Scott. 1970. *Industry and Trade in Some Developing Countries*. Oxford: Oxford University Press.

Loasby, B. 1976. *Choice, Complexity and Ignorance*. Homewood, IL: Richard D. Irwin.

Lucas, Robert E. 1988. "On the Mechanics of Economic Development." *Journal of Monetary Economics*, 22: 2-42.

Maddison, Angus. 1982. *Phases of Capitalist Development*. Oxford: Oxford University Press.

Malthus, Thomas. 1926 [1798]. *First Essay on Population*. London: Macmillan.

_____. 1968 [1820]. *Principles of Political Economy*. New York: Augustus Kelley.

Marshall, Alfred. 1920. *Principles of Economics*. London: Macmillan.

Marx, Karl. 1936 [1847]. *The Poverty of Philosophy*. London: Macmillan.

Marx, Karl, and Friedrich Engels. 1968. *Selected Works*. London: Lawrence and Wishart.

Mason, Edward. 1984. "The Chenery Analysis and Some Other Considerations." In *Economic Structure and Performance: Essays in Honor of Hollis B. Chenery*, edited by M. Syrquin, L. Taylor, and L. Westphal, 3-21. New York: Academic Press.

Masterman, Margaret. 1976. "The Nature of a Paradigm." In *Criticism and the Growth of Knowledge*, edited by Imre Lakatos and Alan Musgrave, 59-89. Cambridge: Cambridge University Press.

Meier, Gerald M. 1984. *Emerging from Poverty: The Economics That Really Matters*. New York: Oxford University Press.

Meier, Gerald M., ed. 1987. *Pioneers in Development*, Second Series. New York: Oxford University Press for the World Bank.

Meier, Gerald M., and Dudley Seers, eds. 1984. *Pioneers in Development*. New York: Oxford University Press for the World Bank.

Mellor, John W. 1976. *The New Economics of Growth: A Strategy for India and the Developing World*. Ithaca, NY: Cornell University Press.

Mellor, John W., and Bruce F. Johnston. 1984. "The World Food Equation: Interrelations among Development, Employment, and Food Consumption." *Journal of Economic Literature,* 22: 531-74.

Michaely, M. 1977. "Exports and Growth: An Empirical Investigation." *Journal of Development Economics*, 4: 149-53.

Michalopolous, C., and K. Jay. 1973. "Growth of Exports and Income in the Developing World: A Neoclassical View." Discussion Paper No. 28. Washington, DC: U.S. Agency for International Development.

Michel, H., and W. Ochel. 1978. "Rural Industrialization in Developing Countries." *Economics,* 18: 42-76.

Miernyk, W. 1965. *The Elements of Input-Output Analysis*. New York: Random House.

Mill, J.S. 1940 [1909]. *Principles of Political Economy*. ed. W. Ashley. London: Longmans, Green.

Millikan, Max, and Donald Blackmer, eds. 1961. *The Emerging Nations: Their Growth and United States Policy*. Boston: Little, Brown.

Moore, Barrington. 1966. *Social Origins of Dictatorship*. Boston: Beacon Press.

Morris, M. 1979. *Measuring the Condition of the World's Poor: The Physical Quality of Life Index*. New York: Pergamon Press.

Mosher, A. 1966. *Getting Agriculture Moving: Essentials for Development and Modernization*. New York: Praeger.

Myint, H. 1958. "The 'Classical Theory' of International Trade and Underdeveloped Countries." *Economic Journal*, 68: 317–31.

_____. 1971. *Economic Theory and the Underdeveloped Countries*. London: Oxford University Press.

_____. 1987. "Neoclassical Development Analysis: Its Strengths and Limitations." In *Pioneers in Development*, Second Series, edited by G. Meier, 105-36. New York: Oxford University Press for the World Bank.

Myrdal, G. 1957. *Economic Theory and Underdeveloped Regions*. London: Gerald Duckworth.

_____. 1968. *Asian Drama: An Inquiry into the Poverty of Nations*. London: Allen Lane.

Nehru, J. 1949. *Speeches,* Vol. 1. New Delhi: Government of India.

Noyola, J. 1965. "El Desarollo Economico y la Inflacion en Mexico y otros Paises Latinamericanos." *Investigación Económica*, 16: 603–48.

Nurkse, R. 1953. *Problems of Capital Formation in Underdeveloped Countries*. Oxford: Blackwell.

_____. 1959. *Patterns of Trade Development*. Stockholm: Almqvist and Wiksell.

Okun, A. 1975. *Equality and Efficiency: The Big Trade-Off*. Washington, DC: The Brookings Institution.

Olson, M. 1965. *The Logic of Collective Action*. Cambridge, MA: Harvard University Press.

_____. 1982. *The Rise and Decline of Nations*. New Haven, CT: Yale University Press.

_____. 1989. "Collective Action." In *The New Palgrave: The Invisible Hand*, edited by J. Eatwell, M. Milgate, and P. Newman, 61-69. New York: Norton.

Palma, G. 1978. "Dependency: A Formal Theory of Underdevelopment or a Methodology for the Analysis of Concrete Structure of Underdevelopment." *World Development*, 6: 881-924.

Paukert, F. 1973. "Income Distribution at Different Levels of Revelopment: A Survey of Evidence." *International Labour Review*, 108: 97-125.

Perkins, D. 1981. "Three Decades of International Quantitative Comparisons." Cambridge, MA: Harvard Institute of International Development.

Pigou, A. 1920. *The Economics of Welfare*. London: Macmillan.

Polanyi, K. 1944. *The Great Transformation*. Boston: Beacon Press.

Prebisch, R. 1950. *Economic Development for Latin America and its Principal Problems*. New York: United Nations.

_____. 1959. "Commercial Policies in the Underdeveloped Countries." *American Economic Review*, 49: 251-73.

_____. 1964. *Towards a Dynamic Development Policy for Latin America*. New York: United Nations.

_____. 1976. "A Critique of Peripheral Capitalism." *CEPAL Review*, 1: 9-76.

_____. 1984. "Five Stages in My Thinking on Development." In *Pioneers in Development*, edited by G. Meier and D. Seers, 175-91. New York: Oxford University Press.

Pyatt, G., and E. Thorbecke. 1976. *Planning Techniques for a Better Future*. Geneva: International Labour Office.

Ram, R. 1987. "Exports and Economic Growth: Some Additional Evidence." *Economic Development and Cultural Change*, 33: 415-25.

Ranis, G. 1988. "Analytics of Development Dualism." In *Handbook of Development Economics*, Vol. 1, edited by H. Chenery and T.N. Srinivasan, 73-92. Amsterdam: North Holland.

Ranis, G. and J. Fei. 1961. "A Theory of Economic Development." *American Economic Review*, 51: 533-65.

Reynolds, Lloyd. 1983. "The Spread of Economic Growth to the Third World: 1850-1980." *Journal of Economic Literature*, 21: 941-80.

Ricardo, David. 1951. *The Works and Correspondence of David Ricardo*, edited by P. Sraffa and M. Dobb. Cambridge: Cambridge University Press.

Robinson, J. 1974. "What Has Become of the Keynesian Revolution?" *Challenge*, 16: 6-11.

Romer, Paul. 1986. "Increasing Returns and Long-Run Growth." *Journal of Political Economy*, 94: 10027-37.

_____. 1990a. "Are Nonconvexities Important for Understanding Growth?" *American Economic Review,* 94: 1002-37.
_____. 1990b. "Endogenous Technical Change." *Journal of Political Economy,* 98: S71-S102.
_____. 1992. "Two Strategies for Economic Development: Using Ideas and Producing Ideas." In *Proceedings of the World Bank Annual Conference on Development Economics*, 63-91. Washington, DC: The World Bank.
Rosenstein-Rodan, Paul. 1943. "Problems of Industrialization in Eastern and Southeastern Europe." *Economic Journal*, 53: 205-16.
_____. 1961. "Notes on the Theory of the Big Push." In *Economic Development for Latin America,* edited by H. Ellis and H. Wallich. New York: St. Martin's Press.
_____. 1984. "Natura Facit Saltum: Analysis of the Disequilibrium Growth Process." In *Pioneers in Development,* edited by Gerald Meier and Dudley Seers, 205-21. New York: Oxford University Press for the World Bank.
Rostow, Walt W. 1952. *The Process of Economic Growth*. New York: Norton.
_____. 1960. *The Stages of Economic Growth: A Non-Communist Manifesto*. Cambridge: Cambridge University Press.
_____. 1971. *Politics and the Stages of Economic Growth*. Cambridge: Cambridge University Press.
_____. 1975. *How It All Began: Origins of the Modern Economy*. London: Methuen.
_____. 1978. *The World Economy: History and Prospect*. Austin: University of Texas Press.
_____. 1984. "Development: The Political Economy of the Marshallian Long Period." In *Pioneers in Development,* edited by Gerald Meier and Dudley Seers, 227-61. New York: Oxford University Press for the World Bank.
_____. 1990. *Theories of Economic Growth from David Hume to the Present*. New York: Oxford University Press.
Rostow, Walt W., et al. 1960. *Economics of Take-Off into Self-Sustained Growth*. London: Macmillan.
Ruggie, J. 1982. "International Regimes, Transactions, and Change: Embedded Liberalism in the Postwar Economic Order." *International Organization*, 36: 379-415.
Schiller, H. 1986. *Information and the Crisis Economy*. New York: Oxford University Press.
Schultz, T. 1964. *Transforming Traditional Agriculture*. New Haven, CT: Yale University Press.
Schumpeter, J. 1934. *The Theory of Economic Development*. Cambridge, MA: Harvard University Press.
_____. 1954. *History of Economic Analysis*. New York: Oxford University Press.

Seers, D. 1963. "The Limitations of the Special Case." *Bulletin of the Oxford University Institute of Statistics*, 25: 77-98.

_____. 1980. "North-South: Muddling Morality and Mutuality." *Third World Quarterly*, 2: 601-93.

_____. 1983. *The Political Economy of Nationalism*. Oxford: Oxford University Press.

Seers, Dudley, ed. 1981. *Dependency Theory: A Critical Reassessment*. London: Francis Pinter.

Sen, Amartya K. 1981a. *Poverty and Famines: An Essay on Entitlement and Deprivation*. Oxford: Clarendon Press.

_____. 1981b. "Ethical Issues in Income Distribution: National and International." In *The World Order: Past and Present*, edited by S. Grassman and E. Lundberg, 464-93. New York: St. Martin's Press.

_____. 1982. "The Food Problem: Theory and Policy." *Third World Quarterly*, 4: 447-59.

_____. 1983. "Development, Which Way Now?" *Economic Journal*, 93: 745-62.

_____. 1988. "The Concept of Development." In *Handbook of Development Economics*, Vol. 1, edited by Hollis Chenery and T.N. Srinivasan, 9-26. Amsterdam: North Holland.

Sen, Amartya K., et al. 1988. *The Standard of Living*. Ed. G. Rowthorn. Cambridge: Cambridge University Press.

Senghaas, Dieter. 1978. "Dissociation and Autocentric Development: An Alternative Development Policy for the Third World." *Economics*, 18: 17-41.

_____. 1982. "Elements of an Export-Oriented and Autocentric Development Path." *Economics*, 26: 7-17.

Shackle, G.L.S. 1967. *The Years of High Theory*. Cambridge: Cambridge University Press.

_____. 1972. *Epistemics and Economics*. Cambridge: Cambridge University Press.

Singer, Hans W. 1950. "The Distribution of Gains Between Investing and Borrowing Countries." *American Economic Review*, 40: 473-85.

_____. 1970. "Dualism Revisited: A New Approach to the Problems of Dual Society in Developing Countries." *Journal of Development Studies*, 7: 60-75.

_____. 1985. "Relevance of Keynes for Developing Countries." In *The Policy Consequences of John Maynard Keynes*, edited by H. Wattel, 128-43. New York: M.E. Sharpe.

_____. 1987. "What Keynes and Keynesianism Can Teach Us About Less Developed Countries." In *Keynes and Economic Development*, edited by A.P. Thirlwall, 70-89. New York: St. Martin's Press.

Smith, Adam. 1971 [1789]. *The Theory of Moral Sentiments*. Ed. D. Raphael and A. Macfie. Oxford: Clarendon Press.

_____. 1937 [1776]. *An Inquiry into the Nature and Causes of the Wealth of Nations*. Ed. Edwin Cannan. New York: Modern Library.

Solow, Robert M. 1956. "A Contribution to the Theory of Economic Growth." *Quarterly Journal of Economics*, 70: 60-94.

_____. 1957. "Technical Change and the Aggregate Production Function." *Review of Economics and Statistics*, 39: 312-20.

_____. 1970. *Growth Theory: An Exposition*. Oxford: Oxford University Press.

_____. 1988. "Growth Theory and After." *American Economic Review*, 78: 307-17.

Srinivasan, T.N. 1985. "Neoclassical Political Economy, the State and Economic Development." *Asian Development Review*, 3: 38-58.

Staley, Eugene. 1944. *World Economic Development: Effects on Advanced Industrial Countries*. Montreal: International Labour Office.

Stigler, George. 1959. "The Politics of Political Economics." *Quarterly Journal of Economics*, 73: 522-32.

Stiglitz, Joseph E. 1988. "Economic Organization, Information, and Development." In *Handbook of Development Economics*, edited by H. Chenery and T. Srinivasan, 93-160. Amsterdam: North Holland.

_____. 1989. "Markets, Market Failure, and Development." *American Economic Review*, 79: 197-203.

Streeten, P. 1974. "Social Science Research on Development: Some Problems in the Use and Transfer of an International Technology." *Journal of Economic Literature*, 12: 1290-1300.

_____. 1982. *First Things First: Meeting Basic Needs*. New York: Oxford University Press.

Sunkel, O. 1960. "Inflation in Chile: An Unorthodox Approach." *International Economic Papers*, 10: 107-31.

_____. 1969. "National Development Policy and External Dependence in Latin America." *Journal of Development Studies*, 6: 23-48.

_____. 1973. "Transnational Capitalism and Disintegration in Latin America." *Social and Economic Studies*, 22: 132-76.

Swan, T. 1956. "Economic Growth and Capital Accumulation." *Economic Record*, 32: 334-61.

Syrquin, M. 1988. "Patterns of Structural Change." *In Handbook of Development Economics*, Vol. 1, edited by H. Chenery and T. Srinivasan, 25-71. Amsterdam: North Holland.

Taylor, L. 1979. *Macro Models for Developing Countries*. New York: McGraw Hill.

_____. 1983. *Structuralist Macroeconomics*. New York: Basic Books.

Timmer, C. 1988. "The Agricultural Transformation." In *Handbook of Development Economics*, Vol. 1, edited by H. Chenery and T. Srinivasan, 276-331. Amsterdam: North Holland.

Todaro, M. 1981. *Economic Development in the Third World.* New York: Longman.

Tyler, W. 1981. "Growth and Export Expansion in Developing Countries: Some Empirical Evidence." *Journal of Development Economics*, 9: 121-30.

United Nations Development Programme (UNDP). 1992. *Human Development Report.* New York: Oxford University Press.

_____. 1994. *Human Development Report.* New York: Oxford University Press.

United Nations General Assembly. 1994. *Macroeconomic Policy Questions: Net Transfer of Resources between Developing Countries.* New York: United Nations.

United Nations Research Institute for Social Development (UNRISD). 1980. *The Quest for a Unified Approach to Development.* Geneva: UNRISD.

Wade, R. 1990. *Governing the Market: Economic Theory and the Role of Government in East Asian Industrialization.* Princeton, NJ: Princeton University Press.

Wallerstein, I. 1974. *The Modern World System.* New York: Academic Press.

Walsh, V., and H. Gram. 1980. *Classical and Neoclassical Theories of General Equilibrium.* New York: Oxford University Press.

Warren, Bill. 1980. *Imperialism: Pioneer of Capitalism.* London: Verso Books.

Watkins. 1963. "A Staple Theory of Economic Growth." *Canadian Journal of Economics and Political Science*, 29: 141-58.

Weber, N. 1930. *The Protestant Ethic and the Spirit of Capitalism.* London: Allen and Unwin.

_____. 1949. *The Methodology of the Social Sciences.* Eds. E. Shils and H. Finch. Glencoe, IL: Free Press.

Weigel, V. 1986. "The Basic Needs Approach: Overcoming the Poverty of *Homo Oeconomicus.*" *World Development*, 14: 1423-34.

Weisskoff, R. 1970. "Income Distribution and Economic Growth in Puerto Rico, Argentina, and Mexico." *Review of Income and Wealth*, 16: 303-32.

Williamson, J. 1983. *The Open Economy and the World Economy: A Textbook in International Economics.* New York: Basic Books.

_____. 1987. "Bancor and the Developing Countries: How Much Difference Would It Have Made?" In *Keynes and Economic Development*, edited by A. Thirlwall, 92-106. New York: St. Martin's Press.

Williamson, J., ed. 1990. *Latin American Adjustment: How Much Has Happened*? Washington, DC: Institute of International Economics.

World Bank. 1983. *World Development Report.* New York: Oxford University Press.

_____. 1989. *Sub-Saharan Africa: From Crisis to Sustainable Growth.* Washington, DC: The World Bank.

_____. 1990. *World Development Report.* New York: Oxford University Press.

_____. 1991. *World Development Report.* New York: Oxford University Press.

_____. 1995. *Monitoring Environmental Progress.* Washington, DC: The World Bank.

Index

About the Author

Wilfred L. David is Graduate Professor of Economics and African Studies at Howard University, Washington, D. C. He holds a Ph.D from Oxford University and has taught at Brooklyn College, the University of Delaware, Fisk, and Vanderbilt universities. He has served as economic adviser to the Government of Guyana and as a consultant to the World Bank and U.S.A.I.D. He is the author of *The IMF Policy Paradigm*, *Conflicting Paradigms in the Economics of Developing Nations*, and *Political Economy of Economic Policy*.